MANGIA, LITTLE ITALY!

Secrets from a Sicilian Family Kitchen

BY FRANCESCA ROMINA

CHRONICLE BOOKS

SAN FRANCISCO

Note: Many of the Italian words and phrases used in this book are in the Sicilian dialect, which varies from village to village.

Library of Congress Cataloging-in-Publication Data:
Romina, Francesca.
Mangia, Little Italy! : secrets from a Sicilian family kitchen /
by Francesca Romina.   p. cm.
Includes bibliographical references and index.
ISBN 0-8118-1533-1 (pbk.)
1. Cookery, Italian—Sicilian style. 2. Italian Americans—New
York (State)—New York—Social life and customs. 3. Little Italy
(New York, N.Y.)—Social life and customs. I. Title
TX723.2.S55R66   1998
641.59458—dc21   97-34027   CIP

Printed in the United States of America.
Designed by Lucy Nielsen.

Distributed in Canada by Raincoast Books
8680 Cambie Street, Vancouver, British Columbia V6P 6M9

10 9 8 7 6 5 4 3 2 1

Chronicle Books
85 Second Street, San Francisco, California 94105

Web Site: www.chronbooks.com

Dedication

To Grandma Josephina, the greatest cook in the world.
Her cooking has caused enough fights and
jealousies from Sicily to America to last two hundred years.
Her food is still the best in the business.

Acknowledgments

A very special thank-you to Louie Di Palo of Di Palo's at 206 Grand Street in New York City, who provided the information on the cheese section in this book. In my opinion he carries the finest ricotta, mozzarella, and other cheeses in New York. ☙ A special thank-you to C & D Bakery in Brooklyn, which has the finest bread around. ☙ And a special thank-you to De Robertis pastry store, which has the finest pastries in New York City. ☙ To Beth Allen, who's a perfectionist in everything she touches. Her expertise in the marketing and style of the proposal sold this book. Thank you for making my book a reality. ☙ To Evie Righter, who spent many long hours assisting me in editing the manuscript. All the information in the chapter introductions, headnotes, and stories is due to her insistence on putting it in. Thanks for everything. ☙ To Mara Reid Rogers, for assisting with this book from the inception to the conclusion in every way. She calls my book "our baby." Thanks for being such a good friend. ☙ To Mary Johnson, who wrote a wonderful first draft of the cookbook proposal. Thanks for starting me off on the right track. ☙ To Bill LeBlond, Leslie Jonath, and Sarah Putman—the editorial staff at Chronicle—and to Sharon Silva, who made my life easy and were a joy to work with. They truly understand Sicilians! Thank you for making this such a terrific book.

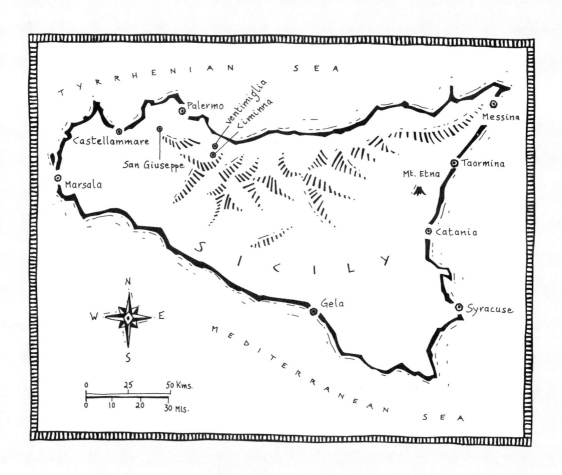

Table of Contents

CHAPTER 3

Brodo e Ova

🐚 Soups and Eggs   41

CHAPTER 6

Pesce

🐟 Fish   127

CHAPTER 7

Carni e Galline

🐦 Meats and Poultry

CHAPTER 8

Verduri e Insalati

🍃 Vegetables and Salads 203

CHAPTER 9

Dolci

Sweets, Fruits, Nuts, and Ice Cream   251

CHAPTER 10

Liquori e Biviri

Liqueurs and Beverages

INTRODUCTION

I learned to cook from my grandma Josephina. But in her kitchen in New York's Little Italy, Grandma passed on more than just culinary traditions. She told me tales from her past, seasoned with superstitions and punctuated by the sounds of chopping, mixing, and sizzling. While the meatballs browned and her seven-hour Sunday sauce simmered, I grew to know the characters in her hometown of faraway Ciminna and the life of nearby Mulberry and Mott streets in their horse-and-buggy days. Grandma's tales and tasks wove themselves together in a uniquely Sicilian fashion. She knew how to add drama to any meal: recalling the ten-foot-wide pizza oven in her childhood home (a mansion no villagers wanted since it was the scene of the most notorious mass murder in Sicily), she set the pizza dough to rise on a wooden board on the bed in her Little Italy apartment.

On Sunday, just the family (anywhere from ten to fourteen people) would gather at Grandma's for dinner. At six-thirty in the morning, she would get up to make the sauce. At two o'clock in the afternoon, the meal would begin. Eight to ten courses later, after night-fall, it would end. The food was sensational!

When I was five years old, I finally got to go shopping with Grandma for our Sunday dinners. It was common for us to stop at twelve different stores. On Saturday, down to the shops we'd go, Grandma pulling her shopping cart along behind her four-foot-ten-inch frame. Everywhere we went, she was known. We'd stop at Di Palo's on Mott and Grand streets for handmade ricotta and mozzarella, drop in next door at Lapariello's at 210 Grand, for Saica olive oil, and then off to Alleva Brothers, just down the street, for *ricotta salata* topped with herbs. At Fretta's on First Avenue and Eleventh Street, we would buy the best pork and sausages in the world. Next, we'd pick up warm Sicilian bread, baked in a hundred-year-old wood-burning brick oven, at Palermo's on Thirteenth Street. Our final stop brought us back to Eleventh Street to De Robertis for pastries and biscotti. Those Saturday afternoons were very special. I miss them still.

Memories of the Saturday morning shopping ritual always make me reminisce about Grandma's massive 100-by-46-inch, double-trestled, mahogany dining room table. It may seem foolish, but over the years I had come to love that table. For everything I had ever learned from Grandma—the cooking, the stories, the lessons in Sicilian mentality—occurred around that table. So one day, I told her that when she died I expected her to bequeath it to me.

She flashed back, her large brown eyes dancing, "Too late, Fren-zee [Grandma's name for me]. I'm giving it to Johnny, your cousin. He just got married and they need a table."

"He's getting the table! He couldn't care less about that table! *Traditore che sei!* [Traitor that you are!] You knew I wanted that table!" Enraged, I slammed the door to her apartment, placing just a minor Sicilian curse on the table on the way out.

Several weeks passed, and I did not speak to Grandma, which is not unusual in our relationship. I heard the table was picked up, repaired, and refinished, and then taken over to my cousin's home. But I consoled myself with the knowledge that the table knows where it belongs and Sicilian curses do not fail.

Two months went by, and the phone rang. "Fren-zee, come over," Grandma said, as if something were up her sleeve.

"What for?" I responded sarcastically.

"I have something to show you. Come over." She hung up.

Mother calmed me down and told me to stop carrying on. After all, it was just an old, beat-up table. But when I entered Grandma's house, she was glistening. "Close your eyes, I have a surprise for you!"

"Oh, for God's sake! I'm not interested in . . ."

"Stop already! Enough! Close your eyes!"

Reluctantly I agreed, and she guided me into her living room. Honestly, this is one of the few times I've stood absolutely speechless. For there was the mahogany table, back where it had lived for sixty-seven years. Shiny and refinished to its original beauty, it was breathtaking. I can't express the joy in my heart and how grateful I was for Sicilian curses. Unappreciated where it was, the table had come back to me.

"What on earth . . . I don't understand!" I retorted.

"Johnny's wife didn't like the table. She said it was too big and she didn't like the antique style. She wants something modern now, and they wanted to sell my table, so I got mad. I said you're not selling my table. Give it back! Now my son Frank is not talking to me. I don't know, I do nothing and no one is talking to me." She turned sharply, *"Tu u fascisti apposta!* [You did this out of spite!] Don't think I don't know. You made this happen. It's strange the way it returned. But," she sat comfortably in her chair, "to tell you the truth, things weren't the same to me without that table. After all, I had it since 1926, when Natale and I married. The table represents everything about life to me."

That was back in 1984. But something occurred to me when that table was gone. The Little Italy Grandma had arrived in was disappearing. Gone were the family stores we visited on our Saturday *girata* (outing); gone was a way of life that had great significance for two generations of Italian Americans; and most importantly, gone was the record of my family's history. This cookbook is a consequence of that realization. And while it is a book about Grandma's food, it is also a memoir about a special corner of New York City at the turn of the century that was about one-half mile square—a place that not only made an everlasting impression on those who lived there, but also changed the way America eats today. It is the story of Little Italy. ꙮ

De Robertis started out as Caffe Pugliese in 1904. Current owner John De Robertis III's grandfather is the third from the left, surrounded by Sicilian bakers and friends.

CUCINA SICILIANA NELLA PICCOLO ITALIA

Certain ingredients are fundamental to the Sicilian Little Italy kitchen. The quality of seasoned bread crumbs, cheeses, herbs and spices, and olive oil determines the flavor of the final dish. If you read this chapter carefully, and stock your kitchen with the proper ingredients, you'll be on your way to becoming a true Sicilian cook. Also included are information on pots and pans and a few basic recipes used throughout the book.

CHEESES

A Sicilian's favorite cheese is usually either *cacio-cavallo* or *incanes-trato*. Also enjoyed is *pecorino-siciliano*, the Sicilian version of *pecorino-romano*, available only in Sicily. Today, many Sicilians substitute romano cheese for the original grating cheeses of *incanestrato* and *cacio-cavallo*, and it is a perfect stand-in.

The tradition began in New York's Little Italy during World War II. Until the war broke out, all of the cheeses listed in this section had been readily available in New York since the turn of the century. But not even letters could reach America once the fighting began, so cheeses were nearly impossible to obtain. Between the two World Wars, Sardinian-Italian cheese makers emigrated to Argentina and began to produce their own version of romano cheese called *sardo*. It was made with cow's milk, which was easily procured, instead of the customary sheep's milk. The wartime prohibition on American trade with Italy opened up a tremendous business opportunity to Argentina: the selling of inexpensive cheeses to America so that Italian Americans would not be forced to pay the high black-market price of Italian cheeses. Thus, Argentine-made romano cheese became the standard substitution. As the years passed, *cacio-cavallo* and *incanestrato* were forgotten by the new generation of Sicilian American children. Even after the war ended, it took many years for Sicilian cheeses to return. Today, most can be found in Italian food shops.

The following cheeses, all Sicilian favorites, are available in this country:

🐎 **Cacio-cavallo (cow's milk)**   The name translates as "horse cheese," after the custom of aging the cheese over a wooden rack with four legs that resembled a horse's back. Pictures in cookbooks of *cacio-cavallo* hanging over an actual horse's back illustrate how the cheese maker transported the cheese for selling throughout the town, not how it was aged. *Cacio-cavallo* is made solely from the milk of modicana cows, the most widespread cow breed in Sicily and one that gives exceptional milk for the making of this cheese. There are two varieties of *cacio-cavallo:* a young one, aged 4 to 6 months, is light yellow, soft, dense, and mild and is used for eating; an older one, aged 12 to 24 months, is extremely hard, darker yellow, and very piquant, and is used for grating. *Cacio-cavallo* is the Sicilian version of provolone.

🐎 **Formaggio fresco (cow's milk)**   In America, this cheese is usually found in a small plastic basket, while in Sicily, a straw basket forms its shape. The cheese is made from fresh curdled milk, which is transferred to the basket, salted, and then left to form its shape for 30 minutes. It should be consumed immediately within hours of purchase for the best flavor, or within a few days at most. *Formaggio fresco* can be made with or without a top crust of salt, and is eaten spread on bread and sprinkled with salt and pepper. The taste of the cheese resembles a hard version of ricotta, while the texture is similar to mozzarella.

🐎 **Incanestrato (sheep's milk)**   *Incanestrato* translates as "in the basket," and is named for the basket in which it is aged and which gives it its distinctive lines that form around the cheese. Made from November to April, the younger *incanestrato*, aged 3 to 9 months, is semisoft, mild, sweet, and eaten with bread. The harder version is aged 9 to 20 months and is dry, grainy, and very piquant. It is used for grating over pasta, soups, and stews. This is my favorite cheese.

☙ ***Mozzarella*** **(cow's milk)** First, there is the buffalo's milk cheese, made from whole milk, that comes from around Naples, in the region of Campania. It was not available in Sicily in the early 1900s. In Little Italy in 1922, Grandma discovered the whole cow's milk mozzarella called *fiore di latte*, and although not Sicilian, it soon became a favorite among Sicilian Americans. The best-quality mozzarella is sold immersed in water. It is known as fresh mozzarella and can be purchased salted or unsalted in any Italian cheese shop. The whole-milk cheese should be made from milk with a butterfat content of at least 45 percent, producing a very white, creamy appearance. It should be soft enough to hold the indentation of your finger, like fresh bread dough, and when sliced, the concentric circles formed from kneading the *pasta filata* (mozzarella string) should be visible. The natural milky juices will cascade down the cheese when it is cut. A lesser butterfat content will yield a dry, rubbery texture. Sicilians enjoy mozzarella as a snack with bread, but it is seldom used in cooking except for pizza or lasagna. For example, it is standard to substitute the more flavorful provolone for mozzarella in veal cutlet parmesan.

☙ ***Pecorino-romano*** **(sheep's milk)** The traditional version (genuine *pecorino-romano*) comes only from the area of Lazio, around Rome. Today, the same type of cheese is produced in Sardinia in large quantities, but they carry only the name *pecorino-romano*, not *genuine pecorino-romano*. Authentic *genuine pecorino-romano* tends to have a slight greenish tint that is not immediately visible to the eye but can be detected upon closer scrutiny. This color is characteristic of the milk produced by the local Lazio sheep. In contrast, the *pecorino-romano* produced in Sardinia is white in color. The cheese should have a firm but grainy texture, yet still retain a moist quality. It should also yield a sharp, pungent, and robust flavor that is slightly salty on the palate, making it excellent for grating and suitable for eating as a table cheese when young. A cheese that has been aged for 2 to 9 months makes a good table cheese, while grating cheeses should be aged for 12 to 18 months. This hard cheese, which is referred to as romano cheese in the recipes in this book, is used in many traditional Sicilian dishes and can be substituted for any Sicilian hard cheese when necessary.

🐚 **Pepato** (sheep's milk)   This is *incanestrato* cheese made with peppercorns and is perfect for spice lovers. The young version is used for eating; the aged version is for grating.

🐚 **Primo Sale** (sheep's milk)   This cheese, a young *incanestrato,* is made once a year in Sicily, in the spring when the ewes give birth and produce a lot of milk. The name means "first salt," which symbolizes the rebirth of Christ, and the cheese is anxiously awaited by Neapolitans each Easter, when a special version of *pizza rustica* is made solely with this cheese. For others, *primo sale* is eaten with bread at Easter. It is not used for grating.

🐚 **Provolone** (cow's milk)   Although not native to Sicily, provolone is a staple in every Sicilian kitchen. There are three types: sweet, which is aged 2 to 6 months; medium-sharp, which is aged 8 to 15 months; and extra-sharp, which is aged 18 to 27 months. As provolone ages, the butterfat evaporates and the cheese dries, releasing a saltier, sharper flavor. When purchasing an aged provolone, note that different seasons produce different textures and flavors. Provolone made from the milk of summer, when the cows are eating fresh grass, is sweeter, drier, and grainier and is slightly yellow. This is my favorite. The fully matured version made from the milk of winter, when the cows are eating alfalfa and hay, is aged for at least 1 year and is white and sharper in flavor. The saltiness of the provolone will not depend on the season or type of milk you purchase, but on how long the cheese is aged. Look for a provolone that is thoroughly speckled with tiny white dots, which denote the butterfat and salt content. These white dots signify a high-quality, properly aged provolone.

🐚 **Ricotta** (cow's or sheep's milk)   As a child in Ciminna, Grandma carried little pails of ricotta from the nearby farm to her waiting mother. She watched the cheese made fresh by a woman who poured the sheep's milk into large pots of boiling whey taken from previously made cheeses like *cacio-cavallo* and *incanestrato,* and then scooped

Louie Di Palo with his parents, displaying mozzarella molded into animal figures—a lost art.

the resulting ricotta into little metal pails to be carted off. The warm ricotta was quickly eaten spread on bread and sprinkled with salt, pepper, or parsley; mixed into pasta with or without sauce; or used as an ingredient in dishes such as lasagna. At Di Palo's in Little Italy, the ricotta is especially handmade for the shop and is still sold in little metal cans with tiny holes to drain off the whey. All ricotta in America is made from cow's milk, which is a good substitute for the sheep's milk version produced in Sicily.

🐑 ***Ricotta salata*** (sheep's milk) Known as *ricotta pecorino salata* in Sicily and as *ricotta salata* in the United States, this air-dried cheese, available in three types, is made from pressing the sheep's milk ricotta to extract a large percentage of its whey. It is then salted and left to age for about 30 days to yield a semisoft table cheese. If pressed further to extract more whey and then salted and aged for about 60 days, a grating cheese is the result. The latter should have a naturally salty flavor, which means that dishes in which it is used will not need any additional salt. It is always grated fresh over the classic linguine with marinara sauce (page 112). The third type, *ricotta salata* with herbs, is rarer. The top crust is drizzled with olive oil and sprinkled with herbs such as rosemary and oregano, then briefly baked. The Italian Food Center on Mulberry and Grand streets in Little Italy carries it only during Easter and Christmas.

Buying, Storing, and Grating Cheeses

When purchasing *cacio-cavallo, incanestrato, pecorino-romano,* or provolone, look for a grainy texture, the sign of properly aged cheese. To buy cheese for eating, search for a piece that drips with a little oil when at room temperature—a product of its natural butterfat content. This epitomizes perfection. If you then decide to grate the cheese, store it in the refrigerator, wrapped in parchment paper, until the excess moisture dries and the cheese hardens, 3 to 7 days.

To store firm cheeses properly, first wrap them in waxed or parchment paper, followed by a second layer of plastic or aluminum foil, and then store them in the refrigerator. To prolong the freshness of mozzarella, store it in a covered container completely submerged in lightly salted water and eat it within a few days. Store fresh ricotta inside a sieve placed in a covered container, a setup that allows the ricotta to continue to drain, extending its life. Italian immigrants used sieve-lined "cheese plates" in the 1900s. Search for them at antique shops. Connoisseurs of mozzarella and fresh ricotta eat them within hours of purchase.

Cheese for grating should always be bought in one piece and grated at home. Stores use an ultrafine disk that reduces the cheese to sand. As a result, it doesn't have much taste and extra spoonfuls are required to flavor a dish. My favorite grater is the old-fashioned type that screws onto a countertop and shreds the cheese into long, thin strips. Electric models are available, but even a mini hand grater will do the job. Technically, cheese should not be grated until it's needed, but if I did that, I would be grating cheese all day long! So I grate one-pound chunks of hard cheeses like romano, *incanestrato*, or *cacio-cavallo* in advance and store them in tightly sealed jars in the refrigerator. Semisoft cheeses like *ricotta salata* and even provolone should not be pregrated, as they lose their taste easily and mold quickly.

SEASONINGS

Basil Forget lemon and purple basils. Sicilians use only sweet basil and they always use it fresh. Tear it with your hands. Cutting it with a knife is considered bad luck in Italy. In the past, basil was found planted in old coffee cans on every fire escape in Little Italy. It grows easily in the winter and the summer if given plenty of water and placed in a sunny spot.

Garlic Despite what you may have read elsewhere, peel garlic cloves with your fingers. Do not crush them first with the flat side of a knife. Also, do not mince the garlic. Using a sharp paring knife, slice the clove lengthwise and then crosswise into small, medium, or large dice. This is the way garlic is to be chopped for the recipes in this book, and the resulting flavor is well worth cutting it properly.

Oregano The only oregano used in this cookbook, and by Sicilians as well, is dried oregano. Fresh oregano is very bland. The full flavor of the herb reveals itself only when it is dried and the leaves are crushed between the palms until powdery. There are three things to keep in mind when buying oregano: 1) The best oreganos to buy are the Greek and Italian varieties since they are the most pungent. Purchase oregano at your local spices store in a clear bag in its natural, unprocessed form, either dried on its own branch or broken up with its sticks. 2) Smell the oregano. If it doesn't have a pungent odor, it's probably stale. 3) If, when crushed, the oregano leaves are soft and powdery, the oregano is fresh. If they remain in hard little bits, the oregano is old and should be discarded.

🔖 **Parsley**   Always use Italian flat-leaf parsley, not the curly American variety. The latter lacks flavor and should only be used for garnish. Parsley leaves are generally chopped coarsely or medium-fine. If they are finely chopped, there is nothing left of the taste. Simply put, Sicilian cooks do not mince. Note, too, that when Sicilian Americans chop parsley, they include the first 2 inches of the stem closest to where the leaves begin, because most of the parsley flavor is contained in the stem. Store fresh parsley sprigs in the refrigerator in a glass half-filled with water; it will keep for about 5 days.

🔖 **Rosemary**   Fresh Italian rosemary branches are often substituted for dried oregano because their taste is similar to that of a mild oregano. Other rosemary varieties found in America have a flowery taste and are never used in Sicilian cooking. Rosemary must always be used fresh off its branch, as it turns bitter when dried. In Sicily, two rosemary branches are clipped from the garden and placed alongside fish, beef, pork, veal, or chicken as it roasts or grills. Write to Fratelli Ingegnoli (see Sources) to obtain Italian rosemary seeds and grow the real thing.

🔖 **Spices**   Sea salt and freshly ground black pepper are pantry staples in Sicily, but in New York's Little Italy, iodized table salt and ground black pepper have long been regularly used for seasoning large pots of sauce or soup. Red pepper flakes and whole red chili peppers flavor many preparations. In Sicily, chili peppers were tied into a braid by my great-grandmother Maria, who used them in her Sunday sauce, on pizzas, or to flavor a pasta with vegetables, a tradition that continues today in Little Italy and throughout the United States.

OLIVE OIL

When Grandma was a young girl in Sicily, she made oil with her father from olives that came from his trees. After he piled them against a wall, he'd throw coarse salt on them and let them stand for several days to soften their skins, then transfer them to a stone press set in motion by a pair of mules. The mules, led by the nose with

Great-grandpa Michele

reins, traveled around and around for hours. Once during this laborious process, a mule refused to budge. Great-grandpa Michele got so mad that he jumped up and bit the mule on the nose, screaming in his ear, "If I work, you work!" Miraculously, the mule's hooves immediately lunged forward and resumed the task. From that press, a delicious extra-virgin olive oil emerged. Its color was pure gold, and its taste was as sweet as honey.

Great-grandpa Michele stored his oil in fifty-gallon ceramic barrels, and what wasn't used at home, he sold and was actually paid in lire. This exchange of lire was unusual around the early 1900s, since people still bartered in Sicily.

Grandma never economized when it came to olive oil; it cost her 25 percent of her paycheck seventy years ago. Here are five things she looks for when buying a good Sicilian extra-virgin olive oil: 1) The color green has nothing to do with the quality of olive oil. Dark green doesn't mean better. Sometimes, although not always, it is the result of the addition of food coloring to fool unknowing buyers. The color of olive oil varies with the depth of color of the olives and the location where they are pressed. If the oil has not been artificially colored, a dark oil simply means that the olives pressed were darker green. These are not better oils. In general, and especially in America, I suggest avoiding very dark green olive oil. It is too often full of additives and heavy. Instead, purchase olive oil that is golden to light green. 2) Some olive sediment should be visible on the bottom of the bottle. It indicates an unfiltered oil and therefore a more natural, more flavorful product. 3) Olive oil should have a little body; that is, it should not be ultrathin when you pour it . 4) Real Sicilian olive oil must be sweet, to impart a sweet taste to the food. 5) The oil should have a light taste. If your olive oil is heavy or greasy, it is of poor quality.

Storing Olive Oil

To economize, buy olive oil in gallon cans. The reason for shipping oil in cans is to protect it from light, which is why it is also packaged in dark bottles. Sunlight or fluorescent light will turn olive oil rancid. Once you open the container, store the oil in its original can in a dark, cool place, transferring it to an oil can or dark, tightly sealed 1-quart bottle as needed. The oil should be used within 4 months of opening. After that it will begin to deteriorate in flavor, although it will still be useful. Keep olive oil away from heat, as it can easily turn it rancid.

Cooking with Olive Oil

Throughout this cookbook, I refer to oiling the pots and pans lightly or generously. To oil a pan lightly, pour in just enough oil to reach the bottom edges of the pan. To oil a pan generously, pour oil in to a depth of about ⅛ inch. When I simply say to oil the pan, add the amount of oil you customarily use, which should fall between the light and generous descriptions.

POTS AND PANS

When I fry, sauté, or boil, I use high-quality stainless steel frying pans and pots with heavy bottoms of copper sandwiched between layers of aluminum. When oven roasting, my favorite pans, and the ones I call for in many recipes, are the black-speckled enamel-on-steel baking pans sold at most department stores. Whatever you roast or bake in these pans will definitely brown better, from veal chops to fish, filet mignon to poultry. They are especially good for baking pizzas and fruit pies, producing a superb brown crust and cutting down on the time in the oven. Do not confuse them with black steel or baker's steel pans.

In addition to the usual assortment of pots and pans found in most kitchens, the following equipment sees heavy use in the Sicilian kitchen: a medium-size (9-inch) frying pan; a large (10- to 12-inch) frying pan with 3-inch sides (excellent for marinara sauces and *cacciatore*); large (8-, 12-, and 14-quart or larger) pots for tomato sauces, pastas, and soups; and, if possible, a 20-quart pot perfect for boiling 2 pounds of lasagna noodles. Finally, never cook tomato sauces in aluminum pots, as they render an iodine taste. Use only stainless steel pots.

Mudrica Condita
FLAVORED BREAD CRUMBS AND BREAD CRUMB COATING

Makes about 2¹⁄₂ cups, enough for coating 2 pounds meat, poultry, fish, or vegetables.

🥄 Sicilian bread crumbs are a staple. They are used to coat everything for cooking from veal cutlets to fish fillets and are often part of a stuffing. The crumb mixture, minus the garlic and parsley, can be made up to 2 weeks in advance and refrigerated until needed, at which point the last ingredients are added.

Begin with day-old Italian bread and grate it on the large holes of a hand grater. To make 1 cup bread crumbs, halve the recipe.

Egg Coating

2 large eggs

4½ tablespoons milk

Dash of salt

Flavored Bread Crumbs

1¾ cups freshly made bread crumbs

½ cup grated romano or *incanestrato* cheese

Scant ½ teaspoon salt

3 large cloves garlic, thinly sliced

½ cup coarsely chopped fresh Italian parsley

Secrets of Success

Leftover crumbs from breading are never thrown away. Instead, Sicilians use them to make delicious little omelets called *froscia piccoli,* which are eaten as a snack or side dish (see variation).

1. To make the egg coating: In a soup plate, beat together the eggs, milk, and salt.

2. To make the bread crumbs: In a dish, combine the bread crumbs, cheese, salt, garlic, and parsley. Mix well.

3. In batches, dip the meat, poultry, fish, or vegetables into the egg mixture, then coat with the crumb mixture. Shake off the excess crumbs.

LITTLE OMELETS VARIATION

Combine the leftover egg and bread crumbs and shape into 3-inch round patties. If the mixture is too soft to form a patty, add more crumbs; if it's too dry, add a few drops of milk. Cook in olive oil in a frying pan over medium heat until golden brown, about 3 minutes on each side. Serve immediately.

For 1 chicken or
fish, about
3 pounds;
serves 4.
For 3 chickens or
fish, about
3 pounds each;
serves 12

Salsa di Limone, Olio, e Aglio

LEMON, OIL, AND GARLIC DRESSING

This dressing is used as a basting sauce for roasted poultry, roasted lamb, grilled chops, baked fish, and shish kebabs. When it is made in Sicily, fresh Italian rosemary branches are often substituted for the dried oregano. If using rosemary, eliminate the oregano completely, and place a long (12-inch) fresh rosemary branch on each side of the meat, fish, or poultry as it roasts or grills. The leaves will fall off during cooking and impart the dressing with their flavor.

I would like to dispel one thing about lemons that has been driving me crazy for years. Sicilians do not eat lemons in salad. In fact, Sicilian lemons are so acidic that they would cause tearing if eaten in salads. Sicilians eat *pirituni*, which look like large lemons but are less juicy and far sweeter. They are strictly salad fruits and are available in the spring and summer in Sicily. No one in the United States has ever heard of *pirituni*, and that includes many Italians from Italy. Therefore, seeing this lemonlike fruit in a salad in Sicily, Italian and American cookbook authors and writers unknowingly have stated for years that Sicilians eat lemons in salads, and all Sicilians have a good laugh at their ignorance. Indeed, Sicilian lemons are so strong that it is common in Sicily to add 1 or 2 tablespoons of cold water to this dressing to dilute its strength.

Secrets of Success

This dressing may be made up to 1 day ahead of time without the garlic, covered, and stored in the refrigerator. Add the fresh garlic right before serving.

For 1 chicken or fish, about 3 pounds; serves 4

Juice of 2 or 2½ lemons (6 or 7 tablespoons)

4 tablespoons extra-virgin olive oil

4 cloves garlic, cut into medium dice

1 teaspoon dried oregano, sticks removed, crushed until powdery

Scant ½ teaspoon salt, or to taste

For 3 chickens or fish, about 3 pounds each; serves 12

Juice of 5 lemons (scant 1 cup)

½ cup plus 2 tablespoons extra-virgin olive oil

10 cloves garlic, cut into medium dice

2 teaspoons dried oregano, sticks removed, crushed until powdery

¾ teaspoon salt, or to taste

1. In a small bowl, combine the lemon juice, olive oil, garlic, oregano, and salt. Mix well. It can be made up to 3 days ahead of time and left refrigerated until needed. If the lemons are too acidic, add 1 to 2 tablespoons water.

Polpetti
MEATBALLS

When Sicilians made meatballs in Little Italy in the early 1900s, they went to a butcher and automatically bought a "meatball mixture." It consisted of ¼ pound ground pork mixed into each 1 pound chopped beef steak. The beef was taken solely from the tail of the T-bone or porterhouse steak, and included its fat. Since the weekday tomato sauce (page 100) included only meatballs, unlike the Sunday sauce with its *braciole* (stuffed pork roast), the addition of ground pork was important, as it imparted a sweet taste to the tomato sauce.

For 1 pound meat

1 pound chopped beef steak from untrimmed T-bone or porterhouse tails

⅓ cup plus 1 tablespoon unseasoned freshly made bread crumbs (page 14)

⅓ cup grated romano or *incanestrato* cheese

1 small yellow onion, cut into medium dice

2 cloves garlic, cut into small dice

5 fresh Italian parsley sprigs, coarsely chopped

¾ teaspoon salt, or to taste

3 or 4 large eggs

Extra-virgin olive oil

For 2½ pounds meat

2½ pounds chopped beef steak from untrimmed T-bone or porterhouse tails

1 cup unseasoned freshly made bread crumbs (page 14)

¾ cup grated romano or *incanestrato* cheese

1 medium-small yellow onion, cut into medium dice

3 large cloves garlic, cut into small dice

12 fresh Italian parsley sprigs, coarsely chopped

1 teaspoon salt, or to taste

8 to 10 large eggs

Extra-virgin olive oil

1 pound meat makes about 9 meatballs; serves 4. 2½ pounds meat makes about 22 meatballs; serves 10

Secrets of Success

True connoisseurs buy meat fresh from a butcher on the day they make the meatballs. Purchase T-bone or porterhouse steak tails (with the fat left on) and have them ground fresh. If your meat is frozen, thaw it thoroughly; the slightest frost makes meatballs tough.

1. To make 9 meatballs: In a large bowl, mix together the meat, bread crumbs, cheese, onion, garlic, parsley, salt, and 3 eggs until the eggs are well incorporated. If the mixture seems dry and not very soft, add 1 more egg. With your hands, make a well in the middle of the meat 2 inches in diameter and 2 inches deep. Fill the well with ¼ cup olive oil.

2. To make 22 meatballs: In a large bowl, mix together the meat, bread crumbs, cheese, onion, garlic, parsley, salt, and 8 eggs until the eggs are well incorporated. If the mixture seems dry and not very soft, add 1 or 2 more eggs, as necessary. With your hands, make a well in the middle of the meat 3 inches in diameter and 2 inches deep. Fill the well with ⅓ cup olive oil.

3. Generously grease your palms and fingers with the oil from the well. Shape the mixture into medium-size ovals—the size of extra-large eggs—coating the meat with the oil from your hands. When the oil in the well has been used, refill the well and repeat until all the meat mixture is used. Cook the meatballs according to the directions in the recipe you are making.

YIELD VARIATIONS

To make ½ pound of meat or 5 meatballs, halve the recipe for 1 pound meat. To make 1¼ pounds of meat or 12 meatballs, use the recipe for 1 pound meat, but increase the meat by ¼ pound, add 4 eggs instead of 3, and use a scant ½ cup bread crumbs. Add a pinch more of herbs, spices, and cheese. To make 1½ pounds of meat or 14 meatballs, use 5 eggs, ½ cup bread crumbs, ½ cup grated cheese, 2 cloves garlic, and an extra tablespoon parsley.

Secrets of Success

Meatballs must be mixed and formed at the last minute. Do not leave them raw in the refrigerator, or the egg will congeal in the meat and render the meatballs tough when cooked. Overmixing will also produce tough meatballs. The more eggs you add, the softer the meatballs. If you overdo it, and the meatball mixture is too eggy, add an extra heaping tablespoon each of bread crumbs and cheese.

Qualche Cosa di Mangiare

A Little

Something to

Munch On

For a true Sicilian, antipasto doesn't exist. When I was growing up, there was always what I would call back-up food in the house—assorted cold cuts, cheeses, roasted peppers, pickled eggplant, olives, anchovies, a loaf of fresh bread. When friends stopped by, some or all of it was automatically set out for a snack. When we ate dinner, these little treats were not removed from the table until we were ready to eat dessert, and whatever was left over became part of the next meal or another snack. Therefore, to "serve an antipasto" sounds unnatural to my ears, and what others consider antipasto is just a way of life in the Sicilian household.

The first time I ever heard the word *antipasto*—literally, "before the meal"—was in a restaurant. It was never used in our home. So in this chapter I am calling those dishes that begin a meal *qualche cosa di mangiare* (a little something to munch on). Recipes include snacks such as Anchovy Fritters and favorite small dishes like Fried Cheese and Olive Salad, all of which we enjoy at all times of the day.

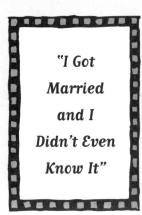

"I Got Married and I Didn't Even Know It"

W HILE WE WERE stuffing peppers, Grandma said in amazement, "Do you know, Fren-zee, even if you were engaged in the 1920s, you couldn't sit down next to a man. You couldn't even hold his hand the day before the wedding."

"That's nuts!" I shouted.

"That's the way it was, and I was married, too!" She made a fist and slammed it on the table. "I didn't even know I was married!"

"Are you totally crazy! How can you get married and not know. These things happen only in the movies." I threw my hands in the air.

"The truth!" Grandma crossed her arms in front of her heart. "It was July 31, 1926, and we went to City Hall just to get a marriage license. The teller asked us for three dollars, helped Natale and me fill out some forms, then told us to go upstairs to the third floor. When we arrived, a justice of the peace said a few words to us, we said yes, and he said we were husband and wife."

"You still didn't get it?" I questioned more intensely.

"No, we still thought this was part of getting the license. And remember, Turidru, my brother-in-law, hated Natale and was hoping to break us up. In those days, I didn't speak or read English. You're in a foreign country and someone puts a few papers in front of you to sign . . . who would suspect? In Sicily, a wedding was in a church with a priest. A few days passed, and my boss at the factory came to me and said, 'Well, Josie, did you go to City Hall and get the license?'

"I said yes, do you want to see it? When my boss read the paper, he got so excited that he began shouting, 'You are husband and wife! This is no license! This is a marriage certificate. If your husband dies, you are the benefactor.'

"I said noooooo! I'm getting married in September. When we showed the papers to Turidru, war broke out! He refused to let Nata *assitata a mia* [sit next to me] even though we were married."

I made a face, suggesting this was ridiculous.

"The truth, Fren-zee. You think I'm lying. If accidentally Natale's chair came near mine when the family was talking, Turidru would say, 'Pipina [my grandma's nickname], get me some espresso in the kitchen.' When I returned, Turidru would be sitting in my chair so I wouldn't be near Natale. The things that went on . . . unbelievable!"

"Why didn't you go with your husband?"

"I was afraid. I thought Turidru would never let me back into the house. Turidru said, 'If you go out, you never come back! The marriage isn't recognized, because it was not in a Catholic church.' He told Natale, 'You say she's your wife, take her and get out!' Natale used to get so mad!" She waved her hand in front of her face. "'That's right—she is my wife and anytime I want, I can take her,' but he never did. It would have been a *disgrazia* [disgrace]! When Turidru saw the Certificate of Marriage— the screaming, the cursing!"

"I bet he had a stroke?" I bounced up and down in my chair.

"And how. 'You did it on purpose!' he screamed. We did it by accident . . . it was the truth. But for spite, he wouldn't even let me talk to Natale until we got married in a church. Turidru told me that even if I saw Natale on the street, I couldn't talk to him. If I did, the wedding was off. He wished me bad luck. He said, 'You want this man, then you get your license and marry him in August and deserve the miserable life you're going to have.' In Sicily, no one got married in August. My mother always said, *'La zita Agostina non si gode la trazzina!'* [The bride who marries in August will have a miserable life of hard luck!] But I'm not stupid. I waited until July 30, when Turidru had to go into the hospital. I planned everything down to the day. On July 31, I went down for my license, and the luck reversed on him. Instead of getting a license, I got married—so I got him first!

"One time Grandpa was waiting for me after work," Grandma informed me seriously. "That day, Turidru asked his friend to spy on me. He told Turidru that a man wearing a gray suit was waiting in front of the factory, and when I came out, we talked. When I went home, Turidru started to beat me with a rope he made into a *trezza* [a braid]. He told my sister, 'I'm going to kill your sister, she *fare i corne*' [she made horns with a man]. He was like a devil—screaming! cursing! 'Natale is American, you can't marry him!'"

"Grandpa was born in Sicily! Right next to you!" I responded, shocked.

"Turidru said Natale had been in America too long. He wanted me to marry a man from my hometown. He'd yell: 'Go home to your father! Let him marry you! I want no responsibility for you!'"

"You were good enough to cook, clean, and pay rent! Why I would have . . ."

"That's all right, Fren-zee, he who laughs last, laughs best. The story isn't over.

"I tricked my brother-in-law, Fren-zee! After grandpa and I were caught seeing each other, I devised a scheme. I told my boss I would only accept calls from a man who gave a certain password. If I didn't hear the password, I refused the call. Twice Turidru had his friend call and impersonate Grandpa. But when I didn't hear the password, I said, 'Natale, I can't talk to you. It's forbidden, so don't call here anymore.'

"Turidru was so happy that I passed the test, he started to treat me better. At the wedding reception, he came over to tell me something. 'Pipina, I have a confession to make. You know the two times you refused to speak to your husband at the factory . . . well, I had someone imitate him, and I was very proud that both times you refused. I arranged the whole thing, because I was trying to call off the wedding, but you passed every test.'

"I laughed in Turidru's face, Fren-zee, and I *fare i corne* [made horns] at him with my hands. I said, '*pigare tu per fissa!* [I took you for a fool!] Ha, ha! *Fare i corne a tu!* I took you for an idiot. You really think you're smarter than me. Never! Natale and I had a password. When your friend called, he didn't give me the password. I knew you were testing me! My boss was in on the whole thing, I spoke to Natale every day. *Fissa ca si!* [Fool that you are!]'

"Turidru's eyes bulged, his face turned beet red, and he became hysterical at the wedding. He kept screaming, '*Tu pigare a me per fissa! Tu pigare a me per fissa!*' [You took me for a fool!] Then he passed out from the attack. He thought he was smart, Fren-zee! He thought he was a fox! But I outfoxed him and I told him right to his face. He was not going to win. If a woman uses her brain, she can always outfox the man! Remember well what Grandma teaches you!" ❧

Great-uncle Turidru and his wife, Grandma's sister Vitina, in New York's Little Italy, 1924.

Peparoli con Sarde Salate e Melanzane

PEPPERS WITH SALTED SARDINES AND EGGPLANT

In Little Italy, this homemade snack is usually made once a year, in the summer, and then eaten in the winter, especially on holidays. In Sicily, every household usually has one jar aging while another one is being served to unexpected guests or eaten as a late-night snack. Note that Sicilian salami is a small, hard salami eaten with bread like pepperoni or used for pickling, since it doesn't fall apart easily. It is found at any Italian cheese shop. Serve the peppers with cheese, olives, bread, and a full-bodied red wine.

2½ pounds long, light green, sweet Italian peppers (each about 4 inches long)

1 pound salted sardines *(sarde salate)*, filleted (page 27),

    or anchovies in olive oil, drained

1 head garlic, separated into cloves, unpeeled

4 cups white wine vinegar

2 eggplants, ¾ pound each, peeled, and cut into ¼-inch-thick rounds

3 large celery stalks, cut into 1-inch pieces

1 bottle (3½ ounces) capers, drained

1-pound piece hard Sicilian salami or any hard dried sausage,

    cut into ¼-inch-thick slices

6 cups extra-virgin olive oil, or as needed

Secrets of Success

To keep this mixture fresh, never stick your fingers into the jar, or the peppers will mold.

1. Cut away the stem from each pepper. Cut a hole in the top and remove all the seeds, leaving the pepper in one piece. Place 1 sardine or 5 anchovies inside each pepper. With the flat side of a knife blade, gently crush the garlic cloves; do not remove the skin. Set aside.

(CONTINUED)

2. In a medium-size pot, bring the vinegar to a rolling boil. In batches, drop in the eggplant slices and cook for about 3 seconds. With a slotted spoon, remove and transfer to a dish.

3. Sterilize a 1-gallon glass jar with a glass-topped rubber stopper. Cover the bottom of the hot jar with the eggplant slices. Top with a few slices of salami, a layer of stuffed peppers, a handful of celery pieces, and 1 teaspoon of the capers. End with 1 clove of the crushed garlic. Repeat the layering until all the ingredients are used up. Pour enough olive oil into the jar to cover all the ingredients and to reach to within 1 inch of the rim. Secure the stopper in the top of the jar. Label the jar with today's date and store it in a cool place for 2 months, or until the peppers are nicely pickled, before eating.

SALTED SARDINES OR SALTED ANCHOVIES WITH VINEGAR, GARLIC, AND OLIVE OIL

Sarde salate and *aliccie salate* are Sicilian specialties found in Palermo's *vucciria*, the central market square that stands where the original Arab marketplace once stood. Good *sarde salate* (salted sardines) should taste like beautiful white anchovies, or *aliccie salate*, which are more difficult to clean due to their tiny size. Both *aliccie salate* and *sarde salate* can be found at most Little Italy food shops. Marinated, the salted sardines run about eight dollars a pound and the salted anchovies about twenty dollars a pound. Ironically, years ago, *sarde salate* were twice the price of the anchovies, but now the costs are reversed since sardines are abundant. Serve as a side dish with roasted meats or sandwiches, provolone, and a full-bodied wine.

6 salted sardines *(sarde salate)* or 10 salted anchovies *(aliccie salate)*

2 cloves garlic, cut into small dice

¼ teaspoon dried oregano, sticks removed, crushed until powdery

2 tablespoons red wine vinegar, or to taste

3 tablespoons extra-virgin olive oil

1. To fillet the sardines or anchovies: With a small knife, scrape off the crusted salt and fish scales. Cut off the tails and heads and discard. Cut a slit along the length of each fish; remove the main bone and discard. Slice in half lengthwise, to separate the fillets.

2. In a small bowl, combine the sardines or anchovies, garlic, oregano, vinegar, and olive oil. Toss gently. Cover and marinate in the refrigerator for at least 3 hours or preferably overnight. Arrange the sardines or anchovies on a platter and serve.

Secrets of Success

Make sure the *sarde salate* and *aliccie salate* are soft and the salt in which they are packed is white. If the sardines or anchovies feel tough and dry, or the salt has turned brown, the fish are old and should be discarded. If there is too much salt on the fish, rinse them in a small bowl of vinegar and pat dry.

Insalata di Olive
OLIVE SALAD WITH FRESH VEGETABLES

This olive salad can be made with store-bought or home-cured olives and should be marinated for at least a full day to allow time for all the ingredients to release their flavors. Olives are served with almost every Sicilian meal, at picnics, and as a light dinner with cheese, crusty bread, hard-cooked eggs, and a hearty red wine.

1 pound Sicilian green olives

½ pound Sicilian black olives

1 small sweet red onion, very thinly sliced, soaked in cold water for 15 minutes, drained, and patted dry

1½ celery stalks, cut on the diagonal into 1-inch-thick slices

1 large red sweet pepper, cut into large dice, or 1 jar (8 ounces) roasted red peppers, drained and cut lengthwise into narrow strips

4 raw small cauliflower and/or broccoli florets, each floret quartered

6 cloves garlic, cut into small dice

⅓ cup red or white wine vinegar

½ cup extra-virgin olive oil

1 teaspoon dried oregano, sticks removed, crushed until powdery

Salt and red pepper flakes, to taste

1. The night before, in a bowl, combine all of the ingredients. Adjust the vinegar, olive oil, and seasonings to taste. Cover and refrigerate for 1 day. Bring to room temperature before serving.

Secrets of Success

If the vinegar is too sharp, don't add more oil. Adjust its flavor by adding a few tablespoons of cold water to dilute its strength, a practice popular in Sicily where the vinegar is often extremely strong.

Grandma Rejects a Suitor

BEFORE MY grandma Josephina was married, she and her sister Vitina worked in a clothing factory on the Bowery. The foreman of the factory was mad about my grandma, and as a consequence did both girls favors, giving them the easier jobs, better lighting, free sodas, and other food privileges no other workers ever had—all in the hope of wooing Grandma. In the summer, when the factory was a steambath, he even provided them with a fan. But Grandma remained cool and was unswayed by his courting. Nothing the foreman did could buy her affection, and he became so upset with her that he took the fan away on the hottest day of the year, in August, gave the sisters the worst jobs to do, and started to abuse them verbally. The sisters quit their jobs and found work elsewhere.

Grandma's moral: "Fren-zee, it's a good thing I didn't marry him. Better to know the devil before the wedding than to regret a mistake for a lifetime." 🐚

Grandma Josephina at Playland in upstate New York, 1936.

Capunatina
EGGPLANT APPETIZER

🐟 Ideal for a holiday gathering, this recipe can be prepared several days in advance.

Extra-virgin olive oil

3 eggplants (about 3 pounds), unpeeled, cubed

2 large yellow onions, cut into medium dice

4 celery stalks, coarsely chopped

1 can (7 ounces) tomato paste

1⅓ cups red wine vinegar

6 tablespoons sugar

1 teaspoon salt, or to taste

4 fresh basil leaves

1 cup green olives stuffed with pimientos, coarsely chopped

½ cup drained capers

Secrets of Success

Prepare the dish
2 days before serving
to allow time for
the eggplant to drain
off excess oil
and to develop its full
flavors.

1. In a large frying pan, heat ⅓ cup olive oil over medium heat. Add eggplant and cook, adding more oil if necessary, until lightly browned on all sides and tender, about 15 minutes. Transfer eggplant to a large colander set over a dish. Cover and store in the refrigerator overnight.

2. The next day, using the same frying pan, heat 4 tablespoons olive oil over medium heat. Add the onions and celery and sauté until golden, about 5 minutes. Add the tomato paste, vinegar, sugar, salt, and basil. Reduce the heat to low and simmer for 10 minutes. Add the olives and capers and simmer for another 10 minutes. Stir in the eggplant and simmer until the eggplant is heated through and the flavors are blended, about 15 minutes longer.

3. Remove from heat, cool, and store in sterilized jars in the refrigerator. Appetizer will stay fresh for up to 2 weeks.

Cosi Fatte di Patate
POTATO PANCAKES

*Makes 12
potato pancakes;
serves 6*

In Sicily during World War I, potatoes rivaled meat in price and availability. Grandma remembers many times during rationing when a potato was substituted for beef or pork in tomato sauce. Soon, however, potatoes became so scarce only the wealthy could afford them.

At the turn of the century, this recipe was called *cosi fatte di patate* (things made of potatoes). Sicilians later renamed it *cazzilli*, and today Americans call these little fried pancakes potato croquettes. The only way to eat them is hot—right out of the pan.

Salt

2 pounds white or red new potatoes (5 or 6 potatoes), peeled

2 or 3 large eggs

½ cup unseasoned freshly made bread crumbs (page 14)

½ cup grated *cacio-cavallo, incanestrato,* or romano cheese

1 medium-small yellow onion, cut into small dice

6 fresh Italian parsley sprigs, coarsely chopped

4 cloves garlic, cut into small dice

Extra-virgin olive oil

1. Half-fill a large pot with salted water and bring to a boil. Add the potatoes and cook until fork tender, about 25 minutes. Drain.

2. Transfer potatoes to a large bowl and mash well. Add 2 eggs, the bread crumbs, cheese, onion, parsley, garlic, and ¼ teaspoon salt. If the mixture feels dry, add 1 more egg. Mix gently with your hands and shape into 12 ovals each about 1 inch wide and 3 inches long.

3. Generously oil a medium-size frying pan with olive oil. Cook pancakes over medium heat until golden brown, about 3 minutes on each side. Drain on a paper towel–lined platter. Serve immediately.

"**Change Your Hair for These Little Things**"

IN THE EARLY 1900s, when Grandma was a child in Ciminna, an ordinary, lonely man who never married and wore shabby clothes tried to make a few extra lire by gathering hair. No one knew his name and no one seemed to know exactly where he lived, but it was said he resided somewhere in the outskirts of town. As he walked the streets, a large basket in his hands, his strident voice cried out, "*Canciari i capelli per i cerini.* [Change your hair for these little things.]" In his handmade straw basket were tangled rubber bands, cords used to make belts, hairpins, matches, and spools of colored cotton.

Grandma told me, "All the children, my mother, sisters . . . when we had a bagful of hair, we'd give it to him. Then we would bargain. Two boxes of matches, hairpins, whatever he had. We'd give him our hair. He'd give us these little things."

"You mean you had to cut off your hair for matches?" I asked, a bit stunned.

"What cut? Fren-zee, you don't understand when I talk. After we combed our hair at night, we never threw the hair away. We saved it in a bag. Sometimes we made it into a big ball."

"But what did he do with it?"

"Wigs . . . eyelashes . . . fake mustaches . . . *per i artisti* [for actors and actresses]. At that time, Sicilian hair was used for the most expensive wigs in the world. After we sold him our hair, we ran to the farm with our matches, where my father, Michele, was waiting for us to cut off the tops of the wheat and make a fire in the earth with some branches from the trees. We'd roast the wheat and eat it. Fren-zee! Like honey . . . delicious . . . right out of its skin!"

"Was it like popcorn? Did you put salt on it?"

She grimaced. "Neah! Popcorn is nothing!" She threw her hands down in disgust. "What salt—in the middle of the farm! You don't need salt. When something is fresh and delicious right from the earth, it's so sweet, you don't need to add anything." Her fingers closed together and she raised her hand to her mouth and blew a loud kiss. 🐌

Grano Brustolito
ROASTED WHEAT

🔥 Fresh wheat can be bought at a farm that makes flour. In Sicily it's abundant, but here you might have to do some hunting. For a touch of tradition, make a small fire with twigs in your outdoor grill or fireplace and roast the wheat for an evening snack.

4 wheat stalks

Salt, to taste (optional)

1. Prepare a fire in a grill or turn the gas jet on your stove top to high. Cut off the wheat stalks 1 foot from the top section of wheat kernels.

2. Holding 1 wheat stalk in your hand, roast the section with the kernels over the fire or gas jet, turning both sides to the flame, until the skins of the kernels turn black and begin to blister, revealing the wheat. Repeat with the remaining 3 stalks.

3. Rub the skins off and eat the hot roasted kernels immediately. Sprinkle with salt, if desired.

FRIED CHEESE

📖 Here are two classic recipes for fried cheese. The first, flavored with herbs, is often eaten as a quick snack. Many cooks have the mistaken notion that only *cacio-cavallo* is traditionally used for this dish. Actually, any hard cheese in the Sicilian household is fried. The second recipe comes from Louie Di Palo of Di Palo's in Little Italy. It is a Sicilian sweet breakfast treat topped with cinnamon and sugar that his grandmother made in Sicily with *ricottone,* a dried ricotta used for frying. Look for *ricottone* at select Italian dairy stores.

Fried Cheese with Herbs

1 tablespoon extra-virgin olive oil

1 pound *cacio-cavallo, incanestrato,* provolone or *ricotta salata* cheese
    cut into 4 slices each ⅓ inch thick

3 large cloves garlic, cut into small dice (optional)

Freshly ground black pepper, to taste (optional)

Dried oregano, sticks removed, crushed until powdery, to taste (optional)

Red wine vinegar, to taste (optional)

1 loaf Sicilian bread, warmed and cut into 2-inch-thick slices (optional)

Fried Cheese with Sugar and Cinnamon

1 cup all-purpose flour

2 teaspoons sugar

2 teaspoons ground cinnamon

1 large egg

2 tablespoons milk

Extra-virgin olive oil

1 pound *ricottone* cheese, cut into 4 rounds each ½ inch thick,
    then each round cut in half

Confectioners' sugar

1. To make fried cheese with herbs: In a medium-size frying pan, heat the olive oil over medium heat. Add the cheese, cover, and cook, turning once, until the slices are a crusty golden brown, about 3 minutes on each side. Transfer to a platter and sprinkle with the garlic, pepper, oregano, and vinegar. Alternatively, eat the cheese spread on heated bread. Serve immediately.

2. To make fried cheese with sugar and cinnamon: In a bowl, combine the flour, sugar, and ½ teaspoon of the cinnamon. In a separate bowl, beat together the egg and milk. Dip the ricotta slices first into the egg bath, and then coat with the flour mixture. Very lightly oil a medium-size frying pan and place over medium heat. When hot, add the ricotta slices and cook, turning once, until golden, about 2 minutes on each side. Transfer to a platter and sprinkle with confectioners' sugar and the remaining cinnamon. Serve immediately.

Olive Fritti
FRIED BLACK OLIVES WITH ONIONS

🌿 A typical evening snack, these warm, plump olives are often accompanied with heated bread and large chunks of provolone, *caciocavallo*, or *ricotta salata* and some roasted peppers. The olives also make an excellent appetizer for a large holiday meal and can be served alongside a platter of cold cuts. They should be cooked right before the guests arrive.

1 tablespoon extra-virgin olive oil

1 yellow onion, thickly sliced

1½ pounds small Sicilian black olives

5 cloves garlic, lightly crushed

½ teaspoon dried oregano, sticks removed, crushed until powdery

1 teaspoon red pepper flakes

½ cup red wine vinegar (optional)

1. In a large frying pan, heat the olive oil over medium heat. Add the onion and sauté until golden, about 10 minutes. Add the olives, garlic, oregano, and red pepper flakes. Cook, shaking the pan occasionally, until the olives plump up, about 3 minutes.

2. Add the vinegar, if using, and continue to simmer until the liquid is reduced by two-thirds. Transfer the olives to a platter and serve hot.

Fanfarichi
ANCHOVY FRITTERS

🐟 I'm often asked about this recipe in my cooking classes, since my students always remember their grandmothers making it for them when they were children. It goes together easily, and if you're in a hurry, you can buy ready-made dough and just knead the anchovies into it.

1 pound homemade or purchased bread dough (page 67)
1 can (2 ounces) anchovy fillets in olive oil, drained and chopped
Extra-virgin olive oil

1. Prepare the dough as directed through Step 3, but allow it to rise a second time on a lightly floured surface, not in the bread pans. Flatten it slightly, sprinkle the anchovies over the top, and knead them into the dough for about 3 minutes. (Do not overknead.) Then roll out the dough ¼ inch thick. Cut into 3-inch squares.

2. In a medium-size frying pan, pour in oil to a depth of ½ inch and heat to 350°F. Add the dough squares, a few at a time, and fry, turning once, until golden on both sides, about 2 minutes total. Transfer to a paper towel-lined platter to drain briefly and serve immediately.

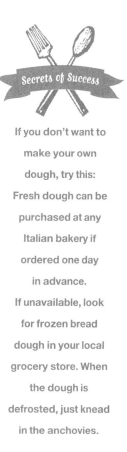

Secrets of Success

If you don't want to make your own dough, try this: Fresh dough can be purchased at any Italian bakery if ordered one day in advance. If unavailable, look for frozen bread dough in your local grocery store. When the dough is defrosted, just knead in the anchovies.

Pane con Olio
HOT BREAD DRIZZLED WITH OLIVE OIL

The first time I was in Grandma's hometown of Ciminna, her niece Rosina served this to me, saying, "I know I have something you have never tasted in America." I shocked her when I told her that both my dad and my grandma had always made this early morning treat for me. I still remember Dad getting up at six o'clock to buy bread right out of the oven of the nearby Italian bakery so he could make this simple dish. We all love it so much that we often reheat fresh bread in the afternoon just so that we can serve it with a light meal. There are many variations on this recipe, two of which I have included, but each region tops the bread with whatever local ingredients are available.

1 loaf Sicilian bread with a good crust, homemade (page 67) or purchased

Extra-virgin olive oil

Salt and freshly ground black pepper, to taste

1. Preheat an oven to 350°F. Slice the bread in half lengthwise and pour a generous amount of olive oil over the cut surface of each half. Sprinkle generously with salt and pepper. Transfer the bread halves to a baking sheet.

2. Place in the oven until very hot, about 10 minutes. Do not allow the halves to toast. Cut into thick slices and eat immediately.

Be as creative as you like. To make this dish more of a meal, prepare as directed and top with favorite cheeses, grilled vegetables, and leftover meats.

CHEESE VARIATION

Prepare as directed. After drizzling with oil, top with grated *incanestrato* cheese or very thin slices of *cacio-cavallo* or provolone cheese. A combination of 2 cheeses is also common, one grated and the other thinly sliced.

SARDE SALATE VARIATION

Prepare as directed, but omit the salt. After drizzling with oil, top with grated provolone cheese and then 3 salted sardines (sarde salate), filleted (page 27) and cut into bite-size pieces. Proceed as directed.

Great-aunt Mica's daughter, Rosina. She was famous in Ciminna for her marvelous breads. They remain the best I have ever tasted.

BRODO E OVA

The Sicilian cook usually begins any large meal with soup, and if there is an antipasto in our heritage, soup is it. Grandma says that chicken soup is served first because it prepares the palate and warms the stomach for the rest of the meal. The poor commonly made their chicken soup with just a few parts— the wings, gizzards, neck—and reserved the whole chicken for the main course. Grandma has been fortunate always to be able to use the whole bird in the soup.

Sicilian soups differ from other Italian soups in that they are not made with chicken or beef broth. Water constitutes the base of a soup, and it is made flavorful by a gentle, slow cooking that allows the flavors of the ingredients to reveal themselves. Some Sicilian soups that are made with vegetables, like *la frittedra*, which combines fava beans and peas, are heavier than the classic chicken soup. They are usually followed by a meat dish such as fried veal cutlets, grilled T-bone steaks, or roasted sausages. A meal like that makes you feel *saziata*—that is, your stomach feels happy and full.

This chapter also contains five egg dishes, including Potato and Onion Egg Pie. Each can accompany a main dish or be served alone.

The Legend of Chickens that Turn into Gold

WE WERE MAKING chicken soup, and as usual, Grandma was driving me crazy with her tales about *la fortunata* [luck].

"To think we're eating chicken, and if you found them, like my neighbor Vincenzo did in Sicily, and had *la fortunata*, you'd be a millionaire," Grandma exclaimed.

"Let's not start with this nonsense again about the *pupo che ballava* [the dancing doll on the mountain— see page 205] disappearing and turning into gold," I replied, frustration rippling through my voice.

"Forget the dolls! *Galline* [chickens]—that's where the big money was!"

"You . . . are . . . nuts!" I yelled out. "Chickens don't turn into gold. This is a legend . . . you of all people! . . . who have helped women give birth, cut up pigs and sheep . . . why, when the woman's husband died next door, she called you instead of an ambulance! And you honestly believe . . ."

Testily, "Were you there . . . that you're so excited and screaming?"

"I know it didn't happen because I have a brain in my head. Your darling neighbor did something illegal and lied. Simple!" I slammed my fist down.

"How could you say that about such a nice man . . . *poooor* . . . like a beggar all his life—until he saw the chickens in his basement."

"Were there any banks robbed around that time?" I asked, searching for clues. "Too obvious. He must have been involved in the crime years earlier . . . pretended to be poor . . . then told this story *di pazzo* [of craziness]."

"Fren-zee! Who are you? Shirl-lock-a [Sherlock Holmes]? One day Vincenzo walked into his basement, he saw chickens and he had no chickens, so he knew it was a vision. He had to have the courage to confront the chickens."

"The courage to confront chickens! Dear God!" I put my head down on the table and covered my ears.

"You laugh, but the chickens represent the devil, so he had to have the courage to confront them and 'the luck' was his. He said nothing to no one, because if you do, you break the spell. He did what others didn't. He fulfilled the legend and didn't run away! Instead, he picked up a stone and threw it at the chickens to kill them. In a minute, the chickens disappeared and in their place were the gold bars. He became a *milionario* overnight. After a few months, he opened a store to sell fabrics, became a very well-respected man in Ciminna, and lived a wonderful life.

"If you go to Sicily and you see a chicken where there isn't supposed to be one, don't tell anyone," her fingers crossed her lips as if to zip them shut. "*State pippa* [keep your mouth shut]. Just quietly get a rock and throw it at the animal, and if it turns into bricks of gold, take the gold, put it in your suitcase and bring it back home."

I spoke so fast, I could barely pronounce the words. "Grandma, if I go to Sicily and start throwing rocks at chickens to see if they turn into gold, they'll put me in Bellevue with all the other nuts in New York!" My heart was palpitating from aggravation.

"In America—but that's the advantage of living in Sicily," she replied, her face and neck leaning over me like a lamppost. "Over there we understand these things." 🐚

Brodo di Gallina
CHICKEN SOUP WITH FRESH VEGETABLES

Chicken soup is served in Sicilian households all year long, even in the heat of the summer. The soup was a sign of wealth in Sicily in the 1900s, so it is always the first course of every holiday and Sunday dinner. When Dad eats chicken soup he wants chunks of fresh vegetables in it. Other family members insist on whole pieces of chicken served on the side. Grandma and I solved the problem by reserving a few chicken parts and presenting a separate platter of chicken and vegetables next to the soup. That way everyone is happy.

1 chicken, 3 pounds, with the liver, gizzard, heart, and neck

1 large yellow onion, sliced

2 large celery stalks, cut in half lengthwise

2 large carrots, peeled and cut in half lengthwise

2 large, ripe tomatoes, quartered

1 small white turnip, peeled and cut in half

10 fresh Italian parsley sprigs, including long stems

5 quarts (20 cups) cold water

1 teaspoon salt, or to taste

1 pound soup pasta such as *bracciletti* (little bracelets), alphabet pasta, or capellini

Provolone, *incanestrato, pepato, cacio-cavallo,* or romano cheese

Secrets of Success

To obtain a very special flavor, cook the pasta right in the broth.

1. In an 8-quart pot, combine the whole chicken, liver, gizzard, heart, neck, onion, celery, carrots, tomatoes, turnip, parsley, water, and salt. Bring to a boil over high heat. Reduce the heat to very low, partially cover the pot, and simmer for 2 hours. After 2 hours, taste the soup, and adjust the salt if necessary. Continue simmering the soup for another 30 to 60 minutes for a total of 2½ to 3 hours, or until the flavors are well blended. Also, check that the water isn't evaporating too quickly. If it is, add 1 or 2 glasses water, or as needed to keep the ingredients covered and adjust the seasonings.

2. Pierce the chicken with a fork to check its tenderness. When it easily falls from the bone, it is done. Once the soup is cooked, transfer the chicken to a platter and set aside. Strain the soup into another 8-quart pot. Transfer all the vegetables to a platter, and cut them into bite-size pieces. Transfer the gizzard, neck, liver, and heart to a plate. Cover both dishes to keep them warm.

3. Bring the strained soup to a boil over high heat. Add the pasta, reduce the heat to medium, and cook until the pasta is tender. (The timing will depend on the type of pasta you use.) Meanwhile, cut up the chicken and remove and discard the skin and bones. Break up the chicken meat into bite-size pieces, and return the pieces to the soup. Simmer until the chicken is hot, about 5 minutes.

4. Ladle the soup into a tureen. Serve with grated cheese, passing a mini hand grater at the table. Accompany with the platter of vegetables and chicken innards.

Brodo di Lenticchie
LENTIL SOUP WITH MACARONI

🖙 Lentil soup is usually made in the winter because it is a hearty dish. A pasta such as *tubettini* or *ditali* (little tubes) is often added once the soup is done, which makes it a one-dish meal that satisfies any good eater.

Since each person prefers a different consistency for his or her soup, I have given you a choice of how long to simmer this one. I always cook the soup for 6 hours because I like the lentils to be creamy, but if you prefer them to have more of a bite, simmer them 4 or 5 hours.

½ pound pancetta or bacon, thickly sliced and cut into 1-inch pieces

1 large yellow onion, sliced

3 carrots, peeled and cut into ¼-inch-thick slices

2 celery stalks, cut into ½-inch-thick slices

4 quarts (16 cups) cold water

1 pound (about 2¼ cups) dried lentils, rinsed thoroughly and
    drained in a colander

4 fresh Italian parsley sprigs, coarsely chopped

Scant 1 teaspoon salt, or to taste

Freshly ground black pepper, to taste (optional)

1 pound *tubettini* or *ditali,* cooked and drained (optional)

Extra-virgin olive oil

Grated romano, *incanestrato,* provolone, or *cacio-cavallo* cheese

1. In a 6-quart pot, sauté the pancetta or bacon, onion, carrots, and celery over medium heat until the pancetta is crisp, about 5 minutes. Add the water, lentils, parsley, salt, and the pepper, if using. Bring the soup to a boil over high heat. Reduce the heat to very, very low, partially cover the pot, and simmer very gently for 4 to 6 hours, depending on the desired consistency. Stir the soup every 30 minutes and adjust all the seasonings every hour, or as necessary. Check that the water isn't evaporating too quickly. If it is, add 1 or 2 glasses water, or as needed, and adjust all the seasonings.

2. Once the soup is ready, stir in the cooked pasta, if using, and heat through. Ladle into individual bowls. Drizzle with olive oil, top with fresh grindings of pepper, if desired, and sprinkle generously with grated cheese.

STORAGE

Before adding the pasta, ladle into 1½-quart containers and freeze for up to 3 months. To serve, thaw the soup, reheat gently, and add freshly cooked pasta. Each 1½-quart container serves 4.

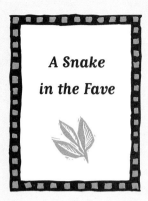

A Snake in the Fave

"How did you harvest *fave?*" I asked Grandma one day as we made *la frittedra*.

"On the farm in the summer, we used to make a big pile of *fave* with their large stalks and, after about two weeks, they dried and we put them in *l'aria* [a barren piece of earth reserved for extracting beans or wheat kernels]. Then my father would take two *vestii* [mules], hold them by the reins, and walk slowly on top of the *paglia* [stalks]. He would walk around and around in circles for hours until all the stalks were broken and the beans were removed. Finally, we'd put the beans in sacks and cart them home. We used to harvest about a thousand pounds or more of *fave.*"

Grandma thought for a minute. "*Fave* were also used for horse feed, you know. One day it started to rain. I was ten years old, and my father told my brother, Vito, and me to run and turn the *fave* so they wouldn't get soaked with water and be ruined. I had a *favuscia* [scythe] in my hand and was turning a bundle of stalks when a large snake jumped up in the air. I had cut it in two. The snake was still alive! Jumping! Then it crawled to the brook. Vito and I began screaming, and we ran away! And that was the last time I ever turned the *fave.*" She clapped her hands together loudly. 🐚

La Frittedra
FAVA BEAN AND PEA SOUP

🐟 Almost every recipe for *la frittedra* includes artichokes as a traditional ingredient. But artichokes are not always available in Sicily, and if you ask around the island, you will find that *la frittedra* is made more often without artichokes than with them. If you have artichokes, you can put them in the soup; if not, there is not a great difference in the taste. The artichokes will fall apart in the liquid, and the soup will turn a murky green.

3 pounds fava beans

3 tablespoons extra-virgin olive oil

1 small yellow onion, thinly sliced

1 pound fresh sweet peas, shelled, or 1 cup frozen or drained,
canned sweet peas

6 fresh basil leaves

½ teaspoon salt, or to taste

Grated *pepato*, provolone, or *cacio-cavallo* cheese

1. First, shell the fava beans: Break each pod open, then, using your fingers, peel away the thin skin covering each bean.

2. In a medium-size saucepan, heat the olive oil over medium heat. Add the onion and sauté until golden, about 3 minutes. Add the fava beans, peas, basil, and salt. Reduce the heat to very low, cover, and simmer until the favas and peas have released some juice, about 15 minutes.

(CONTINUED)

3. Add just enough water to cover the beans and peas, raise the heat to high, and bring to a boil. Reduce the heat to very low, partially cover the pot, and simmer until the favas are completely dissolved and the soup is reduced to the consistency of medium-thick split-pea soup, about 2 hours. Stir the soup every 20 minutes, and adjust the seasonings of basil and salt as necessary. If the soup becomes too thick after 1 hour, add an additional cup or so of water, or as needed.

4. Ladle the soup into individual bowls and sprinkle generously with grated cheese.

ARTICHOKE VARIATION

Add 2 small artichokes, cleaned and quartered (page 207), with the fava beans. Prepare as directed.

My great-uncle Mike (left) with his cousin Dominick in Chicago in the 1920s. When Mike visited New York, my grandma would always make him this soup, which was one of his favorites.

Brodo di Pisedri
PEA SOUP

This soup was taught to my father by his mother, Ciccina. To her, the longer the peas cooked, the better they tasted. Don't worry, as this is not a soup one needs to stand over. Stirring occasionally and checking the level of water is all the attention it needs.

3 tablespoons extra-virgin olive oil

1 large yellow onion, sliced

3 carrots, peeled, sliced ¼ inch thick, and each slice quartered

2 celery stalks, cut into ½-inch-thick slices

4 quarts (16 cups) cold water

1 pound dried green split peas, rinsed thoroughly and drained in a colander

1 pound ham bone with some ham on it

¾ pound smoked ham steak, ½ inch thick, cut into small dice

4 pancetta or bacon strips, cut into 1-inch pieces

¾ teaspoon salt, or to taste

Grated provolone, *ricotta salata, pepato,* or *cacio-cavallo* cheese

Freshly ground black pepper, to taste (optional)

Secrets of Success

For the best-tasting pea soup, simmer for 8 hours on the lowest heat possible.

1. In a large pot, combine the olive oil, onion, carrots, and celery over medium-high heat. Sauté until the onions are lightly browned, about 5 minutes. Add the water, peas, ham bone, diced ham, pancetta or bacon, and salt. Raise the heat to high and bring the soup to a boil. Then reduce the heat to very low, partially cover the pot, and simmer for 5 to 8 hours. Once every hour, stir the soup, then taste and adjust all the seasonings. Also, check the thickness of the soup periodically to make sure it's not thickening too quickly. You will need to add 1 or 2 glasses of water 2 or 3 times during the simmering of the soup.

2. Ladle the soup into individual bowls and sprinkle generously with grated cheese. Top with freshly ground black pepper, if using.

Frittata di Sparagi
ASPARAGUS EGG PIE WITH PROVOLONE

A frittata is an open-face omelet in which vegetables are fried and eggs are poured over them to create a shallow pie. It can be eaten hot or cold as a snack, as part of a light meal with a sandwich, as a side dish, or as an especially good buffet dish.

When choosing asparagus, purchase the thinnest and greenest ones possible, as they are generally the most tasty and tender. It is not necessary to parboil the very thin asparagus for this dish, but if thick-stalked asparagus are used, they must be precooked to ensure tenderness.

1 pound thin asparagus

Extra-virgin olive oil

Salt and freshly ground black pepper, to taste

2 large eggs

2 tablespoons milk

2 tablespoons grated *cacio-cavallo* or romano cheese

1 cup shredded provolone cheese

1. Cut off the hard ends of the asparagus (2 to 3 inches), then peel away any tough skin on the stalks with a knife or vegetable peeler. Tie all the asparagus in a bunch with kitchen string. Fill a small, tall stockpot with water to a depth of 3 inches and add the asparagus, tips up. Cover and bring to a boil over high heat. Reduce the heat to medium-low and steam just until the stalks are tender, about 10 minutes. Drain well.

Secrets of Success

To make a wonderful frittata, purchase good-quality vegetables, and do not overboil them, since they will also be fried.

2. In a medium-size, nonstick frying pan, heat 3 tablespoons olive oil over medium-high heat. Add the asparagus and fry, turning on all sides, until lightly browned, about 3 minutes. Sprinkle with salt and pepper.

3. Meanwhile, in a small bowl, beat together the eggs, milk, grated *cacio-cavallo* or romano cheese, and a pinch of salt. Raise the heat to high and pour the eggs over the asparagus. Gently shake the pan back and forth, allowing the eggs to set but not stick. Reduce the heat to medium, cover the pan, and cook until the eggs are set and no longer runny on the surface, about 2 minutes.

4. Put a plate face down over the pan. Holding the plate firmly, invert the pan and plate together so the frittata falls onto the plate. Return the pan to low heat. Immediately slide the frittata, uncooked side down, back into the pan. Sprinkle the top evenly with the provolone. Cover, and cook until the provolone melts and the bottom is lightly browned, about 1 minute. Slide the frittata onto a serving plate, cut into wedges, and serve hot or cold.

Frittata di Patate e Cipolla
POTATO AND ONION EGG PIE

📖 This classic frittata is a good way to use up leftovers.

Extra-virgin olive oil

2 potatoes, peeled and cut into ¼-inch-thick slices

1 large bell pepper, seeded and cut into ½-inch strips

1 yellow onion, cut into ¼-inch-thick slices

Salt and freshly ground black pepper, to taste

2 large eggs

2 tablespoons grated *incanestrato* or romano cheese (optional)

2 tablespoons milk

1. Lightly oil a medium-size, nonstick frying pan and place over medium heat. Add the potatoes, bell peppers, and onion and cook, stirring and turning often, until the potatoes are browned and fork tender, about 15 minutes. Sprinkle with salt and pepper.

2. Meanwhile, in a small bowl, beat together the eggs, cheese (if using), milk, and a pinch of salt. Spread out the potatoes, peppers, and onion slices in the pan. Raise the heat to high and pour the eggs over the vegetables. Gently shake the pan back and forth, allowing the eggs to set but not stick. Reduce the heat to medium, cover the pan, and cook until the eggs are set and no longer runny on the surface, about 2 minutes.

3. Put a plate face down over the pan. Holding the plate firmly, invert the pan and plate together so the frittata falls onto the plate. Return the pan to low heat. Immediately slide the frittata, uncooked side down, back into the pan. Cover and cook until the bottom is lightly browned, about 1 minute. Slide the frittata onto a serving plate, cut into wedges, and serve hot or cold.

Secrets of Success

Since potatoes, peppers, and onions were so abundant in Sicily, this was eaten as an inexpensive meal, side dish, or sandwich filling. Oftentimes, just potatoes and eggs were used. Nearly any frittata can be enhanced by adding 2 heaping tablespoons of your favorite grated cheese to the beaten eggs.

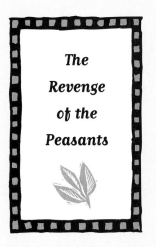

The Revenge of the Peasants

WHILE I WAS slicing an onion for a frittata, Grandma told me about Don Paolo, Grandpa Natale's father and my great-grandfather, a nobleman—in other words, a very wealthy man—who demanded great respect in his hometown of Ventimiglia.

He owned a dairy farm that had twenty-five goats and cows. With the milk from his livestock, his workers produced many cheeses, including ricotta, *incanestrato*, and *cacio-cavallo*. One night a group of envious peasants came onto his land and poisoned all his animals. He arose the next morning to find almost all of his goats and cows dead on the grass and in the barn. Those that were still alive had fallen and were writhing in pain. They had to be destroyed immediately. That night was the last night of his life.

Don Paolo never recovered from his loss, although in an attempt to begin anew he came to America. Lacking the discipline to work, he was unable to hold a real job for any length of time. He died at forty-two of a broken heart—a man once called Don out of respect and honor. 🌿

Salsiccia, Cipolla, e Ova con Formaggio

SAUSAGE, ONION, CHEESE, AND EGG SANDWICH

🐗 I ate this common breakfast treat several times a week when I was a child. It's still a standard in Sicily, where it is made both with and without the sausage.

1 tablespoon extra-virgin olive oil

1 small yellow onion, cut into ¼-inch-thick slices

2 Sicilian sausages, cut into ¼-inch-thick slices

2 large eggs

2 tablespoons grated *cacio-cavallo*, provolone, or romano cheese

Salt and freshly ground black pepper, to taste

Sicilian bread, enough for a sandwich, or an Italian roll

1. In a small frying pan, heat the olive oil over medium heat. Add the onion and sausage and cook, turning as needed, until the onions are golden and the sausage slices are browned and cooked on both sides, about 5 minutes.

2. Meanwhile, in a small bowl, beat together the eggs, 1 tablespoon of the cheese, and a dash of salt. Pour the eggs over the sausages and onion and allow them to set for a few seconds, then scramble until very soft curds begin to form.

3. Remove the pan from the heat and allow the eggs to finish cooking while you continue to scramble. Spoon the mixture over 1 slice of the bread (or half of the roll), and sprinkle with the remaining cheese and the pepper. Top with the remaining bread slice (or the top of the roll). Serve hot.

Olive con Ova

SAUTÉED BLACK OLIVES WITH EGGS

This is one of Grandpa Natale's favorite breakfasts. He used to make this dish for himself, since he was an expert at cooking eggs. A small jar of olives was kept in the back of the refrigerator just for his morning eggs, and he threw a small tantrum if any of us kids ate them. Here's the recipe his mother made for him when he was a child in Ventimiglia in 1897. Serve with *pane rotundo* (Sicilian round bread).

1 tablespoon extra-virgin olive oil

7 Sicilian black olives

2 large eggs, lightly beaten

1. In a small frying pan, heat the olive oil over medium heat. Add the olives and sauté until they plump up, about 2 minutes.

2. Pour the eggs over the olives. Allow the eggs to set for a few seconds, then scramble gently, without disturbing the olives too much. Serve at once.

Secrets of Success

A little secret for making great scrambled eggs is to stir them lightly in a dish before adding them to the pan, for a fluffier texture.

Grandma's Wedding at Webster Hall

O N SEPTEMBER 12, 1926, Grandma Josephina and Grandpa Natale were married. The reception took place at what was at the time the most expensive hall in New York City—Webster Hall on Eleventh Street, between Third and Fourth avenues.

Grandma bought her dress at the bride's shop on Clinton Street. Her gigantic bouquet, almost larger than her tiny four-foot-ten-inch frame, consisted of white lilies with matching cascading ribbons. It was made especially for her by her friend Don Gabriele Nigliaccio, a florist on Christie Street between Stanton and Houston streets. That bouquet cost about forty-five dollars—one week of Grandpa's pay at the factory near the corner of Stanton Street where he sewed pants for a living.

Grandpa Natale made all the arrangements. The wedding menu included traditional Sicilian sandwiches made of Italian hams, salami, and cheeses, arranged on tiered trays. No wine was served, which was the custom. Instead a row of flavored sodas—lime, grape, cherry, cream, orange, lemon—stood at the center of the banquet table. Hundred-pound burlap sacks of the finest-quality *noci* (walnuts), *mandorle* (raw white almonds), and *pinozzi* (peanuts) lined the back wall. All the pastries came from Casale Pasticceria on Houston Street, but the three-tiered *cassata* wedding cake, filled with cannoli cream and topped with fondant icing, although assembled without the traditional green marzipan, was

Grandma Josephina and Grandpa Natale on their wedding day, 1926. The bouquet was so large it took two people to hold it—it cost one week of Grandpa's pay!

made for Natale by his friend from Montelione's Pasticceria on Christie and Houston streets, a shop known for its wedding cakes.

Three hundred people attended Grandma's wedding. Half were uninvited. One invited family brought another two families, one invited friend brought five uninvited friends, and so on. The "crashers" never came near the bride or groom. They never gave a gift; instead, they ate and then left in a hurry. Grandma knew crashers were common at every wedding, but she had never seen so many at one time in her life—and at her own wedding! All she remembers saying to Grandpa, comically, was, "Nata, who the hell are all these people? They're all eating for free! What's it going to cost you?"

Grandpa merrily replied, "Don't worry, Josie, it's a *festa* [festival]! Let them eat!" Their home would be filled with that sentiment throughout their lives. 🐝

Froscia di Vitina

VITINA'S STUFFED EGG CREPES IN TOMATO SAUCE

🐟 For many years, meat was not eaten on Friday in the house of Grandma's sister Vitina for religious reasons. Vitina would make this dish as a second course for dinner almost every Friday night. The first course was a green vegetable with pasta like escarole (page 121) or a vegetable with sauce like Eggplant from Ciminna (page 228).

Sauce

3 tablespoons extra-virgin olive oil

1 large clove garlic, cut into small dice

1 can (16 ounces) whole tomatoes with juice, well crushed with a fork

1 tablespoon grated *cacio-cavallo* or romano cheese

½ teaspoon dried oregano, sticks removed, crushed until powdery

2 fresh basil leaves

¼ teaspoon salt, or to taste

¼ teaspoon sugar

Egg Crepes

4 large eggs

4 tablespoons milk

4 tablespoons extra-virgin olive oil

1 yellow onion, thinly sliced

4 tablespoons small chunks *cacio-cavallo, pepato,* or romano cheese

4 tablespoons grated provolone cheese

4 teaspoons flavored bread crumbs (page 14)

2 fresh Italian parsley sprigs, coarsely chopped

4 fresh basil leaves

Salt, to taste

Grated provolone or romano cheese and chopped fresh
Italian parsley, for garnish

Secrets of Success

Although crepes
are traditionally
made with flour,
I have called these
omelets crepes
to indicate how thin
they should be made.

1. To make the sauce: In a medium-size frying pan, heat the olive oil over medium heat. Add the garlic and sauté until golden, about 1 minute. Add the tomatoes, cheese, oregano, basil, salt, and sugar. Stir the sauce, then taste and adjust the seasonings, if necessary. Bring the sauce to a boil, reduce the heat to low, and simmer for 5 minutes. Remove from the heat. Set aside.

2. To make the crepes: In a small bowl, beat together 1 egg and 1 table-spoon of the milk. Set aside. In a medium-size, nonstick frying pan, heat 1 tablespoon of the oil over medium heat until hot. Pour the egg into the pan, tilting the pan quickly to coat the bottom evenly. Cook until the bottom is golden brown, about 30 seconds. Transfer to a dish. Repeat with the remaining eggs, milk, and oil, making 4 crepes in all.

3. Down the center of each crepe, place a few onion slices, 1 table-spoon of the cheese chunks, 1 tablespoon of the provolone, 1 teaspoon of the bread crumbs, one-fourth of the parsley, and 1 basil leaf. Sprin-kle the fillings with salt. Roll up the crepes and place seam side down in the sauce. Bring the sauce to a boil over high heat, then reduce the heat to low and simmer gently for 10 minutes to heat through.

4. Transfer the crepes to a platter and spoon the sauce over them. Sprinkle generously with grated cheese and chopped parsley.

PIZZA E CALZONE

Even when I was only eight years old, I was fascinated by Grandma's pizza making. Over the years I recorded some of her secrets, which I now pass on to you.

First, she always sets her dough on a large wooden board placed on top of her bed, covers it loosely with aluminum foil, and then tops it with a woolen blanket. Wood is porous and thus allows the dough to breathe so it can rise properly. The modern method of placing dough in a metal or glass bowl to rise does not permit it to expand to its fullest. Grandma never rolls out dough. Instead, she places it in a baking pan, then spreads it out by dimpling it with her fingertips. This technique ensures fluffiness. In Sicily, no one ever rolls out dough for a pizza, since cooks there believe it ruins the dough's texture. But note that it is necessary to roll out dough in certain instances: for topping a stuffed pizza or for shaping a calzone or a Neapolitan pizza.

Since in the past it was common for Grandma to make pizza or *cudririuni* (individual small pizzas) several times a week, she usually bought freshly made dough at the local *panetteria* (bread bakery), either the famous Bivona's on Elizabeth Street in Little Italy, or at Best Quality on Second Street and First Avenue, where it was often made on a moment's notice—just for her. Until this day, Bivona's and Best Quality are spoken of fondly and considered the best bread stores in Little Italy during its heyday of the 1920s to the 1960s.

Grandma's pizza sauces are many. They are always spicy and include sautéed onions. She is very precise about how each one is made and what type of tomatoes are to be used: cooked or uncooked, strained or unstrained, chunky or puréed. And she uses a black-speckled enamel-on-steel pan for baking the pizza to guarantee a rich brown crust. It produces the closest approximation of the crust her mother made in her brick oven in Ciminna.

The Sicilian pizza recipes in this chapter come from both sides of the family. They range from Grandma's sister Mica's recipe for Pizza with Black Olives and Onion to a special Christmas pizza called *Nfriulata*, made by my paternal grandma, Ciccina. And lastly, there is a special-occasion Sicilian Calzone Pie that I created for serving many guests easily.

Great-grandma Maria's Old Brick Oven

WHILE MAKING PIZZAS one day, I asked Grandma how she used to bake pizzas years ago in Sicily.

"My mother used to make pizzas and all her bread in a brick oven ten feet wide," Grandma stated emphatically.

"Ten feet! Grandma, that's bigger than ovens in the pizzerias! You can't mean ten feet!"

"We had the house of Cacaladritta, one of the wealthiest men in Ciminna."

"What color was the oven?"

"Maroon-colored bricks lined the bottom of the oven. Then she used to make a fire with *lagna* [tree branches] from the olive or almond trees. It gave a certain flavor to the dough. When she saw it was red hot inside, she would throw the dried pits and skins of olives or grapes, leftover from making oil and wine, on top of the wood. The flames would shoot up in the oven from the oil in the olive skins, or the alcohol in the grape skin. The oven door was made out of metal, and it wasn't attached either. It was so big, Fren-zee, that it took a couple of us to lift it to close the oven. We had the real wood-burning ovens in the old days. It was a production to light one. We only lit it two or three times a week, at the most—on Wednesdays my mother baked bread and pizza, and always on Sunday to make roasted chicken or meat."

"Ughhhh! I can't stand the taste of ashes on the bottom of my pizza. We went down to Little Italy to one of those brick-oven pizza parlors, and the bottom crust was full of coal ashes. Disgusting!"

"What are you talkin' about, Fren-zee, what ashes? After thirty minutes, my mother would remove all the wood and ashes with an oven broom. Then she took a damp rag, attached it to a long handle, and wiped the inside of the oven. It was spotless! Only then would she put her bread dough and pizzas into it. What's this nonsense about ashes on the crust of the pizza? If my father saw one ash, the pizza would go in the garbage. My mother used a *paletta* [a professional wooden pizza shovel] to put the pizzas in the oven, just like in the pizzerias here. We only made *cudririuni* [small personal pan pizzas] in those days. Each of us kids had their own little pizza. We made maybe twenty pizzas every Wednesday."

"But you said you used to have pizza more than once a week, and fresh bread for your father every day, if you only lit the oven twice a week . . ."

"There were ten kids, I'm the youngest, and most were married. They each had a small brick oven, so each day of the week one of them would light the oven. Monday, my sister Angelina would bake, and Tuesday, my sister Mica would bake. They'd all save a little dough to make pizza or bread for my father. He was so *fus-see!* He always had to have fried onions on his pizza or he wouldn't touch it—golden olive oil, garlic, oregano, chunks of fresh tomatoes off the vine, *sarde* [salted sardines], and lots of cheese." She thought back, and tilted her head, "I used to watch my mother scurry up to the farm of San Michele—holding up her long, black skirt with one hand and a hot pizza in the other hand—just so my father could have fresh pizza while he gardened. Ah, those were the days, Fren-zee. Too bad you never tasted her pizza: everything fresh from the farm. To tell you the truth, the pizza you make tastes more like my mother's than mine does, and she was the best cook of us all!

"I just paid you a good compliment, Fren-zee." She then sat down and crossed her arms, finished with her story. ☙

Left to right: Great-grandma Maria and Great-grandpa Michele, with their sons Nicolo and Vito, 1924.

Pane di Palermo
PIZZA DOUGH OR BREAD FROM PALERMO'S BAKERY

Makes about 3 pounds dough

🍴 "What's your favorite bread?" asked Angelo, former owner of Palermo's bakery in New York City and now owner of C & D Golden Loaf at Thirteenth Avenue and Seventy-Second Street in Brooklyn. Angelo's nickname is The Master because of his bread-making skills.

"The one that's very long, about four feet, that you make for the holidays."

"Did anyone ever tell you that you have excellent taste? It's a little-known secret that the bigger the bread, the better the taste! When the bread takes longer to cook, the flavor stays inside the dough, which makes the bread taste better."

Secrets of Success

Professional bakers measure all dry ingredients on a baker's scale for accuracy, and always use fresh yeast—never dried—for making bread.

1½ pounds bread flour

6 ounces semolina flour

1¼ ounces fresh yeast

1½ ounces sugar

3½ cups warm water (110°F to 115°F)

1½ ounces solid vegetable shortening

1½ ounces salt

1½ teaspoons extra-virgin olive oil

1 cup sesame seeds, for making bread

1. In a large bowl, combine the flours and set aside. In a small bowl, combine the yeast, sugar, and water. Cover and let stand for 5 minutes. Combine the shortening and salt in the bowl of an electric mixer equipped with a dough hook. Mix on the lowest speed for 2 minutes, then add the yeast mixture. Slowly, add 1¼ pounds of the flour mixture. Knead on low speed for 5 minutes. If the dough seems very sticky after 5 minutes, add as much of the remaining flour as is necessary for

the dough to lose its stickiness. Continue kneading until the dough forms one piece and picks up all the flour from the bottom and sides of the bowl and leaves it clean. Then add the oil (to clean the bowl and coat the dough) and knead 6 seconds more.

2. To make bread: Flour the dough on the top and bottom and transfer to a wooden board in a draft-free area. Cover loosely with aluminum foil and 2 thick towels. Let rise until doubled in bulk, 1 to 1½ hours.

3. Divide the dough into 3 equal pieces and shape each piece into a loaf 13 inches long. Roll the top of each loaf in the sesame seeds and fit them into three 13-by-4-by-3-inch bread pans with rounded bottoms and open ends. Cover each pan loosely with aluminum foil and 2 thick towels. Allow the dough to rise again until doubled in bulk, about 1 hour. Press the dough with your finger. If the dough bounces back, it is ready to be baked. If the indentation remains in the dough, it is not ready. Meanwhile, preheat an oven to 400°F.

4. Just before the loaves are to be baked, using a razor blade, make 2 diagonal slits in the top of each loaf. Brush the loaves with cold water and place in the oven. Bake, brushing with cold water once after about 10 minutes and again after 20 minutes, until the crust is well browned, almost 30 minutes.

5. To make pizza: Remove the dough from the mixer, dust with flour, and let it rest for 15 minutes. Then, on a wooden board, divide the dough into desired portions, leaving space between the pieces to allow room for rising. Cover loosely with aluminum foil and 2 thick towels and allow the dough to rise until doubled in bulk, 1 to 1½ hours. Follow directions for the particular pizza recipe you are making.

Secrets of Success

To make only 1½ pounds of dough, simply halve the 3-pound recipe.

Meeting Grandma's Sister Mica

W HEN I FIRST WENT to Ciminna, Grandma's hometown, I had the honor of meeting one of the finest and kindliest ladies I've ever known, my great-aunt Mica, who was a youthful ninety-two. Her face was exceptional, with beautiful navy blue, almond-shaped eyes that shone through alabaster skin, a straight, fine nose, and a perfectly shaped mouth. Her hair was long and gray, never dyed, and she wore it in *u tuppu* [a hair bun] held together by long, black hairpins. Dangling navy blue ceramic earrings were her only adornment, used to offset her radiant eyes. I often told Mica how beautiful she was, and although humble, she would have me in stitches over stories about her youth and great beauty.

"Grandma told me that out of her eight sisters, Lena was the most beautiful and you were second," I teased one day.

"Lena?" Mica said, shocked. "Lena was a beauty, it's true, but if you saw me, you saw Lena. When I walked down the street, people would shout 'Lena! Lena!' and wave. And do you know who it was? Me. We were sisters who looked alike, one and the same, except I was more beautiful." She arose and handed me a slice of the onion and olive pizza she had just made for me.

As I took a bite, I exclaimed, "Tastes just like Grandma's!"

"My pizza tastes just like my sister's," Mica said, smiling confidently. "But of course, you like her cooking best. Pipina and me, we are sisters, aren't we? When you eat her food, you eat my food. We are one and the same.

"You! You look just like me when I was young!" she added, staring and pointing a sharp finger. "I get a funny feeling inside. I think I'm seeing myself when I was just married. Especially with your hair in *u tuppu*. You should always wear it up, you know, or else people talk," she persisted.

"About what? Anyway, it's much more comfortable down."

"It's too sexy down. Long, black hair should be kept up or they might think you're . . . you know . . . not a good girl," she finally blurted out.

"They think I'm a *putana* [whore] because my hair is down!—nooooo!"

"Shhhh! *Si! Si, è vero.*" [Yes, yes, it's true.]

"Well, Mica, then let them think I'm a bad girl!"

She laughed, stuck her head out the door to make sure no one was watching us speak such scandalous talk, slapped her knee, threw back her head, and laughed so heartily that she almost fell off her chair.

"You really think I look like you. Well, then, the argument is over. You are definitely more beautiful than your sister Lena."

She rose and waved a scolding finger in my face, "I knew you'd see it my way. I never lie." 🐢

MICA'S PIZZA WITH BLACK OLIVES AND ONION

In America, all Sicilian pizzas are now considered deep-dish pizzas. Sicilian pizzas are thicker than what Americans normally eat; therefore, the oven temperature must not be higher than 400°F, which is lower than the traditional pizza-baking temperature of 475°F. At the higher temperature, the crust of a Sicilian pizza will burn before the inside of the dough is cooked. When I make pizza, I always use 1½ pounds dough, which yields a crust about 1 inch thick.

My great-aunt Mica, for whom this pizza is named, passed away about ten years ago. Until the day she died, she wrote to Grandma that she wanted me to return to see her and that she would never forget me. I still remember the day I left Ciminna. She stood there, the tears rolling down her face, her son Michele holding her up by the waist on the broken cobblestone steps of the little town. Waving her white handkerchief at me she shouted over and over, "Good-bye, Franca, I think I'll never see you again." That was the last time I saw Mica. Here's the pizza she made for me in Ciminna in 1981.

1½ **pounds pizza dough, homemade (page 67) or purchased**

2 **pounds plum tomatoes**

1 **teaspoon dried oregano, sticks removed, crushed until powdery**

2 **fresh basil leaves**

Salt, to taste

Pinch of sugar

1 **large sweet red onion, very thinly sliced**

¼ **cup extra-virgin olive oil**

¼ **pound small Sicilian black olives, halved and pitted**

6 **heaping tablespoons grated** *incanestrato* **or romano cheese**

Secrets of Success

If you prefer a thinner-crusted pizza, follow the recipe and bake the pizza in the same pan, but use only 1 pound dough. Although black olives are traditional with this pizza, you can substitute a 3-ounce jar of anchovies in olive oil or salted sardines (*sarde salate*; see page 27) for the olives.

(CONTINUED)

1. Prepare the dough.

2. Bring a large pot half-filled with water to a boil. Add the tomatoes and cook for 20 seconds. Remove them from the water and peel off the skins. One at a time, cut the tomatoes coarsely over a large bowl, dropping the pieces into the bowl and capturing all the juices. Crush the tomatoes well with a fork, then stir in the oregano, basil leaves, salt, and sugar. Set aside.

3. In a small bowl, soak the onion in cold water to cover for 15 minutes to remove the sting, changing the water twice. Drain and set aside.

4. Preheat an oven to 400°F. When the dough has doubled in bulk, generously oil the bottom and the sides of a 13-by-9-inch black enamel-on-steel baking pan with some of the olive oil. Fit the dough into the baking pan and, with your fingertips, spread the dough using a dimpling motion.

5. Spread all but 4 tablespoons of the tomato sauce over the dough, then top with the onion slices and olives. Drizzle with the remaining olive oil, and sprinkle evenly with the grated cheese. Spread the remaining 4 tablespoons tomato sauce over the pizza, covering all the cheese.

6. Bake on the middle rack of the oven until the bottom crust is well browned, about 30 minutes. Cut into rectangular slices and serve.

A Pizza Rivalry

WHEN I RETURNED to America from meeting Great-aunt Mica, I told Mica's story to my grandma, who was anxiously awaiting the news from Sicily.

"What, is Mica kidding? Who's she trying to fool? Lena had beautiful long, blonde hair. She was very fair, very busty, and a little plump. Mica had jet black hair and was always slimmer, with a nicer body. How could you take bright blonde hair for jet black?" She threw her hands in the air. "Unless these people couldn't see and needed glasses? Oh, Fren-zee, you really make me laugh! *La gelosia*, that's what I say. They were always jealous of who was more beautiful. To me, Lena was."

Then suddenly Grandma tilted her head back reminiscently and turned to me, "You know, once in a while, when you put your hair up in *u tuppu*, I get a chill in my body. I think I'm seeing Mica. You look just like her." She folded her hands and placed them under her breasts. "With your black hair and your *occhi celeste* [blue eyes]," her hand touched her heart, "I think sometimes I'm sitting and talking to my sister when she was young."

"You know Grandma, Mica said the exact same thing, that I looked just like her when she was young. So the argument is over! Mica was definitely more beautiful!"

"Well Fren-zee," Grandma retorted, "we are sisters, aren't we? When you speak to Mica, you speak to me. We are one and the same." Her voice raised, *"La verita, Fren-zee! Cu fa la pizza chiu meglio io o Mica?"* [The truth! Who makes better pizza, me or Mica?]

"You, Grandma." I answered without thinking. Her arched back relaxed into the old wooden chair as she adjusted her garter a few inches above her knee. Her grin was as broad as the Cheshire cat's. 🐾

Pizza di Nonna
GRANDMA'S PIZZA

🔖 This recipe provides you with two additional options. The basic recipe is Grandma's original thick Sicilian pizza. Following it is a variation for *cudririuni*, which were popularized in Chicago and Little Italy by Sicilians who opened pizza parlors. These were the standard pizzas made in Sicily at the turn of the century into the early 1900s. Since families were large, it was easier to make everyone his or her own pizza than to fight over toppings. In Italian, the word for a small pizza is *pizzetta*; however, a *pizzeta* is traditionally thinner than these small Sicilian pies. Finally, there are directions for the large, thin-crust Neapolitan pizza, which Grandma discovered when she arrived in Little Italy.

1½ **pounds pizza dough, homemade (page 67) or purchased**

1 **can (21 ounces) whole tomatoes with juice**

1 **teaspoon dried oregano, sticks removed, crushed until powdery**

½ **teaspoon sugar**

⅓ **teaspoon salt**

4 **fresh basil leaves**

Extra-virgin olive oil

11 **heaping tablespoons grated** *incanestrato* **or Romano cheese**

4 **yellow onions, thinly sliced**

½ **pound fresh mozzarella cheese, cut into ⅛-inch-thick slices**

1. Prepare the pizza dough.

2. In a large bowl, crush the tomatoes well with a fork. Stir in ½ teaspoon of the oregano, the sugar, salt, basil, 2 tablespoons olive oil, and 2 heaping tablespoons of the grated cheese. Set aside.

3. In a medium-size frying pan, heat 2 tablespoons olive oil over

medium heat. Add the onions and sauté until golden brown, about 10 minutes. Stir in 5 tablespoons of the tomato sauce, 1 heaping tablespoon of the grated cheese, and ¼ teaspoon of the oregano. Reduce the heat to low and simmer for 10 minutes. Set aside.

4. Preheat an oven to 400°F. When the dough has doubled in bulk, generously oil the bottom and sides of a 13-by-9-inch black enamel-on-steel baking pan. Fit the dough into the baking pan and, with your fingertips, spread the dough using a dimpling motion.

5. Drizzle and spread 1 tablespoon olive oil over the dough. Top with the mozzarella and sprinkle with 3 heaping tablespoons of the grated cheese. Spoon the tomato sauce without the onions over the dough, leaving a ½-inch border around the edge. Top with the onion and tomato sauce mixture. Sprinkle with the remaining ¼ teaspoon oregano and the remaining 5 heaping tablespoons grated cheese.

6. Bake on the middle rack of the oven until the bottom crust is well browned, about 30 minutes. Cut into rectangular slices and serve.

CUDRIRIUNI VARIATION

Makes two 9-inch pizzas; serves 4

Proceed as directed for Grandma's Pizza. In Step 2, substitute a 28-ounce can whole tomatoes for the 21-ounce can. Adjust the seasonings. In Step 4, divide the dough in half and, using your fingertips, fit the dough into two 9-inch cake pans. Divide the sauce and all other ingredients into 2 equal portions for topping the pizza. Add mozzarella and grated cheese to each pizza.

NEAPOLITAN PIZZA VARIATION

Makes one 14-inch pizza; serves 4 to 6

Proceed as directed for Grandma's Pizza. In Step 4, lightly oil a 14-inch round pizza tray in place of the rectangular pan. On a well-floured work surface, roll out the dough into a 14-inch round. Fit the dough into the pan. Proceed as directed.

Pizza Siciliana

FRANCESCA'S PIZZA WITH MOZZARELLA

Although the sauce for this pizza is cooked for 35 minutes, it still yields a chunky yet juicy sauce, which was Grandpa Natale's favorite. This recipe makes 2 pizzas, but if you want to make only 1 pizza, use 1½ pounds dough and freeze the remaining sauce for up to 3 months.

Sauce

5 tablespoons extra-virgin olive oil

3 large yellow onions, cut into ¼-inch-thick slices

1¼ teaspoons salt, or to taste

6 cloves garlic, sliced

1 can (35 ounces) whole tomatoes with juice, well crushed with a fork

1 tablespoon dried oregano, sticks removed, crushed until powdery

5 fresh basil leaves

Pizza

3 pounds pizza dough, homemade (page 67) or purchased, divided in half

1½ pounds fresh mozzarella cheese, cut into ⅛-inch-thick slices

¾ cup grated *incanestrato* or romano cheese

1. To make the sauce: In a medium-size pot, combine 4 tablespoons of the oil, the onions, and ¼ teaspoon of the salt. Sauté over medium heat until the onions are golden, about 10 minutes. Move the onions to one side of the pot and add the remaining 1 tablespoon oil and the garlic. Reduce the heat and cook until the garlic is golden, about 1 minute. Stir in the tomatoes, oregano, basil, and the remaining 1 teaspoon salt. Taste and adjust the seasonings. Bring the sauce to a boil over high heat. Then, reduce the heat to medium, partially cover the pot, and simmer for 35 minutes. Stir occasionally. When the sauce is done, remove from the heat. Scoop out ½ cup and reserve.

Secrets of Success

For proper texture when making any pizza, always slice—never grate—the mozzarella, and always grate the *incanestrato* or romano cheese into long, thin strips. If the cheese is reduced to a sand, it will lose its taste on the pizza. Also, never crush the tomatoes in a blender when making sauce, or the sauce will dry up during baking.

2. To make the pizza: Preheat an oven to 400°F. When the dough has doubled in bulk, generously oil the bottom and sides of two 13-by-9-inch black enamel-on-steel baking pans. Fit half of the dough into each baking pan and, using your fingertips, spread the dough using a dimpling motion.

3. Spread half of the tomato sauce over the top of 1 pan of dough, top with half of the mozzarella slices, and sprinkle with half of the grated cheese. Spread ¼ cup of the reserved tomato sauce over the pizza, covering all the cheese. Repeat to make 1 more pizza.

4. Bake on the middle rack of the oven until the bottom crusts are well browned, about 30 minutes. Cut into rectangular slices and serve.

PIZZA WITH MOZZARELLA AND MUSHROOMS

In a frying pan over medium-high heat, sauté ½ pound fresh mushrooms, sliced, in 1 tablespoon extra-virgin olive oil until lightly browned, about 10 minutes. Drain off any leftover oil. Scatter the cooked mushrooms over the mozzarella on 1 pizza. Proceed as directed.

PIZZA WITH MOZZARELLA AND DRIED SAUSAGE

Slice ½ stick *salsiccia secca* [dried hot or sweet sausage] ¼ inch thick. Scatter the sausage slices over the mozzarella slices on 1 pizza, then proceed as directed. Buy dried sausage that has not been aged for more than 21 days, or it will be too hard to eat when baked. Dried sausage that has been aged longer is for eating, not for cooking. Although pepperoni may be substituted for dried sausage, it is not to be confused with it. The former is a cheap, mass-marketed version of dried sausage, and tastes totally different than the real thing. Any good-quality Italian pork butcher or *salumeria* carries dried sausage.

Pizza di Sarde Salate
PIZZA WITH SALTED SARDINES

When my father was a child, *sarde salate* cost two for a dime. Now they cost eight to twelve dollars a pound. He recalls preparing the fish for his mother's pizza by scraping off the salt with his small pocket knife while she made the dough. Since you will never find a pizzeria that tops pizza with *sarde salate,* you will have to bake this pizza at home.

1½ **pounds pizza dough, homemade (page 67), or purchased**

1½ **pounds plum tomatoes**

3 **cloves garlic, sliced**

1½ **teaspoons dried oregano, sticks removed, crushed until powdery**

3 **fresh basil leaves**

½ **teaspoon salt, or to taste**

2 **sweet red onions, thinly sliced**

3 **salted sardines (***sarde salate***), filleted (page 27) and cut into bite-size pieces, or 2 cans (2 ounces each) anchovy fillets in olive oil, drained and cut into bite-size pieces**

¾ **cup grated** ***incanestrato, cacio-cavallo,*** **or romano cheese**

Extra-virgin olive oil

Secrets of Success

To soften the onions during the baking and to allow their sweetness to come through, slice them extremely thin and place them over the dough first, then cover with the sauce.

1. Prepare the dough.

2. Bring a large pot half-filled with water to a boil. Add the tomatoes and cook for 20 seconds. Remove them from the water and peel off the skins. One at a time, cut the tomatoes coarsely over a large bowl, dropping the pieces into the bowl and capturing all the juices. Crush the tomatoes well with a fork, then stir in the garlic, oregano, basil leaves, and salt. Set aside for 15 minutes.

3. In a bowl, soak the onion in cold water to cover for 15 minutes to remove the sting, changing the water twice. Drain and set aside.

4. Preheat an oven to 400°F. When the dough has doubled in bulk, generously oil the bottom and the sides of a 13-by-9-inch black enamel-on-steel baking pan. Fit the dough into the baking pan and, with your fingertips, spread the dough using a dimpling motion.

5. Spread the onions over the dough, then top with the sauce, spreading evenly. Dimple the dough with your fingertips and place small pieces of salted sardine or anchovy in the indentations. Sprinkle the pizza with the grated cheese, then drizzle with 4 or 5 tablespoons olive oil. Using the back of a spoon, spread the oil over the pizza, moistening all the cheese.

6. Bake on the middle rack of the oven until the bottom crust is well browned, about 30 minutes. Cut into rectangular slices and serve.

Nfriulata di Natale
CHRISTMAS EVE PIZZA

Makes 1 double-crust pizza; serves 10

🦐 At our family's house, the cooking for Christmas Eve begins with this special pork and spinach pizza. Old-timers from Little Italy and Sicily remember this seasonal pie, but the tradition has been lost in most of Sicilian America. Most people think Sicilians serve a meal of seven different fishes for Christmas Eve, and many do. Both sides of my family came from Sicily's interior, however, and neither ever heard of serving seven fishes until they came to America. Instead, they began the Christmas season with this pizza. Today, on Christmas Eve, we serve a pizza menu of *nfriulata*, Pizza with Salted Sardines (page 78), and Pizza with Mozzarella and Dried Sausage (page 77), and we follow it with *baccalà* (salted cod) in tomato sauce with olives, fried veal cutlets, and roasted fresh sausages.

This large pizza has two crusts, a thick bottom crust and a thinner one on top. It is stuffed with chopped pork, fresh spinach, spices, tomato sauce, and cheese. The temperature is kept lower than for most pizzas in order to cook both crusts fully without burning.

Secrets of Success

The pork in this recipe must be coarsely ground with the same disk used for making Italian sausage. If it is ground too fine, the dish will be ruined.

2½ pounds pizza dough, homemade (page 67) or purchased,
   divided into 1½ pounds and 1 pound

Extra-virgin olive oil

1 very large yellow onion, cut into medium dice

2 pounds boneless pork, unseasoned, ground as for Italian sausage

1 can (16 ounces) whole tomatoes with juice, well crushed with a fork

1 tablespoon dried oregano, sticks removed, crushed until powdery

Salt and freshly ground black pepper, to taste

½ cup grated *incanestrato* or romano cheese

1¼ pounds spinach, cooked and well drained

1. Prepare the dough.

2. Generously oil a 6-quart pot with olive oil and place over medium heat. Add the onion and sauté until golden, about 10 minutes. Add the pork and cook, stirring, until browned, about 10 minutes. Reduce the heat to medium-low and stir in the tomatoes, oregano, salt, and pepper. Simmer for 1¼ hours, until the flavors are blended. During the last 15 minutes of cooking, stir in 3 tablespoons of the grated cheese and then the spinach. Remove from the heat and set aside.

3. Preheat an oven to 350°F. When dough has doubled in bulk, generously oil the bottom and sides of a deep, 16½-by-11-inch black enamel-on-steel baking pan. On a well-floured surface, roll out the 1½-pound piece of dough into a rectangle the size of the pan. Fit the dough into the pan, stretching it gently into the corners and ½ inch up the sides. Immediately top the dough with the pork mixture, spreading it evenly and leaving a ½-inch border uncovered around the edges. Sprinkle with the remaining grated cheese.

4. Next, roll out the 1-pound piece of dough into a rectangle a little larger than the bottom piece of dough. Cover the pork mixture with the dough. Pinch the edges of the 2 dough layers together. Brush any excess oil from the sides of the pan over the top layer of dough to assist browning.

5. Bake the pizza on the middle rack of the oven until the top and bottom crusts are well browned, 40 to 45 minutes. Every 15 minutes, check the bottom crust to make sure it's not burning. If it is, reduce the heat to 325°F. If the top layer is not browned and the pizza is completely cooked, place the pizza under a preheated broiler for a few seconds to brown. Cut the pizza into 4-inch squares and serve.

Torta di Calzone
CALZONE PIE

🐦 I made this large calzone one day when I was expecting company and didn't feel like doing a lot of work. It was a big success. It also surprised everyone, since my guests weren't quite sure what was inside.

2 pounds fresh ricotta cheese

1 pound pizza dough, homemade (page 67) or purchased

Salt, to taste

4 fresh Italian parsley sprigs, coarsely chopped

½ pound boiled ham, thinly sliced

½ pound fresh mozzarella cheese, cut into ⅛-inch-thick slices

½ cup grated romano, *cacio-cavallo,* or *incanestrato* cheese

Extra-virgin olive oil

Secrets of Success

You must drain the ricotta before beginning this recipe, or it will release too much water during the baking process, and your crust will be soggy and ruined.

1. Place the ricotta in a colander set over a dish, cover, and allow to drain for 2 hours (or overnight) in the refrigerator.

2. Prepare the dough. Preheat an oven to 375°F. When the dough has doubled in bulk, lightly oil a deep, 9-inch metal pie pan. With a lightly floured rolling pin, roll out half the dough into a round large enough to line the pie pan, and overhang the rim by 1 inch. Spoon in half of the ricotta, sprinkle with salt, and then scatter with half of the parsley. Top with half of the ham, half of the mozzarella, and then sprinkle with ¼ cup of the grated cheese. Repeat the layering with the remaining ingredients. Roll out the remaining dough into a round large enough to cover the pie and place it over the filling. Pinch the edges of the top and bottom crusts together, fluting them.

3. Brush a thin layer of olive oil on top of the dough. Bake until the bottom and top crusts are well browned, 40 to 50 minutes. Let the pie rest for 20 minutes before cutting into slices to serve.

An Old Sicilian Joke

UNCLE MIKE, a colorful wise guy, likes to recount this old Sicilian joke called *Basta no Fume* (As Long As You Don't Smoke). It was famous in Little Italy from the 1920s to the 1950s, and it describes the Sicilian mentality toward women. His friend Giuseppe, who owned a fruit store, used to laugh and say, "Okay, Mikey, gotta picture this. A woman who everyone knew was poor was seen showered in diamonds, wore minks, and rode around all day in a limousine. One day, one guy seeing this says to the other guy, 'Where did she get the money for the car and all those jewels?' The friend answered, 'She's a *putana* [a whore], but a high-class one!' To which, the other man replied, '*Basta no fume, basta no fume* [just as long as she doesn't smoke].'"

"You see, Fran-cee," Uncle Mike shook his head in amazement. "From the turn of the century until the 1950s, in Sicily as well as in Little Italy, there was nothing cheaper a woman could do than smoke—not even prostitution."

PASTA E SALSA

Not one of my cooking classes ever goes by without several of the students asking me for my recipe for the seven-hour Sunday sauce or for the secret of how to make soft meatballs, homemade pasta, or Grandma's old-fashioned lasagna. For me, these foods are the foundation of Sicilian cooking.

Grandpa Natale ate only spaghetti and lasagna. He would never eat ravioli or any other kind of pasta, because he considered it beneath him. In the old days in Sicily, shops made fresh spaghetti and the flat *pasta di casa*, which resembled fettuccine, and at day's end, the leftover dough that had hardened was reshaped with disks into *ziti*, *penne*, and *babalucci* (snails) to sell at a cheaper price than the fresh spaghetti or *pasta di casa*. Since Grandma's sister Concetta made fresh pasta in Ciminna, I know this is not a myth. In fact, it was common knowledge throughout Sicily that these little pasta shapes were nothing other than recycled stale dough. Anyone who considered themselves upper class refused to eat them, although children adored the cute shapes. In other words, to get an old-timer to eat anything other than spaghetti or *pasta di casa* was impossible. In my cooking classes, Italian American students often tell me their grandfathers never ate anything but spaghetti, and their grandmothers had to make special dishes just for them. Now they know why.

Detailed instructions for making our seven-hour sauce, which must be cooked over the lowest of heat and nurtured, are given in this chapter. Don't run an errand while it's on the stove. It is like a child demanding attention, and must be stirred and seasoned throughout the day.

You'll find an interesting history of meatballs in the cuisine of Little Italy, along with a list of secrets to guarantee the softest of textures, in the recipe on page 18. In the *Pasta di Casa* recipe, there are instructions on how to make both medium-size and large-size ravioli filled with ricotta, egg, grated cheese, and parsley, just as they were originally made in the 1900s in the pasta stores that lined Little Italy's Grand Street.

My lasagna recipe was created by Grandma in 1944, and you may be surprised to discover the true history and original name of the dish in America. Then onto pasta and fish sauces such as Mother's Clam Sauce, a red sauce for pasta with sardines, and Marinara Sauce. Finally, there are the pastas with vegetables, the true mainstays of Sicily. There's hardly a bean or vegetable that can't be combined successfully with pasta. Although the origin of the combination was with poor peasants having to substitute a vegetable for meat, the story has reversed. Nowadays, in most restaurants you will pay the same amount of money for pasta with vegetables as for pasta with meat. At home, however, these dishes are extremely inexpensive to make. My favorites are *Perciatelli* with Squash and Pasta with Escarole. And let's not forget the two most famous pasta dishes made without tomato sauce, Pasta with Oil and Garlic and Pasta with Grated Cheese, Salt, and Pepper. Both of them are peasant dishes, very Sicilian, and everyone's favorites.

Forget about the time it takes to make tomato sauce, lasagna, and pasta, because the taste will linger in your memory for years. It is not without justification that these are my most requested recipes.

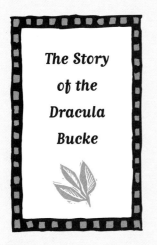

The Story of the Dracula Bucke

WHILE GRANDMA stirred the tomato sauce, she told me the story of Francesco, who climbed into Sicily's high terrain in 1915. In Ciminna, a legend existed about a hidden mountain cave that contained a treasure chest filled with jewels and gold. The villagers believed that a vampire—a Dracula *bucke* (bogeyman)—dwelled in the cave and lured his victims inside by offering them the treasure, then sucked their blood. Many entered the cave, but none returned. Their bodies were never found.

Only one man, Francesco, ever survived to tell the story of the cave. He was walking by it one day and, being an atheist and nonbeliever in such nonsensical tales, decided to look in. He was astonished to see a treasure chest overflowing with jewels, gold coins, and diamonds. Making a torch with wood, he walked into the dark cavern, but when he reached the treasure, the lights began to dim. His eyes bulged as he stuffed his pockets with the gems. But then the last ray of sunlight unexpectedly disappeared and Francesco's torch extinguished itself.

Hours passed as Francesco tried desperately to find his way out, but he could not. Nightfall came and went. Still he was disoriented. Another day passed, and still he walked in circles. Growing weaker from the lack of oxygen, he decided there was only one thing to do: return to the cave what did not belong to him. He emptied all his pockets and placed the rubies, diamonds, gold coins, and even a tiara back in the chest. Magically, the sunlight reappeared, and he found his way out, only twenty feet from where he stood.

Baffled and close to suffocation, he dragged his tired body out of the cave. Falling as he reached the opening, he heard loud, raucous, evil laughter. A man in a black cape was standing beside him. Petrified, he ran for his life, never looking back.

A few hours later, safe in Ciminna, Francesco thought it all must have been a hallucination. But when he entered his home, his family and friends announced that they had been searching for him for two full days.

Francesco's moral: "Do not take things that do not belong to you, or you may have to pay for them with your life."

Pasta con Aglio e Olio

PASTA WITH GARLIC AND OLIVE OIL

When my parents were children living in Little Italy, they ate this dish often. It was always served during the week, since the Sunday sauce was reserved for the weekend. It remains a standard first course in every Little Italy restaurant, where it is usually followed by a meat course of Breaded Veal Cutlets (page 174), roasted sausage, or grilled porterhouse steak. If you prefer to eat your pasta dry, as many people do, eliminate the water in the recipe.

1 pound linguine, spaghetti, or spaghettini

¾ cup extra-virgin olive oil, or to taste

Cloves from ½ to 1 head garlic, to taste, cut into small dice or sliced medium-thick

Salt, preferably freshly ground, to taste

Grated romano, *incanestrato, pepato, ricotta salata,* or provolone cheese

Freshly ground black pepper or red pepper flakes, to taste

1. Cook and drain the pasta, reserving 1 cup of the water. Transfer the pasta and water to a large bowl.

2. Just before the pasta is cooked, in a large frying pan, heat the olive oil over medium heat, then add the garlic and salt. Sauté just until the garlic is golden, about 1 minute. Pour the oil over the pasta and toss. Serve topped with grated cheese and black pepper or red pepper flakes.

Secrets of Success

If available, buy young, light purple garlic, which is slightly hot and full of flavor. Use a good-quality olive oil with a fruity flavor. A poor-quality oil will make this dish taste greasy.

Pastasciutte
PASTA WITH GRATED CHEESE, SALT, AND PEPPER

The very poor didn't have any tomato sauce or stew for their pasta, so in difficult times they ate *pastasciutte*, which consisted of just the pasta with a little pasta water, salt, and pepper. If the peasant was lucky enough to have olive oil and cheese, they were added for extra flavor. Originally, *pastasciutte* was only eaten by the very poor, but the dish was so tasty, it quickly became incorporated into the wealthy man's diet. It was my great-grandfather's favorite dish, which he ate regularly as a first course. Many famous cooks insist that *pastasciutte* simply means any and all types of dried pasta, but this is untrue in our heritage. To Sicilians, *pastasciutte* has always meant either this recipe or Pasta with Garlic and Olive Oil (page 88), a fancier version. Serve with any meat dish, fried vegetables, or Asparagus Egg Pie with Provolone (page 52).

1 pound linguine, spaghetti, or spaghettini

Extra-virgin olive oil

Salt, preferably freshly ground, to taste (optional)

Freshly ground black pepper, to taste

Grated *ricotta salata,* romano, *incanestrato, cacio-cavallo,*
   or provolone cheese (optional)

1. Cook and drain the pasta, reserving 2 cups pasta water. Transfer the pasta to individual dishes along with a little of its water, the amount depending on each person's taste. Drizzle with olive oil and season with salt and pepper, or eliminate the salt and top with the grated cheese.

Secrets of Success

Since the dish is plain, grated *ricotta salata* cheese was traditionally used because its saltiness flavored the pasta. Often Sicilians ask one another, "Do you want your pasta *sciutte* (meaning dry, with a little water) or *sciutte, sciutte* (meaning dry, dry, without any water)?" Eliminate the water entirely if you want it *sciutte, sciutte.*

Children Shouldn't Trust Too Much

L A ZIA CICCINA (Aunt Frances) was a beautiful and kind woman and a *paesana* (friend from the same hometown) from Ciminna. She was also Grandma's sister Angelina's godmother. When she made Little Italy her home in 1930, everyone in the family gave her the respect of calling her *La Zia* (Aunt), and it was in New York that she taught Grandma how to make fresh pasta.

Frances's mother died when she was six years old, and necessity forced her to prepare the family dinners. While still a child, she became well known in Ciminna for making delicious pasta. All the neighbors would stop by and look in on little Frances, but their motives were cruel. Frances often recounted tales to Grandma of how people robbed her home while pretending to play or look in on her. Her father then put a large padlock on all the wheat and other food, and several neighbors never returned. ✺

Ravioli e Pasta di Casa
RAVIOLI AND PASTA AS THEY ARE MADE IN THE HOME

🐦 The pasta dough recipe comes from Frances, but the ravioli filling comes from Carmella, Grandma's neighbor in Little Italy, and the same woman who taught Grandma how to make Bird's Nest (page 272). Since Grandma had a gigantic dining room table, Frances and Carmella would ask to borrow the table to roll out their dough. The two met, became friends, and developed this recipe, which is twofold. You can either make fresh pasta dough and shape the dough as desired, or use the dough to make homemade ravioli (see page 93).

Ravioli filling for 50 large ravioli

1 pound fresh ricotta cheese

1 large or 2 small eggs

5 tablespoons grated *cacio-cavallo* or romano cheese

8 fresh Italian parsley sprigs, coarsely chopped

¼ teaspoon salt, or to taste

Ravioli filling for 70 small ravioli

1½ pounds fresh ricotta cheese

1 large or 2 small eggs

½ cup grated romano or *cacio-cavallo* cheese

11 fresh Italian parsley sprigs, coarsely chopped

⅓ teaspoon salt, or to taste

Pasta

4 to 4½ cups all-purpose flour

½ teaspoon plus 1 tablespoon salt

2 large eggs

1 to 1½ cups warm water (110°F), or as needed

2 tablespoons extra-virgin olive oil

Secrets of Success

Using warm water instead of cold makes pasta dough softer.

1. If you are making ravioli, first make the filling: Choose the size of ravioli you wish to make, then spoon the ricotta into a colander set over a dish. Cover, and place in the refrigerator to drain for 2 hours. Once the ricotta has drained, transfer it to a bowl and add the egg(s), cheese, parsley, and salt. Mix well, cover, and refrigerate until needed.

2. To make the dough by hand: Combine 4 cups of the flour and the ½ teaspoon salt in a sifter, then sift onto a wooden board. Make a well in the center and add the eggs. Using a fork, mix the eggs into the flour. Slowly begin mixing in 1 cup of the warm water, a little at a time, just until a dough begins to form. Using your hands, and continuing to add the 1 cup water, begin kneading the dough. If after 1 cup of the water has been added the dough feels dry or hard, add an extra ¼ cup warm water. Knead until very smooth, about 15 minutes.

3. To make the dough with an electric mixer: Combine the flour and ½ teaspoon salt in a sifter, then sift into a large bowl. Fit the mixer with the paddle attachment, add the eggs, and mix on low speed until the mixture resembles little peas. Replace the paddle with a dough hook. Slowly pour in 1 cup of the warm water until a soft dough forms. If the dough feels dry or hard at this stage, add the remaining ¼ cup warm water. Continue to knead the dough with the dough hook until smooth, 12 to 15 minutes.

4. Form the dough into a large ball, cover with a damp cotton towel, and let rest in a draft-free area for 20 minutes. The dough will be more pliable after it rests. If the dough feels dry or hard after 20 minutes, add an extra ¼ cup warm water. Whether you add water or not, knead the dough again, by hand or mixer, until very smooth, 5 to 10 minutes.

5. Line 2 large baking sheets with waxed paper and dust the waxed paper with flour. Form the dough into a large oval loaf about 11 by 7 inches. Cut off a 1-inch-thick slice of the dough. Pass the slice through a manual pasta machine set on the first setting. Next, sprinkle the

bottom of the dough with the remaining ¼ cup flour, then fold the dough into thirds. Pass the dough through the rollers again. Repeat this process on the first setting a total of 8 times.

6. Adjust the pasta machine to the second setting. Do not fold the dough into thirds. Pass the dough through the rollers once. Then, adjust the setting to number 3, and continue in the same manner, passing the dough through the rollers once each on the third, fourth, and fifth settings. Transfer the resulting pasta sheet to 1 of the prepared baking sheets. Repeat until all of the dough has been rolled out, arranging the sheets in a single layer on the baking sheets. To make ravioli sheets, stop at the fifth setting; do not put pasta through the cutter. Go to step 8.

7. To make *pasta di casa*, fettuccine, or linguine: Select the cutter width you want, and pass the pasta sheets through the cutter on the fifth setting, then stop. Dough passed though the sixth setting is too thin for regular pastas, but fine for making *capellini* (angel hair pasta) for soups. If you are unable to cook the pasta immediately, sprinkle it with extra flour, toss gently, cover well, and freeze for up to 3 days.

8. To make ravioli: Pass the dough sheets through setting number 5. Lightly oil and then flour a ravioli mold with large or small indentations. Place 1 sheet of dough over the ravioli mold, the part with the round or square cut-out shapes. Position the other half of the mold, with the round or square indentations on it, over the dough, and press down gently to form the indentations in the dough for the filling. Gently separate the 2 mold pieces. If making small ravioli, fill each indentation with 1 heaping tablespoon of ravioli filling. For large ravioli, use 1½ heaping tablespoons of filling for each indentation.

9. Place a second sheet of dough over the ravioli. Using a rolling pin, roll back and forth over the dough several times until all the edges

Secrets of Success

Never stack fresh pasta or ravioli; it will stick badly, ruining it completely. For the finest taste, cook fresh pasta on the day it is made. Although it will lose some freshness, it is acceptable to cook fresh pasta or ravioli within 2 or 3 days, but no longer than that. Serve the pasta or ravioli topped with your favorite tomato sauce. Sprinkle generously with your grated cheese and grindings of fresh pepper.

around the ravioli are cut and the ravioli can be separated. Tilt the ravioli mold on its side and tap it from behind; the ravioli will pop out.

10. Line 1 or 2 large baking sheets with waxed paper and sprinkle with flour. Transfer the ravioli to the prepared baking sheets and sprinkle extra flour over the top. Cook immediately, or freeze for up to 3 days.

11. To cook the ravioli or fresh pasta: Bring a large pot of water to a boil and add the 1 tablespoon salt and the olive oil. If cooking ravioli, add them and boil until they rise to the surface, about 5 minutes (1 or 2 minutes longer if frozen). If cooking fresh fettuccine or most other long pastas, boil for 2 or 3 minutes (1 or 2 minutes longer if frozen). Fine pastas need to cook only 1 or 2 minutes, even if frozen. Sicilians use a large slotted spoon to remove the ravioli and a spaghetti fork (large fork with slightly curved tines) to scoop out the long pastas. As they are removed, transfer them to individual dishes.

Great-grandma Maria with her sons, in 1916. Her Sunday sauce was considered the best in Little Italy.

Salsa
SEVEN-HOUR SUNDAY TOMATO SAUCE

Makes about 6 quarts, enough to sauce 4 pounds pasta or one 2-pound pan of lasagna; serves 12

I began helping Grandma make this tomato sauce when I was three years old. Years ago we made it with fresh tomatoes from the vegetable stands on Mott and Mulberry streets. We boiled the tomatoes, and strained them by hand through a *stringituri* (flat disk colander). Canned tomatoes were used only when fresh ones were out of season. Today, flavorful fresh tomatoes are expensive, so using canned tomatoes year-round has become common.

Traditionally, we gather to *bagna pane* (bathe the bread), which is the Sicilian ritual of dipping bread into the pot of sauce. Everyone in the family insists that his or her mother makes the best tomato sauce, and heated battles regularly ensue. Once my uncle and his wife fought so loudly over the subject, they almost came to blows. When my father walked through the door unknowingly, my uncle grabbed him excitedly by the arm. "The truth, who makes the best tomato sauce?"

Innocently, Dad replied, "Of course, it's your mother. There's not even a question." My aunt threw her arms in the air, exasperated. "All right, all right! Nobody makes tomato sauce like your mother. She's the greatest cook in the world!"

Vindicated, Uncle Phil placed his finger right in her face and shouted, "You said it, kid—not me!"

When Sicilian Americans make this sauce, it is customary for them to measure the water with the empty cans from the tomato paste and whole tomatoes. My recipe is written this way, but I've also added the equivalent in cups to help you measure more quickly. Serve this tomato sauce with your favorite fresh pasta noodles or homemade ravioli (page 91), or use it to assemble a 2-pound pan of lasagna (page 108).

(CONTINUED)

Secrets of Success

If possible, make the tomato sauce 1 day ahead of serving to allow the herbs and spices time to settle and enhance the overall flavor.

Extra-virgin olive oil

6 cloves garlic, sliced

1 teaspoon sugar, or as needed

6 cans (6 ounces each) tomato paste

1½ tablespoons dried oregano, sticks removed, crushed until powdery

1 teaspoon salt, or to taste

8 fresh basil leaves

12 tomato paste cans water (9 cups water)

3 cans (35 ounces each) whole tomatoes with juice, strained of seeds

1½ to 2 whole tomato cans water (6½ cups water)

1 recipe Meatballs made with 2½ pounds meat (page 18)

1 recipe Stuffed Pork Roast for Seven-Hour Tomato Sauce (page 99)

½ to ¾ pound beef stew meat, cut into large cubes

1 pound sweet or hot Italian sausages

1. Generously oil a 12-quart stainless steel pot and place over medium heat. Add the garlic and sauté until golden, about 1 minute. Vigorously stir in 1 teaspoon sugar and the tomato paste. Then add ½ tablespoon of the oregano, ½ teaspoon of the salt, and 4 basil leaves. Reduce the heat to very low, cover the pot, and simmer, stirring occasionally, for 5 minutes. The paste should be bubbling. After 5 minutes, stir in the 12 paste cans of water. Bring the tomato sauce to a rolling boil over high heat. Cover the pot, reduce heat to very low, and simmer until extremely thick, about 20 minutes.

2. Next, add the strained whole tomatoes and 1½ tomato cans water. Add the remaining 1 tablespoon oregano, ½ teaspoon salt, and 4 basil leaves. Bring the sauce to a rolling boil over high heat, then reduce heat to very, very low. The surface of the sauce should be barely rippling. Prop a wooden spoon under the lid to keep the pot half covered.

3. Meanwhile, prepare the meatballs and the pork meat. Generously oil a medium-size frying pan and place over medium-high heat. In batches, add the meatballs and the pork roast and brown on all sides.

Secrets of Success

Always cook the tomato sauce in a stainless steel pot; aluminum can inflict an iodine taste on tomato sauce. If the tomatoes are sour, add 1 cup sweet red wine to remove the off-taste. To ensure the sweetness of the sauce, Grandma always adds 1 teaspoon sugar while sautéing the garlic, plus all the leftover oil and scraped bits from browning the meats. If there is too much salt or sugar in the sauce, add a glassful of water at a time until the saltiness or artificial sweetness disappears, and allow the sauce to cook down again.

As they are browned, add them to the tomato sauce. (Do not stir the sauce for 40 minutes after the meatballs are added. They need time to set or they will break apart.) Next, brown the beef cubes and the sausages, then add them to the sauce with any leftover oil and scraped bits from the frying pan. All the meats should be added to the tomato sauce within the first 2 hours of cooking and must be covered by the sauce. If they are not, add just enough water to cover them.

4. Every hour, taste the tomato sauce and adjust all the seasonings as necessary. Slowly stir the tomato sauce every 30 minutes, being careful not to break the meatballs. If the tomato sauce is bitter after 6 hours, add 1 more teaspoon sugar, stir, cook for a few minutes, and retaste; adjust the sugar as necessary. The tomato sauce should cook a total of 7 hours, and the consistency should be thick but not mudlike. Once the sauce is done, scoop off any excess oil that has settled on top and discard. The appearance of the oil signifies a deliciously sweet sauce, a result of the pork and beef releasing their flavorful fats.

To Store Tomato Sauce

You must store the meats and the sauce in separate bowls to prevent the meatballs from absorbing the sauce. If only a portion of the tomato sauce is used, freeze the rest for up to 3 months. Unlike refrigerated sauces, the meatballs can be frozen right in the tomato sauce without any absorption problem. Freeze the sauce in 1½-quart plastic containers with a few meatballs and pieces of pork. One container of tomato sauce combined with 1 pound pasta will serve 4 people.

To Defrost Tomato Sauce

Defrost the tomato sauce overnight in the refrigerator. Alternatively, place the container of frozen sauce into a pot of hot tap water for 30 minutes to begin the thawing process, then reheat the semifrozen tomato sauce over very low heat. It will easily defrost.

Sunday Dinner

FOR SICILIANS, *Pranzo di Domenica* (Sunday dinner) is the most sacramental part of their life, as well as the most special time of the week. At Grandma's house, it only included the immediate family and relatives from Sicily who were visiting. Friends were never invited. Everyone traipsed in around midday, except the women who were helping Grandma cook, like my mother and me. We arrived shortly after nine o'clock mass to assist, but Grandma never needed much help. She was always well organized and accustomed to cooking for large numbers of people. By three o'clock at the latest, we would begin our first course of chicken soup, always followed by her Sunday tomato sauce with pasta. Several hours later, we ended the ceremony with espresso, anisette, *cannoli*, and ½-inch-thick Nestle's chocolate bars.

The place of honor at the table always went to Grandpa, the patriarch of the family. He ate his spaghetti from the traditional *spillongo* (oval platter), with Grandma by his side. Around him, like his own troops in an army, sat all his children and grandchildren. Often we kids were placed at a separate table set up in the living room, where we were entertained by television. Since we were waited on and able to watch our cartoons, none of us complained.

Although the meal was primarily the same every Sunday, it was never boring. The menu only changed if there was a seasonal vegetable Grandma found at the market, like *cardune* (cardoons), or if the London broil at the butcher shop looked exceptional and was substituted for the customary club or T-bone steaks. It was unthinkable for anyone to bring food to Grandma's house. She would have considered it an insult, implying that she was not doing her job properly of cooking for *la familia*. What was permitted were gifts of cookies, pastries, candies, or *gelato*.

There was great tradition in this dinner, and more than anything else, it kept the family together. When Grandpa Natale died, the family scattered, which proves that there must always be one person, a head of the family, who demands respect and honor. ॐ

Braciole di Maiale Grande per la Salsa
STUFFED PORK ROAST FOR THE SEVEN-HOUR TOMATO SAUCE

🐚 To most Italian Americans, *braciole* are thin pieces of beef or pork rolled around a stuffing. But in Ciminna, my great-grandmother Maria would cook one large piece of pork roast for *braciole*, which was standard in Sicily. Sicilians consider the smaller, thinner *braciole* found in America to be a Little Italy invention.

1 recipe (6 quarts) Seven-Hour Sunday Tomato Sauce (page 95)

     made with 2½ pounds Meatballs (page 18)

1 boneless pork loin center cut, 2 to 2½ pounds

Salt and freshly ground black pepper, to taste

2 large cloves garlic, cut into medium dice

4 slices provolone or *cacio-cavallo* cheese, each 2 by 2 by ¼ inch thick

Grated romano or *incanestrato* cheese

6 slices medium-small yellow onion

3 fresh Italian parsley sprigs, large thick stems removed

4 fresh basil leaves

1 meatball, fried until cooked through and broken into chunks

1 Sicilian sweet sausage, fried until cooked through and broken into chunks

1 hard-cooked egg, peeled and quartered

1. Prepare the tomato sauce through Step 3.

2. Meanwhile, cut a deep, lengthwise slit along the center of the pork, and open it flat. Sprinkle the meat with salt and pepper. Across the center of the meat, layer evenly the garlic, cheese slices, 2 teaspoons grated cheese, onion slices, parsley sprigs, basil leaves, meatball, sausage, and egg quarters. Reshape the pork into its original form and tie it with kitchen string at 1-inch intervals. Secure each end with 2 toothpicks.

(CONTINUED)

3. Brown and cook the pork roast as directed in Step 3 for the tomato sauce. When the sauce is ready, transfer the pork roast to a platter. Cut off the strings, remove all the toothpicks, and allow to rest for 10 minutes. Cut into slices ½ inch thick. Drizzle with the tomato sauce and top with grated cheese.

Salsa di Semane
WEEKDAY TOMATO SAUCE

Makes about 1¹⁄₂ quarts, enough to sauce about 1¹⁄₂ pounds pasta; serves 4

🐖 This standard weekday sauce was made by all the Sicilians in Little Italy. It was a quick sauce and, unlike the Sunday sauce, it often did not contain meat. If meat was added, it was usually in the form of meatballs. But since tomato sauce requires pork for sweetness, the meatballs used in the weekday sauce were always made with ¼ pound chopped pork mixed into every 1 pound chopped beef. If no meatballs were used, a pork chop or sparerib was commonly added for sweetness.

Extra-virgin olive oil

3 large cloves garlic, cut into medium dice

2 cans (6 ounces each) tomato paste

6 fresh basil leaves

¾ teaspoon salt, or to taste

2 teaspoons dried oregano, sticks removed, crushed until powdery

4 tomato paste cans water (3 cups water)

1 can (35 ounces) whole tomatoes with juice or tomato purée, strained of seeds

**1 recipe Meatballs (page 18) made with ½ to 1 pound meat,
     including chopped pork (optional)**

1 pork chop or sparerib (optional)

1 teaspoon sugar, if needed

1. Generously oil a medium-size pot and place over medium heat. Add the garlic and sauté until golden, about 1 minute. Stir in the tomato paste, 3 basil leaves, half of the salt, and half the oregano. Stir vigorously. Once the tomato paste begins to boil, reduce the heat, cover the pot, and simmer for 5 minutes, stirring occasionally. The mixture should become very thick and dark. Stir in the 4 paste cans of water and bring the sauce to a rolling boil over high heat. Reduce the heat to medium-low, cover the pot, and let cook for 15 minutes.

2. Meanwhile, prepare the meatballs, if using. Lightly oil a medium-size frying pan, and place over medium-high heat. Brown the meatballs on all sides and transfer to a plate. Add the pork chop, if using, to the pan, brown on both sides, and remove from the heat.

3. After the tomato paste mixture has cooked for 15 minutes, stir in the strained tomatoes and the remaining basil, salt, and oregano. Then add the meatballs, the pork chop, and all the oil, drippings, and scraped bits from the frying pan. Cover the pot, bring the sauce to a rolling boil, and boil for 2 minutes. Reduce the heat to very low. Prop a wooden spoon under the lid to keep the pot half uncovered, and cook gently until thick, 1½ to 2 hours. While the sauce is cooking, stir it every 20 minutes, being careful not to break the meatballs, and taste and adjust all the seasonings as necessary. If the sauce is bitter after 1 hour, add the sugar.

SAUCE FOR VEAL CUTLETS PARMESAN (PAGE 175)

Prepare as directed, but omit the meatballs and pork. After oiling the pot, sauté 2 large yellow onions, sliced ⅓ inch thick, over medium heat until golden, about 10 minutes. Add only 1 can (6 ounces) tomato paste and 1½ cups water. Then add 1 hot or mild dried sausage or pepperoni (about 10 ounces), cut into ¼-inch-thick slices, and simmer the sauce for about 1¼ hours. It should have a medium-thick consistency when ready.

Some Opinions on Estratto

G RANDMA ON *estratto:* "In Ciminna we made *estratto* all the time. It was easy! We made it in our backyard. We had the land, the sun, and the room. But in America it was a big production and I made it only a few times. Then my cousin Frank, as a joke, threw two stones into it as it sat on the roof. To me what he did was a disgrace to my cooking. I had a big fight with Frank and never made it again. And every time I hear the word *estratto*, I think of that fight."

Mother on *estratto:* "It was like a crazy thing making *estratto*. Up and down the roof for the sun. I never even cared for it that much. But it was to the Sicilians what caviar is to the French. It was the 'in' thing to make. Along Houston, Elizabeth, and Mott streets in the late summer all you would hear about was people making *estratto*. It was a *smania* [a mania]."

Father on *estratto:* "My mother made it a few times. I used to have to carry those boards on my back up the steps to the roof, then down. *Estratto* made the sauce very dark red and thick. I liked it, but in the city it was too much work. You need a backyard to make *estratto*."

Uncle Paul on *estratto:* "Mikey and I used to carry the boards, covered with thirty-two pounds of tomatoes, on our backs up to the roof. Then we'd bring the *estratto* back home when the sun went down. It was work. Every day we used to stir the tomatoes, and finally after a few weeks they would get thick like mud. Then if it rained, your grandma would call out the window, *'L'estratto—Paul-eeee! Mi-keeee!'* We kids knew to run back home and go to the roof and bring down the boards. And if you were lucky and everything went

Uncle Mike as a child.

right!" he popped up like a weasel, grabbed a spoon and held it high in the air, and hit his other hand on the table hard, "You got one tablespoon."

"One tablespoon!" My cousin Robert and I shouted hysterically as we listened to him speak.

"Don't laugh!" replied Uncle Paul immediately. "That's if everything went right. But if it rained or water got into it, it was over. You kids have no idea what we used to go through for food in those days. Everything's easy today—in a can. In the old days, we used to keep the *estratto* in a small ceramic jar in the closet over the sink. I would climb on the sink, take the jar down, and sneak some to eat. Your grandma would see me, come running from the living room, and hit me with a wooden spoon, 'Get down from there! *L'assalo ire l'estratto! L'assalo ire l'estratto!'* [Leave the *estratto* alone!] But I loved that damned *estratto*," his voice cracked slightly. "I would eat it by the spoonfuls, and it was worth getting hit for." 🐾

Estratto
SICILIAN TOMATO PASTE

✒ *Estratto* is the original tomato paste, the mother of tomato paste as we know it today. It imparts a dark maroon color and gives a rich flavor of tomato and basil to sauces. It should not be confused with the toothpaste tubes of *estratto* sold at gourmet food stores, which is definitely not *estratto*, but recycled tomato paste. Save your money!

Here's a bit of history: Students in my cooking classes ask me how tomato sauce was made in Sicily at the turn of the century when the tomato season was over. It was with *estratto*, which was prepared and stored in ceramic jars for the winter. The regular Sunday sauce could not be made without fresh tomatoes, but a tomato sauce made with lots of water and *estratto* rendered a thinner but acceptable sauce for most people. *Estratto* was also used to make red-based stews or to add a touch of flavor to anything in which a tomato might have originally been used. Sun-dried tomatoes were not used in the winter. Southern Italians consider them a low-class food and unpleasantly rubbery. Many southern Italians and Sicilians have never even heard of sun-dried tomatoes. And for all the contemporary talk about plum tomatoes, you'll be shocked to know they did not exist in the early 1900s in Ciminna, and Grandma didn't even see them in Palermo when she went to school there in the teens. The only kind of tomatoes used to make sauce in those days were the large, red beefsteak tomatoes, which Grandma says were as sweet as honey. The first time she saw plum tomatoes was in America in Little Italy in the early 1920s.

In the old days *estratto* was not refrigerated, but it was used constantly. Therefore, for the sake of safety, store it in the warmest part of the refrigerator for up to 4 months. If some still remains after that time, discard it and make a fresh batch.

Secrets of Success

If you're using tomato paste along with *estratto* in a sauce, use only 1 teaspoon to 1 tablespoon *estratto*, or the sauce will become too thick too soon. *Estratto* must be made on hot, dry, summer days, when the sun is very strong—at least 90°F. Check the weather forecast for the coming 2 weeks before beginning this recipe.

30 pounds beefsteak or plum tomatoes, cut into large chunks

Salt, to taste

6 fresh basil leaves, or to taste

Extra-virgin olive oil

1. Place the tomatoes in a 12-quart pot over very low heat. Cook, stirring every 3 minutes to prevent sticking, until the skins become soft and split, about 45 minutes. While the tomatoes are cooking, using a potato masher, crush them into smaller chunks.

2. In batches, pass the tomatoes through a food mill fitted with the disk with the smallest holes, then return them to the pot. Add the salt, keeping in mind that *estratto* should taste a little salty. Bring the tomatoes to a boil over high heat, reduce the heat to low, and simmer for 2 hours more, stirring every 5 minutes. After the tomatoes have reached a consistency the thickness of crushed tomatoes, spoon the mixture in a thin even layer onto a large wooden board (about 4 feet by 8 feet) or about 12 large platters.

3. Transfer the board or platters outside and set them, uncovered, in the strong sunlight (90°F or hotter) until sunset. During the day, stir the mixture 6 times. Then, bring the board or platters into the house and cover them loosely with plastic wrap. The next morning, uncover and repeat the process. Do this for 14 consecutive days. Each day the mixture will dry a little more in the hot sun.

(CONTINUED)

4. No water is added to this dish. If it begins to rain, immediately bring the *estratto* indoors, then return it to the outdoors as soon as the sun shines. If it rains for 1 day, store the *estratto*, covered, in the driest area of your home. If the estratto has dried halfway, for 7 days or more, spoon it into large bowls, cover well, and refrigerate for up to 2 days. If, however, the *estratto* is still very liquid and you have 1 whole week of rain, the dish will be ruined. The liquid tomato chunks will spoil after only a few days in the refrigerator, so discard them and begin the recipe again.

5. On the 14th day, stir in the basil. At this stage the *estratto* should be a dark, rich maroon and as thick as mud. Spoon it into a large ceramic or glass jar with a tight-fitting lid. Stir in 4 tablespoons olive oil, then pour in enough olive oil to form a layer ½ inch thick on the top. Do not stir in this oil. Cover the top of the jar with plastic wrap and seal with the lid. If the *estratto* begins to dry out, stir in a little more oil and pour additional oil on top.

Note: When making *estratto*, the yield is about 10 to 1, that is, 30 pounds of tomatoes will yield about 3 pounds of *estratto*. Since you use only 1 or 2 tablespoons when making a sauce, this amount will last for months. To make less *estratto*, simply halve the recipe, but I think it's foolish to do all this work for a smaller quantity.

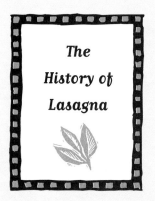

The History of Lasagna

LASAGNA IS CONSIDERED one of Sicily's most elegant dishes. Developed in the town of Modica on the southern tip of the island, the recipe, which contained a generous amount of meats and was made with the slow-cooked Sunday tomato sauce, was enjoyed only by wealthy Sicilians. What I didn't know when I began to write this book was that my grandma was actually one of the inventors of the lasagna made in Little Italy today. Here is the conversation I had with her about the history of this famous dish.

"What lasagna!" Grandma laughed. "In those days, there was no such thing as lasagna. It was called *pasta infornata* [pasta baked in the oven]. Years later, it was called lasagna after the shape of the pasta used to make it. Most of us were dirt poor, Fren-zee, when we came over, and lasagna was only for the very wealthy. People hardly ever made it sixty years ago. If you asked, nobody knew what it was! It was only served at the weddings of the wealthy, at baptisms, and for special occasions. The first time I tasted it was at *cugina* [cousin] Vitina's wedding. Grandpa liked it, a shock! So I went home and made it in my own way. People in the neighborhood heard about it, so one by one they knocked on my door, '*Signora*, we heard you make a baked pasta with ricotta, mozzarella, and a delicious tomato sauce. Would you teach us?'

"Who do you think taught the people in my area how to make lasagna?" she asked, grinning complacently. "Grandma," she said, pointing to herself.

"You mean, you're the one who set the standard and taught people how to make lasagna in Little Italy?"

"Not everybody, but a lot of people passed through my door, then taught others."

"Why you should be famous!" I began shouting. "To think you were one of the originators of lasagna in Little Italy—Grandma this is big, really big! But!" I turned sharply while a feeling of pride swelled in my heart, "I bet they don't make it as good as you do!"

"Well, Fren-zee," she giggled, sitting down, "now that's another story entirely." She adjusted her garter and crossed her little legs, contented at my compliment. 🌿

Lasagne al Forno
BAKED LASAGNA

🍴 Here's Grandma's original 1942 lasagna recipe, my all-time favorite dish. Note: A pan measuring about 15 by 9½ inches and 4 inches deep will hold this 2-pound lasagna. To make 1 pound of lasagna, halve the recipe and freeze leftover sauce (see page 97).

1 recipe Seven-Hour Sunday Tomato Sauce (page 95) made with

    2½ pounds Meatballs and Stuffed Pork Roast

1 tablespoon salt

2 tablespoons extra-virgin olive oil

2 pounds lasagna noodles (32 noodles)

4 cups cold water

3 pounds fresh ricotta cheese

1½ pounds fresh mozzarella cheese, cut into ¼-inch-thick slices,

    then quartered

3½ cups or more grated romano cheese

1. Make the tomato sauce, including the meatballs and pork roast. Ladle half of the tomato sauce, without the meatballs or pork, into a large bowl. Set aside.

2. Bring a 14-quart or larger pot of water to a boil and add the salt and olive oil. If you do not own a large pot, use two 8-quart pots and boil 1 pound of noodles in each. Add noodles to the boiling water and cook until tender. Drain the noodles in a colander and then return them to the pot in which they were cooked. Add the cold water to cool the noodles and prevent them from sticking together. As they are needed, remove 3 noodles at a time, and return them to the colander to drain.

Secrets of Success

Since making lasagna can be time-consuming, I suggest preparing the tomato sauce one day ahead, and then assembling the lasagna the next day. Ask anyone who makes a great lasagna what the secret is and they'll reply, "Be sure to add enough of everything."

3. In another large bowl, combine the ricotta and 4 cups of the tomato sauce. Break 2 pounds of the meatballs into large chunks and add them to the bowl. If the ricotta mixture seems dry or looks too white, stir in 1 or 2 more cups of tomato sauce. Reserve the extra meatballs for the top layer.

4. Preheat an oven to 350°F. Spread a generous layer of the reserved tomato sauce (without the meatballs) on the bottom of the pan (see recipe introduction for dimensions). Line the bottom with a layer of noodles, fitting them edge to edge and making sure they do not overlap (about 4½ noodles per layer). Spread a generous amount of ricotta mixture evenly over the noodles. Evenly top with some of the mozzarella pieces, and then with ½ cup of the romano cheese. Next, spread a generous amount of tomato sauce over the top, completely covering the lasagna. Repeat the layering until all the ingredients are used up and you reach the top of the pan. (You will have 7 layers.) Cover the last layer with extra tomato sauce. Break the reserved meatballs into large chunks and spread them on top. Sprinkle with mozzarella and grated cheese to create a beautiful-looking lasagna.

5. Bake the lasagna, uncovered, on the middle rack of the oven for 45 to 60 minutes. To check, use a spatula to lift a corner section. If the mozzarella is completely melted in the center layers, the lasagna is done. Let stand for 10 minutes before serving, then cut into squares. Place the *braciole* on a platter, snip the strings, and slice. Serve with the lasagna.

Secrets of Success

Use noodles with curly edges; they are the traditional lasagna noodles of Little Italy. Do not use noodles with ridges through them; they're too thick and gummy and will ruin the taste of the dish. Always add a few tablespoons of oil when boiling the noodles, or they will stick badly.

Salsa di Vongole di Mamma
MOTHER'S CLAM SAUCE

Makes about 4
quarts, enough
to sauce 3
pounds pasta;
serves 8 to 10

This sauce can be cooked with other types of fish, such as shrimp, crabmeat, or calamari, but Mom prefers making it with clams. It does not have an overly fishy taste, so you may want to add another cup of clam juice during the last hour of cooking. Linguine is traditionally served with this sauce, but spaghetti and spaghettini are also acceptable. As opposed to the rest of Italy, Sicilians have always used cheese when preparing their fish dishes. Here, I recommend serving grated *ricotta salata* or *incanestrato*. Both cheeses impart extra flavor to the clams and complement the pepper in the sauce.

Secrets of Success

Using a sieve lined with paper towels instead of cheesecloth removes the dirt, sand, and grit from the clam juice properly. In Sicily, tiny "pasta clams" are used for this dish. In America, New Zealand cockles, which are half the size of littlenecks, can be substituted.

8 dozen New Zealand cockles, shucked and left whole with liquor reserved;

    5 dozen littlenecks, shucked and halved with liquor reserved; or 4 dozen

    cherrystone clams, shucked and coarsely chopped with liquor reserved

Extra-virgin olive oil

6 cloves garlic, sliced

4 cans (6 ounces each) tomato paste

6 tomato paste cans water (4½ cups water)

2 cans (28 ounces each) tomato purée, strained of seeds

1¾ tomato purée cans water (6¼ cups water)

8 fresh basil leaves

4 tablespoons dried oregano, sticks removed, crushed until powdery

1 tablespoon salt, or to taste

2 teaspoons red pepper flakes or cayenne pepper or 3 dried chili peppers,

    coarsely chopped

1. Line a medium-size sieve with 2 white paper towels. Position the sieve over a bowl. Pour the reserved clam liquor through the sieve. Discard the paper towels, rinse the sieve, and repeat the procedure 3 more times, using 2 new paper towels each time. At this point the liquor should be clear and free of sand; if it is not, repeat the filtering until it is. You should have about 2 cups. Set aside.

2. In an 8-quart pot, combine ⅓ cup olive oil and the garlic and place over low heat. Sauté until the garlic is golden, about 2 minutes. Add the tomato paste and, using a wooden spoon, stir the mixture constantly for 3 minutes. Stir in the 6 paste cans of water. Bring to a boil, then reduce the heat, cover, and simmer for 15 minutes. Stir in the tomato purée, the 1¾ purée cans of water, the basil, oregano, salt, pepper, and 1½ to 2 cups reserved liquor, depending on the taste. Bring the sauce to a boil and add 4 tablespoons olive oil. Reduce the heat to very low so the surface of the sauce is barely rippling. Prop a wooden spoon under the lid to keep the pot half uncovered, and cook gently until medium-thick, about 4½ hours. While the sauce is cooking, stir it every 30 minutes, and taste and adjust all the seasonings as necessary. Add the clams during the last hour.

Storage

Because this sauce contains fish, it should be refrigerated and used within 3 days. Smell the sauce; if it smells rancid, discard it. Freezing the leftover sauce in 1-, 2- or 3-quart containers is preferred. It will keep for 1 month.

Salsa Marinara
MARINARA SAUCE

🐟 This sauce is the centuries-old invention of Sicilian fishermen who came into port and needed a quick tomato sauce that was easy to make on board. Topped with grated *ricotta salata*, linguine tossed with marinara sauce has become one of the most famous dishes throughout Sicily, Little Italy, and now the whole United States. Despite popular belief, fishermen did not put their fish into the sauce. Instead, they sold their fish, because if they ate their catch, it translated into less money in their pockets.

If you want to make this sauce the way the fishermen made it centuries ago, here's the original recipe: Prepare as directed below, but substitute 2½ pounds fresh tomatoes, cut into small chunks, for the can of whole tomatoes. Place the tomato chunks with their skins and seeds in the frying pan, and as the sauce simmers, crush the tomatoes with a fork. During the cooking, the tomato skins will curl; remove them with a fork and discard. If the fresh tomatoes are too dry, add ¾ cup water to the sauce. Otherwise, water is never added.

Secrets of Success

To make marinara sauce come out perfect, plan to cook the sauce for 1 minute for every 1 ounce of tomatoes used.

1 can (35 ounces) whole tomatoes with juice, unstrained and unseeded

Extra-virgin olive oil

5 cloves garlic, sliced

2 teaspoons dried oregano, sticks removed, crushed until powdery

Salt, to taste

6 fresh basil leaves

1 pound linguine

Grated *ricotta salata*, *pepato,* or romano cheese

Freshly ground black pepper or red pepper flakes, to taste

1. Pour the tomatoes and their juice into a medium-size bowl. Using a slotted spoon and working in batches, remove the whole tomatoes to a separate dish. Crush them well with a fork or potato masher. (Do not

put the tomatoes in a blender or food processor or the texture will be ruined.) The tomatoes should be left in small chunks. Return the tomatoes to the bowl. Set aside.

2. Generously oil a large frying pan with olive oil and place over medium heat. Add the garlic and sauté until golden, about 1 minute. Add the tomatoes, oregano, salt, and basil. Bring to a boil, reduce the heat to medium-low, and simmer until the sauce is medium-thick and has a chunky consistency, about 35 minutes.

3. Meanwhile, cook and drain the linguine. Transfer the pasta to a platter, spoon a little sauce over the top, and toss well. Top with grated cheese and pepper, and serve the remaining sauce on the side.

Pasta con le Sarde
PASTA WITH SARDINES

Serves 4

𓂀 In Sicily, this dish is traditionally made for St. Joseph's Feast Day, which falls on March 19. A *tavoletta* (large spread of many dishes) is put out, and this is one of the few times when family and friends are encouraged to bring something homemade to eat, and thus share in the dinner preparation. People roam from house to house and eat a little from each buffet as they visit.

Most cooks know *pasta con le sarde* as a dish without tomatoes, but there were always two versions. Here, I have chosen to include the tomato-based one since I've never seen it printed. The use of fried bread crumbs in place of cheese originated with the peasants, since cheese was far too expensive for them. The resulting taste was spectacular and the texture delightfully crunchy. It soon became a standard throughout Sicily. This tradition continues at the table of St. Joseph.

(CONTINUED)

Note that there are two types of fennel, *finocchio dulce* (sweet fennel), which has a very strong taste of licorice, and *finocchio* (wild fennel), which is the regular leafy kind that tastes like a vegetable, not a candy. Sadly, neither of these two tastes exist in America, so we must make do with what we have. If available, purchase wild fennel, not sweet fennel, for St. Joseph's Feast Day. Since it costs $110 a bushel, only a few gourmet stores carry it. You can also buy the Italian seeds (page 330) and grow the wild fennel yourself. If wild fennel is unavailable, substitute sweet fennel (see note below). In New York City, Balducci's carries wild fennel in March. If it's California grown, it's $5 per pound. If it's grown in Sicily, it's $20 per pound.

Secrets of Success

Fry the bread crumbs at the last minute, or they will become soggy.

½ **pound fresh sardines (about 6 sardines), each 6 inches long,**
   filleted (page 136)

6 **tablespoons extra-virgin olive oil**

1 **large clove garlic, cut into medium dice**

1 **can (6 ounces) tomato paste**

5 **tomato paste cans water (3¾ cups)**

1 **teaspoon dried oregano, sticks removed, crushed until powdery**

4 **fresh basil leaves**

Salt

3 **tablespoons golden raisins**

3 **tablespoons pine nuts**

1 **bunch wild fennel or sweet fennel (see note), stalks separated and trimmed**

3 **tablespoons extra-virgin olive oil**

1 **pound *perciatelli* or *bucatini* (long pasta with a hole in the middle)**

½ **cup unseasoned bread crumbs, homemade (page 14) or purchased**

Grated *ricotta salata, incanestrato, pepato,* romano, or provolone cheese

1. Cut the sardine fillets into 1-inch pieces. In a medium-size pot, combine the olive oil, garlic, and sardines over medium heat. Sauté, stirring frequently with a wooden spoon to smash the sardines and garlic together, until a paste forms, about 10 minutes.

2. Stir in the tomato paste and 5 cans water. Add the oregano, basil, ½ teaspoon salt, raisins, and pine nuts. Stir well and bring the sauce to a rolling boil. Next, reduce the heat to very low so the surface of the sauce is only barely boiling. Prop a wooden spoon under the lid to keep the pot half uncovered, and simmer until the sauce is medium-thick, about 1 hour. While the sauce is cooking, stir it every 15 minutes, and taste and adjust all the seasonings as necessary.

3. As soon as the sauce begins to simmer, bring a large pot of water to a boil and add ½ teaspoon salt. The wild fennel will take 5 to 15 minutes to cook, and the sweet fennel will take 35 to 45 minutes. Add the fennel and cook until the leaves and stalks are fork tender. Using a slotted spoon, transfer the fennel to a platter, and cut the leaves and stalks into bite-size pieces. Add the fennel to the sauce and reserve the fennel cooking water in the pot.

4. Return the pot of fennel water to a boil. Add 1 tablespoon of the olive oil. Cook and drain the pasta. Transfer the pasta to individual dishes.

5. Meanwhile, 5 minutes before serving, heat the remaining 2 tablespoons olive oil over medium heat. Add the bread crumbs and a little salt to taste. Stir constantly until the bread crumbs become a rich brown and are crispy, about 5 minutes. Transfer to a small bowl. Although it's traditional to use only the bread crumbs on the pasta, many Sicilians prefer grated cheese with or without the bread crumbs. I suggest serving both.

Note: If substituting sweet fennel, purchase a bunch with very leafy tops. Use the leafy tops and the long, thin stems. Remove the white bulbs, wrap them in plastic wrap, and refrigerate for a snack.

The Curse of the Woman in the Red Dress

WHILE PREPARING PASTA one afternoon, Grandma told me about Don Ciccio Lutari, the wealthiest man in Ciminna. He owned a great deal of farmland, and the townspeople considered him a knight, riding around, as he always did, on his magnificent white horse. Many times he would pass a convent up on a hill where he noticed a very pretty young nun, Filomena, who peered back at him through the shutters of her window. One day he tipped his hat and waved at her, and she waved back. The next day, he waited for her to come out of the convent, and when she was in the doorway, he picked her up in his arms, threw her over his horse's back, and rode off.

It was one of the biggest scandals in Ciminna. The sisters of the convent ran to the police and demanded that Don Ciccio be arrested for kidnapping, but because he was a noble, and owned the whole town, the police feared him and did nothing. After several days passed, Don Ciccio came riding into town to announce he and the nun were married. The town finally calmed down. The two of them adored each other and lived a very happy, quiet, and content life. But during the birth of her third child, Filomena died at the age of only twenty-six. Don Ciccio was heartbroken and inconsolable. The townspeople believed that she died so young and in such an unfortunate way because God took her for leaving the convent.

About two years later, Don Ciccio Lutari met another pretty woman. Her name was Rosetta, and she was extremely poor, but very kind in spirit, with malice toward none. For twenty years she lived with him—raising his children as if they were her own—always believing Don Ciccio's promises to marry her. After three years of living with him, he gave her some property and money to secure her future, then several years later cruelly tricked her into returning them by promising jewels and that she was to be his wife, which would ensure her half of all his property. But the Don never had any intention of marrying Rosetta.

One day, the Don's married son came to live in his father's house, and the young man's wife, learning by vicious rumor that Rosetta was not really her husband's mother, refused to eat with her. The children, who had thought Rosetta was their

116

real mother for twenty years, turned on her after all she had done for them. Instead of immediately stopping their show of disrespect, the Don united with his children, attacking her for living with him without marriage. He no longer needed Rosetta: her beauty was fading and his children were grown. She was just another mouth to feed. Finally, to torture her, the Don asked Rosetta to leave the table and eat in the next room with the servants. She humbly agreed for she was destitute, but soon the Don began treating her like a servant, ordering her to scrub floors and clean the barn for her food and shelter. He even refused to allow her to join him on his arm as his woman.

Rosetta was furious at Don Ciccio Lutari for treating her like dirt. They fought constantly, and eventually she moved out of his house to live with her sick, elderly mother, but not before putting a curse on her former lover: "Now I'm nothing after twenty years of service. I'm just a servant! For treating me like a *putana* [whore]— you wouldn't marry me, used me, robbed the little property and money you gave me—I curse you, Don Ciccio Lutari! You're going to die like a dog, all alone!" she screamed, as she packed her clothes. "No one will bother with you. No one will speak to you. You will cry for help, but no one will come, and when you die, I will wear a bright red dress and ring the bells of the church high on the hill. I will laugh heartily and dance in my red dress while I sing, *"Veve ka ta latu! Boom! Boom! Veve ka ta latu! Boom! Boom!"* (This is a very disrespectful ditty that is sung to disgrace the person who died. It means Hooray! You're dead! You died and I'm alive. I'm thrilled that you are dead!)

The Don shrugged his shoulders, and responded coldly and imperiously, "I am the richest and most famous man in the town and I will never be alone. I bark and people jump. My great wish has always been to be honored like a knight, and when I die, I will have the grandest of funerals. And it will come true, for all will mourn the loss of Don Ciccio Lutari, and they will line the streets of Ciminna and cry tears of sorrow."

"We will see, for a curse is now upon your head," Rosetta retorted knowingly, then made the sign of the *malocchio* (evil eye) with her hands, and slammed the door to the house that had been her home for the last twenty years. She was never to return.

Several years passed, and the plague called *spannola* came to Ciminna. Rosetta lived like a pauper, surviving on leftover scraps of food that Don Ciccio had his servants bring her from his farm. Then one day, the Don woke up with a high fever. Like so many others, he was stricken down by the plague, and everyone deserted him. Not one of his darling children, not one of his loyal servants—despite all the money he offered them—would go near him. Don Ciccio was left all alone in the house screaming for just a glass of water because his mouth was parched and blistered. No one dared enter his home.

It was said that the Don's cries for Rosetta could be heard for blocks, but Rosetta did not come. When his son who started all the trouble for Rosetta heard that his father was dying, he paid a servant one year's pay to go into the house to rob his father of the gold he had hidden under the floorboards and in the mattresses. When Don Ciccio, writhing in pain, saw the man robbing him, he kept hollering: "Your curse came true! Rosetta! Your curse came true! Help me, Rosetta! Help me!"

Rosetta waited patiently, and when the Don's cries for help were no longer heard coming from the house, she put on her bright red taffeta dress and slipped on a ruffled red petticoat underneath. It is said that the whole town waited anxiously for Rosetta, and as she marched out of her home and headed toward the long, tall steps to the church of San Francisco high on the hill, the townspeople followed her. Lifting her red skirt, Rosetta began her climb, her skirt echoing a rustling sound as the taffeta swept along the cobbled steps. The crowd stared; Rosetta kept walking. The crowd cheered; Rosetta remained undisturbed. The crowd shouted for revenge; Rosetta marched like a trained soldier. Triumphantly, she reached the top of the hill, pushed open the doors to the church, clutched her hands tightly around the heavy snakelike cord, pulled down with all her strength, and rang the bells of San Francisco. She then ran outside and began to dance, click her heels, and sing the ditty of great disgrace. Each person who had watched her walk, passed by Rosetta and nodded to her in respect as she sang out loud, *"Veve ka la latu! Boom! Boom! Veve ka la latu! Boom! Boom!"*

The Don left Rosetta nothing. The children she had raised as her own never bothered with her again, and they were glad she was shut out of their inheritance.

But Rosetta was satisfied, for her curse had come true. The villagers, too, were happy, for they felt the Don had finally received his comeuppance, and the story of the curse is remembered in Ciminna to this day. Not only did the Don die alone, but no one would even dare touch his body to bury him. Instead, he was left in his house for more than a week, rotting like an old, dead dog surrounded by his priceless possessions. His wish for a noble funeral fit for a knight was never to come true.

Grandma's moral: "Never live with a man before getting married, or you'll end up with nothing." 🐝

Pasta con Broccoli o Cavolifiore
PASTA WITH BROCCOLI OR CAULIFLOWER

🐟 In Sicily and in Little Italy during the early 1900s, this dish was made in the spring and summer when fresh vegetables were in season. Today, broccoli and cauliflower can be found year-round. In the old days, this pasta was a common part of the weekday meal, served either as a first course or main dish about once a week. The large bowl of pasta was placed in the center of the dining room table, and a small carafe of olive oil, a pepper mill, and cheese were set along the edges, an arrangement that allowed diners to serve themselves easily.

1 pound spaghettini or spaghetti

1 head broccoli or cauliflower, 1½ to 2 pounds

1 teaspoon salt, or to taste

1 whole head garlic, cloves separated and sliced medium-thick

Extra-virgin olive oil

Freshly ground black pepper or red pepper flakes

Grated *ricotta salata, incanestrato, pepato,* romano, or provolone cheese

1. Break the spaghettini or spaghetti in half, then break each half in half again. Cook and drain the pasta.

2. While the water is heating for the pasta, remove the green leaves from the broccoli or cauliflower. Peel away the hard exterior of the stems, and if the stems are long, cut them into 2-inch pieces. Cut the rest of the broccoli or cauliflower into small florets. Fill a medium-size pot with water and bring to a boil. Add 1 teaspoon salt and the broccoli or cauliflower. Boil until the florets and stems are fork tender, about 5 minutes. Transfer the vegetables and 2½ cups of the cooking water to a large bowl. Add the garlic and toss gently.

3. Transfer the cooked pasta to individual dishes and, using a ladle, top with as much broccoli or cauliflower water and as many florets and chopped stems as each person likes. Set out olive oil, black pepper or red pepper flakes, and grated cheese for each diner to add to taste.

VARIATION

Substitute *perciatelli*, *bucatini*, *ditali*, or medium-size *tubettini* for the spaghettini or spaghetti. They are all traditional in Little Italy and give variety to the dish.

Pasta con Scarola
PASTA WITH ESCAROLE

Serves 4

🌱 Pasta with escarole is my personal favorite pasta-and-vegetable dish, and in the past it was usually served once a week in most Little Italy households. This dish is sweet from the escarole, yet hot and spicy if you use red pepper flakes. If escarole is unavailable, substitute chicory, which looks and tastes similar.

Secrets of Success

1 pound young escarole or chicory, trimmed

3 quarts (12 cups) water

Salt

½ pound spaghetti

½ cup extra-virgin olive oil

6 large cloves garlic, sliced

2 overripe tomatoes, peeled and cut into chunks (optional)

Freshly ground black pepper or red pepper flakes

Grated *incanestrato, pepato, cacio-cavallo,* romano, or provolone cheese

(CONTINUED)

Buy a head of young, light green escarole. It has a sweet taste and small, nearly white leaves in the center. The leaves of mature escarole are darker green at the center and are often wider and longer.

1. Separate the escarole leaves. Transfer them to a large pot filled with cold water. Toss the leaves several times, discard the water, and repeat this process 4 times. Then clean each leaf under cold running water. Making small stacks of the leaves, cut them crosswise into 2-inch-wide pieces.

2. In a medium-size pot, combine the escarole, water, and 1 teaspoon salt. Bring to a boil, reduce the heat to medium, cover, and cook, until the leaves are tender, about 10 minutes. Using a slotted spoon, transfer the escarole to a large bowl, cover, and set aside. Reserve the water.

3. Break the spaghetti in half, then break each half in half again. Return the escarole water to a boil, add the spaghetti, and cook until tender. Drain the pasta, reserving 3 cups of the water.

4. Return the pasta, escarole, and the 3 cups water to the pot and place over medium heat. Stir in 1 teaspoon salt. Simmer for a few minutes until the escarole is hot.

5. Meanwhile, in a medium-size frying pan, combine the olive oil and the garlic and place over medium heat. Sauté until the garlic is golden, about 2 minutes. Add the tomatoes, if using, and simmer for 5 minutes. Transfer the contents of the frying pan to the pasta and escarole and stir well. Taste and adjust with salt if necessary. Transfer to individual dishes. Serve with a small carafe of olive oil, black or red pepper, and grated cheese on the side. Allow each person to drizzle on extra olive oil and sprinkle as desired with pepper and grated cheese.

Perciatelli con Cucuzza
PERCIATELLI WITH SQUASH

Serves 4

🐟 Although this dish is now a family favorite, I rarely ate it until Grandma's sister Mica prepared it for me in Ciminna. As soon as I came home I made it, and all my Sicilian-born relatives said they had forgotten how delicious this dish was. The pasta and squash on their own are bland, which is why you need a sweet olive oil and lots of pepper and cheese to make this dish tasty. If you have only poor-quality oil, I suggest making another dish.

Extra-virgin olive oil

2 pounds green summer squashes, peeled and cut into ½-inch-thick slices

Salt

1 pound *perciatelli, bucatini,* linguine, or fettuccine

6 cloves garlic, cut into medium dice or sliced

Freshly ground black pepper or red pepper flakes

Grated *ricotta salata, incanestrato, cacio-cavallo,* provolone, or romano cheese

1. Generously oil a large frying pan with olive oil and place over medium heat. In batches, cook the squash, turning as needed and sprinkling with a little salt, until browned on both sides, about 4 minutes total. Transfer to a dish.

2. Meanwhile, cook and drain the pasta. Transfer the pasta to a large bowl and keep hot. Measure the amount of oil remaining in the frying pan from cooking the squash and add enough oil to measure 1 cup. Add the garlic to the pan and sauté over medium heat until the garlic is golden, about 2 minutes. Return the squash slices to the frying pan and mix well. Remove from the heat.

(CONTINUED)

3. Transfer the pasta to individual plates and top with the squash-and-oil mixture. Sprinkle generously with pepper and grated cheese.

"WET VERSION" VARIATION

Many Sicilians will not eat dry pasta. They prefer their pasta wet. Simply reserve 2 cups of the pasta water before draining the pasta, and stir it into the cooked pasta before adding the oil and squash.

Pasta con Pisedri e Cipolle

PASTA WITH PEAS AND ONIONS

Serves 4

In the summertime in Sicily, peas are extremely sweet and abundant, so pasta and peas are a natural marriage. Made with or without tomato sauce, this dish is a standard offering in every hotel dining room on the island.

Extra-virgin olive oil

3 cups shelled fresh sweet peas, or 1 can (16 ounces) petite peas, drained

1 small yellow onion, very thinly sliced

Salt, to taste

¾ pound chicory or escarole, trimmed, carefully rinsed, and leaves cut into 2-inch-wide pieces (see Pasta with Escarole, Step 1, page 122), optional

12 fresh basil leaves

1 pound spaghetti, spaghettini, or linguine

Freshly ground black pepper, to taste

Grated *incanestrato, cacio-cavallo,* romano or provolone cheese

1. In a small pot, combine 5 tablespoons olive oil, the peas, and the onion. Place over medium-low heat and cook, stirring frequently, until onion is translucent, about 15 minutes. Add water just to cover the peas, season with salt and basil, and bring to a boil. Reduce the heat to very low and simmer until peas are ultratender and flavorful, about 1 hour. Stir the peas every 10 minutes to avoid sticking. (If the water evaporates after 30 minutes, add 1 more cup, or as much as is necessary). Remove from the heat and transfer to a large bowl, including all the water.

2. Meanwhile, fill a medium-size pot with water, bring to a boil, and add the chicory or escarole, if using. Cook until the leaves are tender, about 10 minutes. Drain, reserving 2 cups of the cooking water. Set the leaves and reserved water aside and keep hot.

3. While the greens are cooking, break the spaghetti in half, then break each half in half again. Cook and drain the pasta.

4. In a large bowl, combine the peas and their water, the spaghetti, and the greens and their water. Ladle into soup plates. Drizzle with olive oil, season with salt and pepper, and top with grated cheese.

VARIATION

To make a side dish of peas with onions, prepare as directed through Step 1; omit all other steps.

PESCE

Fish

I would like to dispel one myth: fish was never the mainstay of the Sicilian diet. Traditionally, it was eaten regularly only by people who lived along the coast. In late 1800s and early 1900s, it took six hours to travel from Ciminna to Palermo. Today, it is a thirty-minute drive. If you lived inland at the turn of the century, fish was available only six to eight times a year, whenever the fishermen decided to make the long trip. Pasta and vegetables were the mainstays in the past, and they still are. In Grandma's day, members of her family weren't that excited about fish. They preferred eating meats and poultry, because in their minds fish was the food of poor fishermen. To find out how fish was sold in Ciminna, see page 129.

Sicilians adore seafood. In my family, we enjoy breaded or sauced fish fillets, but our all-time favorite dish is baked fresh sardines, a preparation that is unfortunately rarely eaten these days since large sardines are seldom available. Tiny sardines, only about three inches long, are sold, but little flesh remains once they are filleted. (To find out the secret of cleaning sardines quickly and easily, see page 136.) Our most treasured fish, of course, are *sarde salate* (salted sardines), one of the great Sicilian delicacies of the early 1900s. When Grandma came to America, every store in Little Italy carried them, but in the 1970s, this king of fishes became difficult to find. Today, however, they are making a comeback at most Italian shops. You'll find a recipe for Salted Sardines with Vinegar, Garlic and Olive Oil on page 27 and one for Pizza with Salted Sardines on page 78.

This chapter includes classic preparations dating back centuries, such as Salted Cod in Tomato Sauce with Black Olives and Baked Bluefish with Lemon, Oil, and Garlic. For an unusual dish seldom made in America, try *Scungilli* with Pepper Biscuits (page 148), a preparation my cousin Gloria re-created after eating it at a seafood restaurant in Little Italy. All these recipes, transported long ago from Sicily to New York, have undergone little, if any, updating. Also, don't be surprised to find cheese in Sicilian fish dishes. Unlike northern Italians, Sicilians believe cheese and fish are complementary. How the rumor started that they don't go together I do not know, but Sicilians don't eat fish any other way.

Finally, the love that seafaring Sicilians have for fish is at its most elaborate on Christmas Eve, when a seven-course dinner of favorite seafood dishes are served, the number of courses symbolizing the seven sacraments of Catholicism. Living inland, Grandma never heard of this Christmas Eve custom until she came to America. To serve this fish feast yourself, select seven complementary recipes from this chapter and from the seafood recipes in the Pasta and Sauce chapter for your holiday celebration.

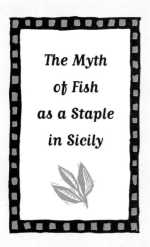

The Myth of Fish as a Staple in Sicily

ALTHOUGH A FISH STORE now stands in Ciminna's market square, in 1916, villagers only ate fish when visited by *pescatori* (fishermen).

"What . . . you think they sold fish like today!" Grandma laughed. "The fishermen came with a hundred pounds of fish or more in large *carteddri* [straw baskets]. They had fish every day because they lived on the water, but in Ciminna fishermen showed up once every two months. The man would come around with a *tambourino* [a large drum] hanging from his neck. He'd march through the streets playing his drum and shouting, '*Chi vuole accattare pesce andate o scaro posto di marchetta che sono venuto i pescatori.*' [Whoever wants to buy fish, go to the marketplace where the fishermen are.] The *genti di mare* [people of the sea] came from the villages of Sciacca and Castellamare with their *carteddri* full of fish."

"With a drum?" I asked shocked. "Don't tell me he sang a song, too!"

"Fren-zee, what do you think! There was no radio or television in those days. The fisherman did it to call attention to himself. And by five o'clock, all the fish had to be sold or else the town *carabiniere* [police] made him throw it away."

"Why couldn't he take his fish back home with him?"

"There was no refrigeration! No ice! Nothing! If the fish weren't sold by five o'clock, they would smell in the heat. But most of the time the fish were sold. It was a production in those days to get fish—a half-day's ride from Castellamare to Ciminna."

"But Castellamare isn't that far from Ciminna," I remarked.

"And they came with a truck, too!" she retorted, flabbergasted. "You see how long it took to drive in those days."

"I didn't know they had trucks in Ciminna in 1916!"

"Of course! You know, with the wheels and *u mulo* [the mule]?"

"That's not a truck!" I screamed excitedly, flinging my hands in the air. "You're talking about a horse and buggy! Grandma! Don't you know what a . . ."

"Well, Fren-zee," she said, interrupting my tantrum, "what did you think a truck was in Ciminna?" 🖋

Shurmu al Forno

BAKED BLUEFISH WITH LEMON, OIL, AND GARLIC

🐟 Summertime in New York City meant fresh fish courtesy of my grandma's neighbor and avid fisherman, Mr. Marshall. She says she can still recall his weekly knock on the door in the 1930s and 1940s, and the two or three large bluefish he'd place in her arms before going silently about his business. This is her favorite fish dish. And for those of you who think bluefish is overly oily and fishy tasting, try this recipe. The lemon dressing removes the fishy taste. If you are making this dish for 4 people, make only 1 bluefish.

2 bluefish, 3 pounds each

6 large cloves garlic, sliced

¾ cup grated *incanestrato,* provolone, or romano cheese

9 fresh Italian parsley sprigs, stems removed and leaves chopped coarsely

2 recipes Lemon, Oil, and Garlic Dressing for one 3-pound fish (page 16), with garlic cloves coarsely chopped rather than cut into medium dice

1. Preheat an oven to 400°F. To clean each bluefish, cut off the head, tail, and fins. Using a knife or fish scaler, scrape the skin smooth of scales on both sides. Using a sharp knife, insert the tip right below the head, and make a clean cut horizontally to the tail. Remove all the innards. Do not remove the backbone. Rinse the cavity of the fish; pat dry.

2. Transfer the fish to a large baking pan. Make 5 deep 3-inch-long slits on both sides of each fish. In a dish, combine the garlic, grated cheese, and parsley. Fill the slits with the mixture, and spoon the remaining mixture into the cavity. Brush both sides of the fish with one-third of the dressing.

Secrets of Success

Add 4 tablespoons
flavored bread
crumbs (page 14) to
the cheese mixture
for extra flavor.

3. Place in the oven and bake until the flesh turns opaque throughout and flakes when tested with a fork and the skin is golden brown, about 35 minutes. Baste frequently with the remaining dressing and pan juices.

4. To serve, using a sharp spatula, cut into large chunks and lift the fish pieces carefully off the main bone.

Pesce Spada alla Griglia
GRILLED SWORDFISH WITH LEMON AND ROSEMARY

Serves 4

🌿 Grilled swordfish is usually eaten in the summer when the fishermen bring in a big catch. When I was in Ciminna, I passed a fish store and was shocked to see the head of a large fish, its sword sticking out of the open door of the shop. It was so gigantic that I had to stop and question the fishmonger. He told me that displaying the head with its sword signified the fisherman's prize catch. A large chunk of the fish was cut off as needed, then the chunk was recut into smaller pieces to sell.

This standard recipe is often served in Sicily with Fried Black Olives with Onions (page 36), Sicilian Potato Salad (page 245), crusty *pane rotundo* (large, round Sicilian bread), and a favorite cheese. The fish can either be grilled, as is usually done in Sicily, or broiled, the more common method in America.

4 swordfish steaks, each ½ pound and 1 inch thick

1 recipe Lemon, Oil, and Garlic Dressing for one 3-pound fish (page 16),
    substituting 2 large fresh Italian rosemary branches for the oregano

(CONTINUED)

1. One day before serving: Place the fish in a nonreactive container. Add the dressing, cover, and refrigerate.

2. To grill the swordfish: Prepare a fire in a charcoal grill. Remove the rosemary branches from the marinade and break each one in half. Place ½ branch on each fish steak. Place on the grill rack and grill, turning once and brushing with the marinade every 2 or 3 minutes, until the fish turns opaque in the center, 4 or 5 minutes on each side.

Alternate: To broil the swordfish, preheat a broiler. Place the fish steaks inside a wire-hinged grill basket. Remove the rosemary branches from the marinade, lay them on top of the steaks, and close the basket. Place a large baking pan under the grill basket to catch the drippings. Broil, turning once, and brushing with the marinade every 2 or 3 minutes, until the fish turns opaque in the center, about 10 minutes total.

The interior of Di Palo's first store, on Mott Street. This is where Grandma shopped when she came to Little Italy in 1922. Note the sardine cans.

Tonno in Agrodolce
SWEET AND SOUR TUNA

🐟 This dish is my father's specialty, as well as one of Sicily's oldest recipes. It was taught to Dad by his mother, and he has fiddled with it for years to bring it to perfection. Serve the tuna with your favorite salad, cheese, bread, and a full-bodied wine.

1 pound tuna fillets, about ¾ inch thick

¼ cup all-purpose flour

3 tablespoons extra-virgin olive oil

1 large yellow onion, sliced

½ cup red wine vinegar

2 heaping tablespoons sugar

3 tablespoons tawny Port or sweet Marsala wine

10 Sicilian green olives, pitted and cut into strips

1. Dredge the tuna in the flour, shaking off the excess. In a large frying pan, heat the olive oil over medium heat. Add the onion and sauté until translucent, about 5 minutes.

2. Push the onion slices to one side of the pan. Add the tuna and cook, turning once, until the fish flakes when tested with a fork, about 3 minutes on each side. Stir in the vinegar, sugar, wine, and olives. Reduce the heat to low and simmer for 5 minutes to allow the flavors to blend. Turn off the heat, cover the pan, and allow the tuna to stand for 10 minutes to absorb the pan juices, then serve.

Secrets of Success

Dad feels the

addition of Port

or Marsala wine

gives the fish just the

right sweet

and sour balance.

Sicilian Grandmas Guard Their Recipes

OLD-TIMERS DO NOT take kindly to cookbooks. They refuse to be told how to do anything, and they never want their secrets revealed. They prefer to die with their recipes and be immortalized in a story that tells of how great a particular dish they made was. My grandma is no different. One day while making sardines with vinegar and onions, I was struggling to clean a sardine when, exasperated, I screamed, "No wonder no one eats these things anymore. They're a real pain!"

Grandma laughed. "So easy."

"Easy!" I got up and peered over her shoulder and realized she had cleaned four sardines—which looked excellent, I might add—while the one I had cleaned was quite ruined. "You cleaned four!" I said, astonished. "I did just one, and there are all these bones in the fish I still have to pick out."

"That's because you're doing it wrong!"

"No I'm not," I argued. I opened the cookbook of a very reputable Italian woman cook. "Here . . . snap off the head, using your fingers . . ."

"Fren-zee, stop reading! Please! Come here." She gestured to me. "The secret is the water. Here!" she said, as she put a pair of scissors in my hand. "Now watch." She cut off the head, fins, and tail, and then cut open the belly. Holding the fish under cold running water, she wiggled her thumbs under the main bone, and within a few seconds, it lifted out easily and the sardine was perfectly clean.

"Wow! Where'd you learn that?"

"My mother taught me . . . that's how we did it in Ciminna!"

"But the book says . . ."

"Fren-zee! Please!" She covered her ears with her hands. "I don't need no *cook-ka-book* to teach me and neither do you. What I've taught you all these years, you can't learn in no *cook-ka-book*. Whatever you need to learn, Grandma will teach you."

"Your mother was brilliant."

"Now you're talkin'! My mother was the best cook in all of Ciminna. The wealthy of the town used to come with fruit, a barrel of wheat, cheese, crystal—whatever God created—just to eat her bread."

"They gave her Waterford for bread?" I asked. "Not bad, Grandma."

"What do you think, there was money in those days? People used to trade. Sometimes they would give her handmade linens, whatever they had, just to taste her sauce or food. She always told me if you put the sardine in water, the bone comes out in a second. Fren-zee!" Grandma yelled. "This woman who wrote the *cook-ka-book* that you wasted your money on as usual, is she Sicilian?" she smirked.

"No!"

"If she was Sicilian, she would know how to do it right in the first place!" She threw her arms in the air. "If people went back to the old ways of Ciminna, there would be no need for no *cook-ka-books!*" She took the book, closed it, and threw it on the table. "My mother could teach her!"

"But Grandma," I started yelling, my arms waving furiously in the air, "I'm writing a cookbook! I'm trying to teach people the old ways of Ciminna! And you're so damned uncooperative!"

Her hands were on her hips now. Her hips were now swaying, and her apron strings hung down over her little rounded belly as she shouted back, "Because you're here, in America. In Ciminna everyone knows how to do these things already!"

"Don't be so smart!" I shot back. "They didn't cook as good as you do over there." My finger was pointing right at her stubby nose.

"Well—what can I say." Her face and voice became angelic. "You win this argument," she grinned. "Let's get back to writing the *cook-ka-book*, even though," she waved her finger in my face, "you should really have opened a pizza store to make a living, because in Ciminna you'd be out of business!"

There are times . . . 🐢

Great-grandma Maria, the best cook in all of Ciminna, in 1924.

Sarde con Aceto e Cipolle
FRIED SARDINES WITH VINEGAR AND ONIONS

🐟 The reason most people don't buy fresh sardines is because they have to clean them. If you think I'm exaggerating, go into any fish store and ask for sardines. They'll tell you, "Nobody wants to clean them. They take too much time, so we don't carry them." They're right. Cleaning sardines according to every cookbook is a breeze. Untrue! But there's hope. Read Secrets of Success for Grandma's quick, easy method.

2 pounds fresh sardines, each about 6 inches long

1 cup all-purpose flour

Extra-virgin olive oil

Salt

2 yellow onions, thinly sliced

1½ cups red wine vinegar

1. Clean each sardine and remove the backbone, leaving the fish in one piece. Rinse well and pat dry. Close up each sardine, reforming it to its original shape. Dredge in the flour, shaking off the excess. Generously oil a large frying pan with olive oil and place over medium heat until hot. Add the sardines, sprinkle with a little salt, and cook, turning once, until browned on both sides, about 5 minutes total. Sardines do not take long to cook. Watch carefully, or they will be dry. Transfer the sardines to a plate lined with paper towels to drain.

Secrets of Success

To clean a sardine, cut off the head, tail, and fins with a pair of kitchen scissors. Next, make a clean cut along the belly horizontally to the tail. Open the fish like a book and remove the innards. Wash the sardine under cold, gently running water. Position your thumbs under the backbone until they come together, then wiggle your thumbs up and down while the water is running over the sardine. The main bone will lift out easily without leaving any tiny bones behind. Pat dry.

2. Meanwhile, place 4 tablespoons olive oil in a medium-size frying pan and place over medium heat. Add the onions and sauté until golden brown, about 10 minutes. Sprinkle to taste with salt. Then add the vinegar and simmer until the vinegar reduces by one-third and the sauce looks carmelized, about 5 minutes. Remove from the heat.

3. Discard the paper towels from under the sardines, and spoon the sauce over the fish. Cover the platter and allow the sardines to stand for 5 minutes to absorb the sauce, then serve.

Sarde al Forno
BAKED SARDINES

🐟 Our family is always on the lookout for fresh sardines to make this classic two-hundred-year-old dish. In 1905, my great-great-grandma Angelina would make this dish for my great-grandma Maria and my grandma when she was a child in Ciminna. Sardines can usually be found at the market during the summer months and the winter holidays. They must be at least six inches long, or there will not be enough meat on them once they are filleted.

2 pounds fresh sardines, each about 6 inches long

1 recipe lemon, oil, and garlic dressing (following)

4 large fresh Italian parsley sprigs, with long stems attached

1 recipe flavored bread crumbs (following)

Fresh Italian parsley sprigs, for garnish

1. Preheat an oven to 400°F. Clean and remove the backbone from each sardine, leaving the fish in one piece (see Secrets of Success, page 136). Rinse well and pat dry.

(CONTINUED)

Serves 4

Secrets of Success

The large parsley sprigs placed beneath the sardines prevent the fish from sticking to the pan.

2. Coat the bottom of a medium-size baking pan (about 13 inch by 9 inches) with 1 tablespoon of the dressing. Lay the parsley sprigs with stems in a single layer on the bottom of the pan, flattening them out and placing each sprig pointing in the opposite direction from the one next to it. Open the sardines like a book. Arrange, cut side down, in a single layer in the pan. Sprinkle the fish with half of the bread crumb mixture, and evenly drizzle half of the remaining dressing over the top. Repeat, making 1 more layer.

3. Place in the oven and bake until the skins of the sardines turn golden brown, 15 to 20 minutes. Baste every few minutes with the pan juices. Watch carefully to prevent burning, or the sardines will be dry. Transfer to a platter and garnish with parsley sprigs.

LEMON, OIL, AND GARLIC DRESSING FOR SARDINES

In a small bowl, combine the juice of 4 fresh lemons (about 12 tablespoons); 1 teaspoon dried oregano, sticks removed, crushed until powdery; 5 tablespoons extra-virgin olive oil; 5 cloves garlic, sliced; and ¼ teaspoon salt, or to taste.

FLAVORED BREAD CRUMBS FOR SARDINES

In a small bowl, mix together ¾ cup plus 2 tablespoons unseasoned freshly made bread crumbs (page 14); 6 tablespoons grated romano, provolone, or *incanestrato* cheese; 3 cloves garlic, diced; ½ cup fresh Italian parsley leaves, coarsely chopped; and scant ½ teaspoon salt.

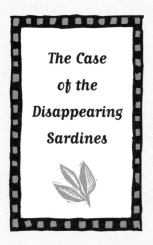

The Case
of the
Disappearing
Sardines

As A CHILD, I was a very poor eater, but one day when I was four years old, Dad recalls that Grandma sent down a tray of baked sardines right out of the oven, a treat my father and mother were anxiously awaiting. My parents, knowing I disliked fish, thought nothing of leaving the sardines on the coffee table in front of me while they finished up in the kitchen. When they returned fifteen minutes later, the tray was nested on a large dish towel in my lap, and I was leisurely finishing up the last sardine while enjoying cartoons on television. "Hmmm! Good, Daddy!" I smiled.

Astonished, and thinking that I had dropped the fish somewhere, Dad fell to his knees and kept searching around the floor, until he screamed, "I'll kill her! The whole tray! A little kid like that. How could she eat the whole tray . . . and she looks sweet, too!"

Mom and Dad at a
Sicilian birthday party
in the 1960s.

Frutti di Mare Fritto

FRIED BREADED COD, FLOUNDER, OR SHRIMP

🐟 Sicilians enjoy this simple preparation of fried breaded seafood sprinkled with lemon or vinegar. You can use this recipe for any white, meaty fish, but even sardines or bluefish steaks taste great prepared this way. For those who dislike fish, the breading takes away any overly fishy taste.

Breaded cod, flounder, or shrimp is a standard in every Sicilian household. Uncle Joe, my dad's brother, used to bake the breaded shrimp drizzled with his favorite white wine (see variation). We often make these fish to accompany roasted meats or linguine with Marinara Sauce (page 112).

To serve fish the old-fashioned Sicilian way, make Grandma's Mixed Salad (page 241) with double the amount of the dressing. Place a portion of the salad on each dinner plate, and top with the breaded shrimp. Pour extra dressing on top and mix lightly. Eat by taking a shrimp and a forkful of salad at the same time. Fish fillets are eaten by topping the fillet with the salad and a few tablespoons of the dressing. The oil, vinegar, and garlic will permeate the fish, giving it a tremendous taste.

1 cup bread crumb coating (page 14)

1 pound fresh cod or flounder fillets, or 1 pound medium-size shrimp,
     peeled and deveined

Extra-virgin olive oil

2 lemons, cut into wedges

Red wine vinegar

1. To make the cod or flounder: Prepare the bread crumb coating. Dip the cod or flounder fillets into the egg bath, and then coat with the bread crumbs. Generously oil a medium-size frying pan with olive oil and place over medium heat until hot. Add the fish fillets and fry, turning once, until golden brown on both sides and the flesh turns opaque at the center and flakes when tested with a fork, about 3 minutes on each side for the cod and about 2 minutes on each side for the flounder. Transfer the fillets to a dish lined with paper towels to drain briefly, then remove the towels. Serve with lemon wedges and a cruet of vinegar. Guests can sprinkle with one or the other, as desired.

2. To cook the shrimp: Prepare the bread crumb coating. Dip the shrimp into the egg bath, and then coat with the bread crumbs. Generously oil a medium-size frying pan with olive oil and place over medium heat until hot. Add the shrimp and fry, turning once, until they turn opaque and curl, about 1 minute total. Do not overcook them or they will be tough. Transfer the shrimp to a dish lined with paper towels and let drain briefly, then remove the towels. Serve with lemon wedges and a cruet of vinegar, as directed for the fish fillets.

BAKED SHRIMP WITH WHITE WINE

Preheat an oven to 425°F. Dip the shrimp into the egg bath, coat with the bread crumbs, and place in a single layer in a large baking pan. Sprinkle the shrimp with ¾ cup sweet white wine. Bake just until the bread crumbs turn golden brown and the edges of the shrimp turn opaque, about 10 minutes.

Fritelle di Piscistoccu
CODFISH CAKES

My father invented these fish cakes by watching what his relatives made when he was a child. The cakes are not overly fishy. For those who prefer a stronger fish taste, use 1½ pounds cod instead of 1 pound, and add an extra pinch of salt, 1 more garlic clove, an additional heaping tablespoon of grated cheese, and an additional egg. These fish cakes are excellent on a buffet table, as they taste good hot or lukewarm.

1 pound white or red new potatoes (about 3 potatoes), peeled and cut in half

1 cup bread crumb coating (page 14)

Extra-virgin olive oil

1 pound fresh cod fillets

½ cup grated romano or *cacio-cavallo* cheese

1 yellow onion, cut into medium dice

3 cloves garlic, cut into small dice

6 fresh Italian parsley sprigs, chopped medium-fine

1 teaspoon salt, or to taste

2 eggs

Fresh Italian parsley sprigs or rosemary branches, for garnish

1. Fill a medium-size pot with salted water and bring to a boil. Add the potatoes and cook until fork tender, about 20 minutes. Drain, then transfer to a bowl. Using a fork, mash the potatoes well. Set aside. Have the bread crumb coating ready.

Secrets of Success

Good-quality cod fillets are very white. Look at the edges of a fillet. If they are brown, the fish is not fresh. Next, look for bones. Choose fillets free of tiny fish bones, or they will turn up in your fish cakes.

2. Meanwhile, generously oil a large frying pan with olive oil and place over medium heat until hot. Add the cod fillets and fry, turning once, until golden brown on both sides and the flesh turns opaque at the center and flakes when tested with a fork, about 3 minutes on each side. Transfer the fillets to a dish lined with paper towels and let drain for 1 minute on each side.

3. Add the fish to the potatoes and mash lightly. Add the cheese, onion, garlic, parsley, salt, and eggs; mix well. Form the mixture into 3-inch round patties each about ½ inch thick. Brush each patty with the egg bath, then coat with the bread crumbs. Repeat until the fish mixture has been formed.

4. Generously oil another large frying pan and place over medium heat until hot. Add the fish cakes and fry, turning once, until browned on both sides and heated through, 2 to 3 minutes on each side. Use a small spatula and turn the fish cakes gently, or they will break apart. Transfer to a dish lined with paper towels.

5. To serve, arrange the fish cakes on a large platter in a single layer. Do not stack them. Garnish with sprigs of Italian parsley or rosemary branches.

Insalata di Pesce
FISH SALAD

🐟 This classic fish salad is prepared throughout Sicily and is often served as a first course in expensive hotels and restaurants. Sicilians who traditionally eat seven different fish dishes on Christmas Eve will always include this as part of their holiday meal. *Scungilli* is the Sicilian term for the large, spiral-shelled mollusk known as conch. It is available canned in most Italian shops.

4 pounds calamari (squid), each about 3 inches long,

    or 3 pounds cleaned calamari rings

1 can (2 pounds) *scungilli,* preferably La Monica brand, drained

1 cup extra-virgin olive oil, or as needed

6 cloves garlic, cut into medium dice

2 pounds shrimp, peeled and deveined

1 pound Sicilian green olives, pitted but left whole

½ cup drained capers

1 large celery stalk, cut into medium dice

8 fresh Italian parsley sprigs, coarsely chopped

1 cup drained jarred Italian mixed pickled vegetables *(giardinieri),* optional

1 cup drained pickled, light green, hot Italian peppers *(peperoncini),* optional

½ cup white wine vinegar, or more to taste

Juice of 2 large lemons, or more to taste

Salt and freshly ground black pepper, to taste

Red pepper flakes, to taste

Small bunch fresh radishes, stems removed

2 lemons, cut into wedges

2 cans (2 ounces each) anchovy fillets, in olive oil, drained, for garnish

3 fresh Italian parsley sprigs, coarsely chopped, for garnish

Secrets of Success

To make this salad
properly, use
excellent-quality
olive oil and vinegar
and good,
fresh lemons.

1. To clean the calamari: Pull the tentacles away from each body and cut off and discard the head. Squeeze out all the membranes and remove the quill-like bone from the body. Rinse under cold running water, inside and out. Pull off the thin mottled skin from the body. Rinse all pieces again; pat dry. Cut the sac crosswise into ⅓-inch-wide rings; leave the tentacles whole. Bring a medium-size pot filled with water to a boil over high heat. Reduce the heat to low, add the calamari and simmer for 1 or 2 minutes until the rings curl. Drain and set aside. If using purchased cleaned calamari, simply cook as directed.

2. Rinse the *scungilli* well under cold running water; pat dry. Slice ½ inch thick, and then quarter each slice to form bite-size pieces.

3. In a very large frying pan with 3-inch sides, heat 1 cup olive oil over medium heat. Add the garlic and sauté until lightly golden, about 1 minute. Add the calamari and *scungilli*, cover and cook for 5 minutes, stirring every 2 minutes. Add the shrimp and cook for 2 minutes longer, stirring continuously. As soon as the shrimp turn opaque and begin to curl, remove them from the heat.

4. Transfer the contents of the frying pan, including the oil, to a large bowl. Add the olives, capers, celery, parsley, and the pickled vegetables and pickled peppers, if using. Toss to mix. Add the vinegar, lemon juice, salt, black pepper, and red pepper flakes. Taste and add more oil, if necessary. Toss well, cover, and refrigerate for at least 5 hours or preferably overnight.

5. To serve, transfer the fish salad to a large platter, mounding it in the center. Surround the platter with radishes and lemon wedges. Decorate the top of the salad by making Xs with the anchovy fillets. Sprinkle with the additional parsley.

Baccalà in Sugo con Olive Neri

SALTED COD IN TOMATO SAUCE WITH BLACK OLIVES

🐟 *Baccalà* is cod that is caught and filleted at sea and then salted in a brine. Once the ship docks, the cod is removed from the brine and allowed to dry. Originally, the cod was salted as a way of preserving fish that could be eaten when times were hard. Nowadays, salted cod is available at gourmet shops and many grocery stores, especially during the holidays.

Grandma remembers eating *baccalà* often in Sicily and later in Little Italy in the 1920s. This dish was always made on Christmas Eve in most Sicilian households, and it is still popular today among old-fashioned Sicilian Americans. Accompany with Potato and String Bean Salad (page 246).

1½ **pounds salted cod fillets**

1 **cup all-purpose flour**

7 **tablespoons extra-virgin olive oil**

4 **cloves garlic, sliced**

1 **can (35 ounces) whole tomatoes with juice, well crushed with a fork**

¼ **pound Sicilian black olives**

1½ **teaspoons dried oregano, sticks removed, crushed until powdery**

3 **fresh basil leaves**

Salt and freshly ground black pepper, to taste

Red pepper flakes, to taste (optional)

1. To prepare the salted cod: Place the cod in a large bowl with cold water to cover for 2 or 3 days, changing the water 3 times a day. To find out when the fish is ready to use, dip your finger into the soaking water. When it no longer tastes overly salty, the cod can be cooked. Drain well and pat dry.

2. Cut the fish into 3-inch pieces. Dredge the pieces in the flour, shaking off the excess. In a large frying pan, heat 3 tablespoons of the olive oil over medium heat. Add the fish pieces and cook just until they begin to turn opaque, about 1 minute on each side. Transfer the fish to a dish lined with paper towels to drain. Set aside.

3. Scrape up the fish bits in the frying pan and push them to one side. Add the remaining 4 tablespoons olive oil and place over medium heat. Add the garlic and sauté until golden, about 1 minute. Add the tomatoes, olives, oregano, basil, salt, black pepper, and red pepper flakes, if using. Raise the heat to high and bring to a boil. Return the fish pieces to the pan, reduce the heat to low, and simmer until the fish is opaque in the center and the sauce thickens, about 20 minutes.

4. Transfer the fish to a platter and spoon the tomato sauce over the top and around the sides.

Scungilli con Frisilli

SCUNGILLI WITH PEPPER BISCUITS

🐟 My cousin Gloria re-created this dish after eating a well-known version of it in a famous clam bar on Mott Street in Little Italy. Although a classic, it is seldom seen in America anymore, but is still popular among Sicilians abroad. The unique use of *frisilli* (Sicilian pepper biscuits, see note) makes this dish highly original and gives it an unusual table presentation.

This recipe can be tricky to make because the sauce requires faithful attention. You must remain near the stove, since water is continually stirred into the sauce. If you walk away, the sauce, which is made solely of tomato paste, will stick to the bottom of the pot and burn. If it burns even slightly, you must begin this dish again, because the burnt taste will permeate the dish.

½ cup extra-virgin olive oil

2 cloves garlic, cut into medium dice

4 cans (6 ounces each) tomato paste

1 teaspoon dried oregano, sticks removed, crushed until powdery

6 large fresh basil leaves

Salt and freshly ground black pepper, to taste

Red pepper flakes, to taste

1 can (2 pounds) *scungilli,* preferably La Monica brand, drained (see page 144)

1 pound black pepper biscuits *(frisilli)* (see note)

1. Rinse the *scungilli* well under cold running water; pat dry. Slice ½ inch thick, and then quarter each slice to form bite-size pieces. Set aside.

Secrets of Success

Using a nonstick pot will prevent the sauce from sticking and burning easily. Use the lowest heat possible; the sauce should be barely rippling on the surface.

2. In a 4-quart pot, combine the olive oil and garlic over medium heat and sauté the garlic until golden, about 2 minutes. Stir in the tomato paste and ½ cup water. Season with the oregano, basil, salt, black pepper, and red pepper flakes. Bring to a boil, then reduce heat to very, very low and simmer, stirring constantly, until all the water has been absorbed by the tomato paste, about 15 minutes. After 15 minutes, stir in another ¼ cup to ⅓ cup water. Return to a boil, then lower the heat to very low again and simmer, stirring constantly, until the water has been absorbed, about 15 minutes. Repeat this process 4 more times, adding ¼ cup to ⅓ cup water every 15 minutes and cooking it down. Taste the sauce every 30 minutes, and adjust all the seasonings as necessary. Cook the sauce for a total of 1¾ hours. After 1½ hours, add the *scungilli* and cook for the last 15 minutes without stirring. Remove from the heat.

3. Place each biscuit under warm running water for 15 seconds, turning constantly. Shake off the excess water. In an attractive, shallow, medium-size baking dish, arrange the biscuits in a single layer. Ladle the *scungilli* and sauce over the biscuits. Spoon the leftover sauce into a small bowl and serve it on the side. Using a spatula, transfer the biscuits with the *scungilli* to each person's plate, and spoon the sauce over the top. Pass the black pepper and red pepper flakes.

Note: *Frisilli* are called biscuits even though they are slices of Sicilian bread. Made with visible pieces of black butcher's pepper, the bread is baked, sliced, and rebaked to produce a hard crust. Sold at Italian bread bakeries, the slices are very hard and must always be passed under warm running water to soften before eating. They are enjoyed for breakfast or a snack and are also sometimes buttered and dipped into espresso.

CARNI E GALLINE

CHAPTER

7

Meats

and Poultry

It is a fallacy to say that Sicilians do not eat meat. Both sides of my family have traditionally considered meat a status symbol. In Sicily, buying meat meant that you were wealthy enough to afford it. The more often expensive meat was on your table, the wealthier you were. Even at the turn of the century, everyone, except for the very poor, ate some beef, veal, pork, or lamb regularly. Meat was purchased in Ciminna either from the few local butchers in the town, or from traveling butchers who set up shop in the main market square. Just like the fishermen, the latter would send out a worker with a large drum hung around his neck. He walked through the town playing his drum and shouting, "Whoever wants meat, go to the market square." Grandma recalls that, "People would run down the cobbled streets, and in a few minutes, the meat was sold. You had to be fast because the butchers only came with one calf, cow, sheep, or pig. So it was first come, first serve."

The millionaires of Sicily always began dinner with a first course of pasta with tomato sauce, followed by an elegant meat course. Nightly, these two dishes constituted what Sicilians called "the way *genti nobili* [noble people] ate." My grandma was considered *alto-borghese* (upper middle income) and ate meat three times a week from the butcher or from a calf, cow, or pig her father raised and slaughtered solely for that purpose. The peasant did not have this luxury, and if he was fortunate enough to own a cow or sheep, he kept it to have milk for making ricotta and other cheeses. Never would he consider killing an animal for the pleasure of having a meat dinner, an act that would deprive him of his future survival.

The opposite was true in the early 1900s in Little Italy. Meat was so plentiful, of such high quality, and so inexpensive that both sides of my family consumed it almost nightly. The best butcher shop in the 1920s in Little Italy, and in all of New York for that matter, was Fiumefreddo at 91 East Third Street. Grandma only bought meat there occasionally because the prices were high, but she says, "You could cut a two-inch high steak with a fork!" Years later the *Daily News* and the first issue of *New York Magazine* named the now-defunct Fiumefreddo the source of the best meat in New York City. We Sicilians had already known that for years.

It was extremely common in the Sicilian household to find two-inch-thick porterhouse and T-bone steaks, one-inch-thick pork or veal chops, prime rib, and even London broil on the dinner table several times a week. These new cuts discovered in America were simply grilled over the open flames of the coal stove or adapted to Sicilian classics: London broil could replace beef stew cubes in Beef Stew with Garden Veg-etables, and the *pizzaiola* sauce tasted terrific over club and shell steaks and veal and pork chops. This led to an expansive repertoire of meat recipes in Little Italy restau-rants. Grandma insists that the quality of meat in the 1920s was so marvelous, nothing else

Dad (left) and his brother Joe eating steaks from Fiumefreddo, once the best butcher shop in all of New York, circa 1960.

was required—not even salt and pepper.

Times have changed. Many cuts of meat were and still are an amusement to Grandma and my father. In the 1920s, for example, all the butchers in Little Italy gave spareribs away as dog food. No one wanted to be seen buying them or eating them because it meant that you were so poor you could not afford real meat, such as a steak. Baby lamb chops were also thought of as food of the lower classes, and they were one of the most inexpensive meats to purchase. Today, in contrast, they are among the most expensive. Milk-fed or not, veal cutlets were the priciest of all meats, and that has not changed.

In this chapter I've included the traditional dishes Sicilians brought over with them from their homeland, like Breaded Veal Cutlets, Stuffed Pork Chops, Veal *Pizzaiola*, and Veal Cutlets Parmesan. The very expensive milk-fed veal cutlets and Italian sausages of today were cooked almost nightly by Grandma in the past and served in addition to the main dish or as an evening snack. Every home that acquired a refrigerator-freezer in the early 1940s had veal cutlets and sausages on hand in the event of unexpected company. The tradition continues to this day, and it is difficult to recall a time when my freezer or my grandma's freezer hasn't been stocked with Sicilian sausages or veal cutlets.

Fried meatballs were another Little Italy household staple, and they were not always prepared with tomato sauce. Meatballs went into the famous Meatball Stew with Squash, or were simply fried and served on a little platter that Grandma still uses.

When I think of meat, I cannot remember a day when Grandma didn't fry meatballs, cutlets, or sausages. It was a way of life. I guess I lived like a queen and didn't know it.

Poultry, in contrast to meats, was nearly always purchased. As a result, it was considered a high-class food reserved for the *alto-borghese* and the *genti nobili*.

At the turn of the century and into the 1930s, chickens were often a means of livelihood for the very poor. Sometimes they even contributed to the income of a middle-class family. They provided eggs, which were sold, and when they hatched offspring, the extra chicks were sold for money or bartered for goods. The people in Sicily who raised chickens hardly ever ate them, since to do so meant eating their income. Therefore, the only time a farm-raised chicken was eaten was when it became lame or old, at which point it was immediately killed and consumed. Even to poultry sellers eating a chicken was considered a luxury.

In America, Grandma bought her chickens live from the chicken market on Canal Street or from her neighbor Pietro. Although they were killed for her, she did have to clean them. First, she'd fill a large pot with water and heat it until it was very hot but not boiling. Next, she'd remove the pot from the heat and place the chicken into it for ten minutes, or until the feathers could easily be pulled off. Then, she'd cut off the head and feet and rinse the bird well inside and out under cold running water. To remove the gamy taste, Grandma filled another large pot with cold water, stirred in several trays of ice cubes, added the chicken, and sprinkled two large handfuls of regular or kosher salt over the top. The chicken was left in the water for a minimum of two hours. During that time, the water and salt were changed twice, and the water had to remain ice cold. Once the chicken was removed from the salted water, it was rinsed, patted dry, and immediately cooked. Even to this day, Grandma would rather buy a freshly killed chicken and take the time to clean it properly than eat a supermarket chicken.

Although game is considered a specialty here in America, in Sicily, it was thought of as extremely ordinary. It was hunted for free in the hills, or, with permission, on the land of a neighbor or relative. Sicilians, in fact, are quite puzzled as to why Americans would pay more for a duck or pheasant with its dark meat and gamy taste than for a delicious freshly killed chicken, which can still be purchased from a kosher butcher or some Chinese butchers. Throughout Sicily, the most elegant poultry dishes are Chicken Cacciatore and Chicken with Lemon, Oil, and Garlic, not pheasant under glass.

A Jealous Husband

ONE AFTERNOON, as Grandma was making beef *pizzaiola*, she told me that her sister Lena was said to be the most beautiful woman in Ciminna and that Lena's husband, Onofrio, was a very jealous man. They had a little boy baby, but sadly the infant died of a weak constitution after living only five months. At the same time, one of the wealthiest couples in Ciminna also had a son, but his mother could not breast feed him because she was ill and the milk in her breasts had dried up. To ensure her son's survival, she asked Lena, who was very bosomy, healthy, and full of milk, to care for her son and breast feed him. Lena, who was brokenhearted over her son's death, felt such pity for the woman, she immediately agreed to her request. That day the child moved in with Lena and she cared for him as if he were her own. As the months went by, the little boy became so attached to her, he came to call her *Maaaa-maaa Leaaa-naaa*.

During this time, Onofrio was in Chicago working on the railroad so that he could send money back home. One day, a fellow worker told him that his wife was having an affair with one of the wealthiest men in Ciminna and that she had had an illegitimate child with him whom she was raising in her home. Outraged, he wrote a letter to Lena saying that he was coming back to Ciminna to knife her and the bastard son to death. Hysterical, Lena told the boy's parents to take the child back immediately. They did. But the little boy only knew Lena as his mother and, feeling she had deserted him, he refused to eat. They tried enticing him in every way, but he would just tighten his lips and bow his head in depression. The parents repeatedly begged Lena to take the boy back, but she refused, fearing her husband's return any day and a double murder. After a week of not eating, the little boy grew very weak. All day long he would ask for *Maaaa-maaaa Leaaa-naaa* over and over again. Finally, his mother burst into Lena's home and begged her to come quickly, as the child was fading away. Shocked that the situation had gone this far, Lena lifted her long dress and ran up the narrow cobblestone streets to the house and grabbed the little boy tightly in her arms. She begged him to live, telling him she'd never desert him again. But the boy was only able to open his eyes, smile gently, and whisper *Maaa-maaa Leaa-naaa*. He then tried to embrace Lena, but dropped his arms and died.

About two days after the boy's death, Onoforio arrived in Ciminna. Seething, he burst through the doorway and accused his wife of *fare i corne* (making horns, that is, having an affair with another man) and "working for money," something women in those days simply did not do. Lena then told him the whole tragic story, explaining that it was all a misunderstanding, borne out of vicious gossip. Onofrio apologized and insisted that he never would have killed the baby. He was just out of his mind with jealousy. He then asked to see the boy and his parents so that he could make amends, but instead found out the child was dead. Onoforio was shocked.

Lena cursed him for hurting an innocent child. The people in Ciminna, knowing the truth, never forgave Onoforio. They disliked him and always remembered him as a vicious, cruel man.

Grandma's moral: "*La gelosia* (jealousy) is a dangerous thing. It can cost innocent lives." 🐢

Great-aunt Lena at seventy-five, in the 1960s.

Pizzaiola di Bifstecca con Marsala

PRIME RIB PIZZAIOLA WITH MARSALA

Here is another of my father's recipes, and a Little Italy invention, since neither butter nor prime rib was available in Sicily at the turn of the century. This simple but elegant dish can be made on the spur of the moment. It only serves 2, but simply double the recipe to serve 4. Accompany with Artichokes Stuffed with Bread Crumbs (page 222) and Fried Potatoes Cut into Little Triangles (page 218).

2 tablespoons butter

1 small yellow onion, cut into medium dice

1 clove garlic, sliced

½ cup fresh mushrooms, rinsed and wiped one by one by hand, then quartered

2 prime rib steaks, 1 pound each

½ cup sweet Marsala or tawny Port wine

3 fresh basil leaves

Salt and freshly ground black pepper, to taste

Secrets of Success

To make an instant great-tasting meat sauce, add sweet wine like tawny Port or sweet Marsala, a little butter, and fresh basil to any leftover meat juices.

1. In a large frying pan, melt 1 tablespoon of the butter over low heat. Add the onion, garlic, and mushrooms and sauté until the onion is translucent, about 3 minutes. Raise the heat to medium, add the steaks, and cook for 3 or 4 minutes. Turn over the meat and add the wine, basil, salt, pepper, and the remaining 1 tablespoon butter. Stir up any browned bits stuck on the bottom of the pan. Continue to cook 3 minutes longer for medium-rare, or until done to your liking.

2. Transfer the steaks to a platter and spoon the sauce over them.

Carne al Forno Piena di Cugina Francesca
COUSIN FRANCES'S STUFFED FILET MIGNON

🐃 This unique version of filet mignon is stuffed with such typical Sicilian ingredients as garlic, provolone and *cacio-cavallo* cheeses, and pancetta. My cousin Frances invented the recipe one evening when company was coming and she wanted a dish she could prepare in advance and roast just before serving. It was a big hit, and this recipe typifies how to "Sicilinize" a French cut of meat. To serve 4, halve the recipe and use a 3-pound filet mignon.

1 trimmed, ready-to-cook filet mignon, about 6 pounds

10 large cloves garlic, quartered

7 tablespoons grated *cacio-cavallo* or romano cheese

½ bunch fresh Italian parsley, coarsely chopped

6 fresh basil leaves, torn into small pieces

¼ pound provolone cheese, cut into small chunks

3 cups onion soup, homemade or purchased

2 large yellow onions, cut into ¼-inch-thick slices

8 slices pancetta, cut in half, or 12 slices bacon

1. With a sharp knife, make a shallow vertical cut down the length of the filet mignon. Then cut in a circular motion to form a spiral, leaving 2 inches of the meat uncut toward the end. The meat should be in a single piece and be cut in a pinwheel pattern when viewed from the end. In a small bowl, combine the garlic, 5 tablespoons of the grated cheese, the parsley, and the basil. Pull the fillet apart slightly. Spread half of the garlic-cheese mixture and all of the provolone along the center of the meat. Press the filet mignon back together, reforming it into its original shape. Tie securely with kitchen string at 2-inch intervals.

2. Preheat an oven to 450°F. Cut 8 slits each 1 inch long and 1 inch deep along the top right side of the filet mignon. Cut 8 additional slits on the left side. Stuff the slits with the remaining garlic-cheese mixture. Transfer the meat to a large, shallow baking pan. Sprinkle with the remaining 2 tablespoons *cacio-cavallo*. Pour the onion soup into the pan and arrange the sliced onions and 5 of the pancetta slices or 8 of the bacon slices around the meat. Place the remaining pancetta or bacon slices over the top of the filet mignon.

3. Roast, uncovered, until the meat is cooked the way you like it. Plan on about 45 minutes for rare, or until an instant-read thermometer inserted into the thickest part registers 135°F, or about 55 minutes for medium, or until the thermometer registers 155°F. Transfer the meat to an oval platter, cover, and let stand for 5 minutes. Remove the string, and cut into 1-inch-thick slices. Spoon the pan juices and onions around the edges of the platter.

Carne di Vaccina con Verdura
BEEF STEW WITH GARDEN VEGETABLES

🐟 In Ciminna, only one calf, cow, pig, or sheep was killed and sold each week at the butcher shop, so in order to buy good cuts of meat, you had to place your order a week in advance. Once the meat from that particular animal was sold, you had to wait until another week passed before you could buy that type of meat again. Sometimes a traveling butcher would visit the town's market square, and meat could be purchased from him, and a few times each year Great-grandpa Michele and families of the *alto-borghese* and higher slaughtered their own calves, piglets, or lambs for the table. Ordinarily, this was done for the holidays.

Although my grandma was considered wealthy in Ciminna, when she arrived on Ellis Island in 1922, she was poor. Even so, she remembers eating meat four times a week because it was so inexpensive in the 1920s. London broil, one of her favorite new meats in New York City, quickly became incorporated into this stew that her mother had taught her as a child. In Ciminna, it was made with beef stew cubes.

3 tablespoons extra-virgin olive oil

1½ pounds London broil, in one piece

6 small potatoes, cut in half

2 yellow onions, sliced

1½ teaspoons all-purpose flour

2 tablespoons hot water

Salt and freshly ground black pepper, to taste

1 teaspoon dried oregano, sticks removed, crushed until powdery

6 fresh basil leaves

Grated *cacio-cavallo*, provolone, *pepato*, or romano cheese

1. In a large pot, heat the olive oil over medium heat. Add the London broil, potatoes, and onions and brown the meat well on all sides, turning frequently.

2. Add just enough water to cover the meat and vegetables. In a cup, using a fork, beat together the flour and hot water until no lumps are visible. Stir the flour mixture into the stew, and season with salt, pepper, oregano, and basil. Raise the heat to high and bring to a boil. Reduce the heat to very low and simmer very gently for 2 to 2½ hours. Stir the stew every 15 minutes, and taste and adjust all the seasonings as necessary. After 1 hour, check the water. If it's evaporating too quickly, add 1 or 2 more cups water, or as needed. The stew is done when the meat is fork tender.

3. Transfer the London broil to a platter. Cut into ¼-inch-thick slices and place a few slices on each plate. Top with the gravy and potatoes. Sprinkle generously with grated cheese and grindings of pepper.

Secrets of Success

The heat must be very low and the surface of the stew must be barely rippling, or the meat will burn on the bottom.

Stu di Polpetti e Cucuzza
MEATBALL STEW WITH SQUASH

🐟 This popular Sicilian stew is among the most requested recipes in my cooking classes. In the 1930s on Mulberry Street, Dad never needed to add bouillon cubes to the stew, since the flavors of the meat and vegetables were much more intense in those days. But now he adds them to give back to the stew its original flavors. He also puts in a pinch of herbes de Provence, which imparts a little Gallic accent, in honor of the French occupation of Sicily during the eleventh and twelfth centuries. One day, when we ran out of chopped meat, we experimented by substituting veal stew cubes for the meatballs. The result was excellent (see variation).

3 tablespoons extra-virgin olive oil

1 large yellow onion, cut into medium dice

2 celery stalks, cut into medium dice

2 carrots, peeled and diced

2 quarts (8 cups) water

3 beef bouillon cubes

2 large, ripe tomatoes, peeled, seeded, and diced,
    or 1 can (8 ounce) tomato sauce

6 fresh basil leaves

Pinch of herbes de Provence

Salt and freshly ground black pepper, to taste (optional)

1 recipe Meatballs made with 1½ pounds meat, unformed (page 18)

4 large red potatoes (about 2 pounds), peeled and cut into bite-size pieces

2½ pounds dark green or yellow squashes or light green zucchini

Grated *pepato, cacio-cavallo,* provolone, or romano cheese

Secrets of Success

When adding
squash to stew,
leave strips of skin
on the squash
to prevent it from
falling apart
during cooking.

1. In a large pot, combine the olive oil, onion, celery, and carrots over medium heat. Sauté, stirring occasionally, until the vegetables are golden, about 10 minutes. Add the water, bouillon cubes, tomatoes or tomato sauce, basil, herbes de Provence, salt, and pepper. Raise the heat to high and bring to a boil. Reduce the heat to low, cover, and simmer for 2 hours.

2. As soon as the stew begins to simmer, prepare the mixture for the meatballs. Form the mixture into 25 balls, each 1 inch in diameter, and add them to the pot. Do not stir the stew for the first 20 minutes after you add the meatballs so they won't break up. Then, stir the stew every 20 minutes, and taste and adjust all the seasonings as necessary.

3. After 2 hours, add the potatoes, and taste and adjust all the seasonings as necessary. Re-cover and simmer for about 1 hour longer, or until the stew is at the desired thickness. Peel off long strips of skin from the squashes so that they have a striped appearance, then cut into bite-size pieces. During the last 20 minutes of cooking, add the squashes. Serve the stew with grated cheese.

VEAL STEW VARIATION

Prepare as directed, substituting 1½ pounds veal stew meat, cut into bite-size pieces and lightly floured, for the Meatballs, and 3 chicken bouillon cubes for the 3 beef bouillon cubes. In Step 1, heat the olive oil over medium-high heat, add the veal, and brown on all sides, turning frequently. Reduce the heat to medium and add the onion, celery, and carrots; proceed as directed.

Lost and Found

IN THE 1890s in Ventimiglia, my great-grandpa Paolo, Grandpa Natale's father, threw a stone at a dog that had tried to bite him. The stone crippled the dog, and the dog's owner had Paolo arrested. He was sentenced to three months in jail in the adjoining town of Ciminna, where Grandma was born. One day, Great-grandpa's neighbor took Grandpa Natale, then only a five-year-old child, to visit his father in jail. The neighbor, caught up in a conversation with a long-lost friend she met along the way, completely forgot about Natale and lost him.

Somehow, the little boy, all alone and six miles from his town, found his way back home, arriving even before the neighbor did. By this time, the two towns of Ciminna and Ventimiglia were looking for the boy, fearing the worst. Natale was eating a sandwich and quietly awaiting the neighbor in his living room, when half the town burst into the house. No one could believe that such a young child could have found his way home so easily. To this day, Grandma insists, as did Grandpa, that the experience trained him to have a particularly keen sense of direction, for no matter where he was, he knew north, south, east, and west and could find his way home instinctively. 🌿

Polpetti Agrodolce
SWEET AND SOUR MEATBALLS

🍴 Dad makes *polpetti agrodolce* often, using a special sweet and sour sauce. The Marsala is his own addition to this ancient recipe, which stems from the town of San Giuseppe. He says it adds just the right balance of sweetness. Over the years, I watched him make this dish, never saying a word. One day about ten years ago, when he was out of the house, I decided to give it a try on my own. After he tasted my version, he pronounced it a little better than his own sauce. Serve the meatballs with Sicilian bread for dipping into the sauce.

1 recipe Meatballs made with 1 pound meat (page 18)

Extra-virgin olive oil

2 large yellow onions, sliced

¾ cup red wine vinegar

2½ tablespoons sugar

2 teaspoons sweet Marsala or Port wine

12 Sicilian green olives, pitted and cut into strips

1. Prepare the meatballs. Generously oil a large frying pan with olive oil and place over medium heat. Add the meatballs and cook, turning as needed, until well browned, about 3 minutes on each side. Transfer to a plate lined with paper towels to drain.

2. Lightly oil another large frying pan and place over medium heat. Add the onions and sauté until golden, about 15 minutes. Add the vinegar, sugar, and wine, stirring until the sugar is dissolved. Add the meatballs and the olives. Reduce the heat to low and simmer, uncovered, for 5 minutes. Turn off the heat, cover the pan, and allow the meatballs to absorb the sauce for 15 minutes before serving.

3. Serve the meatballs with the sauce spooned over the top.

Secrets of Success

Making the sauce in 2 separate pans eliminates the bits of fat leftover from frying the meat that can make the sauce a little greasy.

Carne Macinata al Forno
SICILIAN MEAT LOAF

Here's a meat loaf made Sicilian style, with Worcestershire sauce adding just a touch of the American pantry. If you want to have tomato sauce with your meat loaf, prepare the Marinara Sauce (page 112) but strain the tomatoes. Cook the sauce only 10 minutes, then pour it over the meat loaf in the oven after it has been cooking for 30 minutes. Serve with bread, Artichokes Stuffed with Bread Crumbs (page 222), and Sicilian Potato Salad (page 245).

1½ pounds ground top beef sirloin

¼ pound provolone or *cacio-cavallo* cheese, cut into small chunks

1 yellow onion, cut into small dice

⅓ cup flavored bread crumbs (page 14)

1 can (8 ounces) tomato sauce

2 eggs

1 tablespoon Worchestershire sauce

½ teaspoon salt

2 tablespoons extra-virgin olive oil

1. Preheat an oven to 350°F. In a medium-size bowl, combine the beef, cheese, onion, bread crumbs, tomato sauce, eggs, Worchestershire sauce, salt, and 1 tablespoon of the olive oil. Lightly oil a medium-size baking pan or medium-size loaf pan with the remaining 1 tablespoon olive oil. If using a baking pan, transfer the meat to the pan and form it into a loaf measuring about 9 by 5 inches. If using a loaf pan, gently press the meat into the pan.

2. Bake until an instant-read thermometer inserted into the center registers 160°F. Let stand for 10 minutes before serving, then cut into 1-inch-thick slices.

Great-aunt Concetta Jilts a Suitor

GRANDMA ONCE TOLD ME about a very wealthy and handsome Sicilian named Giovanni, who wanted to marry her sister Concetta. It was 1914, and he was suddenly drafted. But to avoid going to war, he pulled out every one of his teeth. Nonetheless, my great-grandfather Michele foresaw an easy life for Concetta and was eager for a marriage to take place. After several visits to the home, Giovanni asked for Concetta's hand, upon which she ran upstairs and locked herself in her room. Her father begged her to come down, but as she reached the edge of the stairs, she shouted out loud to her father in front of Giovanni, "I will not marry a man without teeth! I would have to make special food for him—two different meals a day! And feed him like a child." She then ran back to her room and slammed the door.

Grandma's moral: "Always marry a man with teeth, Fren-zee. Sicilian women have enough hard work to do and don't need any more!" 🌿

Coscia di Agnello con Limone, Olio, e Aglio
LEG OF LAMB WITH LEMON, OIL, AND GARLIC

Many Sicilian families traditionally eat lamb on Easter Sunday and other very special occasions. This recipe has been used in Sicily for centuries and is still made in Little Italies all over America. I suggest using a domestic spring lamb; avoid using New Zealand lamb, which has a gamy taste. Order the meat in advance from your local butcher. Vegetables such as corn on the cob, string beans, and broccoli make good side dishes.

1 leg of spring lamb, 6 pounds, trimmed of fat and four 3-inch square fat pieces reserved

10 large cloves garlic, quartered

4 tablespoons extra-virgin olive oil

1½ cups Lemon, Oil, and Garlic Dressing (page 16)

4 large potatoes, peeled and cut into 1-inch-thick slices

Secrets of Success

A spring lamb, which is also called young or baby lamb, is milk-fed and no more than 5 months old.

1. Preheat an oven to 500°F. Cut 20 slits, each 1 inch long and 1 inch deep in the top of the leg of lamb. Cut 20 more slits on the bottom of the leg. Insert the garlic slivers into the slits. Coat the bottom of a large roasting pan with the olive oil, then transfer the lamb and reserved fat to a large roasting pan.

2. Roast, uncovered, for 15 minutes at 500°F. Baste with the dressing, then reduce the heat to 350°F. Roast for 2 hours longer for rare lamb, or until an instant read thermometer inserted into the center registers 145°F; for 2½ hours longer for medium, or 160°F; or for 3 hours longer for well done, or to 170°F. During the last 1¼ hours of roasting, add the potatoes to the pan. Baste the lamb and potatoes with the dressing and pan drippings every 20 minutes.

3. Transfer the lamb and potatoes to a large platter and allow the lamb to stand for 10 minutes before carving. Skim the excess fat off the pan juices and pour the juices into a gravy boat. Carve the lamb into slices and pass the gravy.

ROSEMARY VARIATION

Prepare as directed, but omit the oregano in the dressing. Substitute 2 fresh Italian rosemary branches, each 12 inches long, for the oregano. Place 1 branch on each side of the lamb in the roasting pan. Proceed as directed.

Mom at her confirmation with her sister, Mary. To celebrate, Grandma found an excellent leg of lamb at the butcher's and made this recipe as part of Mom's confirmation meal.

STUFFED VEAL ROAST WITH PANCETTA, CHEESE, AND GARLIC

Here's a dish my mother first made when she was a teenager. She seldom made it after that, until it had to be retested for this book. Following some trial and error, we turned out a veal roast that literally melted in one's mouth, and we've been making the recipe ever since. It's a one-pan meal and will serve 4 people well. If you have a first course of pasta, it will serve 6 generously. It is a dish to prepare for guests, because you can stuff the veal the day before and make the bread crumbs, then there's little left to do. Serve with Asparagus Egg Pie with Provolone (page 52) on the side.

3 tablespoons extra-virgin olive oil

2 yellow onions, thinly sliced

Salt

1 veal roast cut from the leg, 3½ pounds

Freshly ground black pepper

½ cup flavored bread crumbs (page 14)

4 cloves garlic, thinly sliced

½ pound pancetta, cut into 1-inch-thick slices, or bacon slices

¼ pound provolone, *cacio-cavallo,* or *pepato* cut into ¼-inch-thick slices

6 fresh Italian parsley sprigs, large stems removed

1 large carrot, peeled and cut into ½-inch-thick slices

1 large celery stalk, cut into ½-inch-thick slices

3 large potatoes, peeled and cut into 1-inch-thick slices

1 pound fresh portobello mushrooms, rinsed, wiped, and cut into ½-inch slices, or white mushrooms, cleaned and quartered

2 cups chicken broth

¾ cup sweet Marsala or tawny Port wine

1½ teaspoons all-purpose flour

¼ cup hot water

1. Preheat an oven to 500°F. In a small frying pan, combine 1 table-spoon of the olive oil, 1 sliced onion, and a dash of salt and place over medium heat. Sauté until the onions are golden, about 10 minutes. Drain off the oil and set the pan aside.

2. Using a sharp knife, make a horizontal cut down the center of the veal roast; do not cut it all the way through. Open the veal up flat like a book. Down the center, sprinkle the veal lightly with salt and pepper and the bread crumbs. Spread the sautéed onion and the garlic over the meat, and lay all but 4 slices of the pancetta over them. Top with all of the provolone slices and 5 sprigs of the parsley. Close the veal, reshaping it into a roast, and tie with kitchen string at 2-inch intervals.

3. Place a medium-size baking pan on the stove top over medium heat. Add the remaining 2 tablespoons olive oil and heat until hot. Add the veal roast and brown on all sides, about 15 minutes. Transfer to the oven and roast at 500°F for 15 minutes. Reduce the heat to 375°F and add the remaining sliced onion and the carrot, celery, and potatoes. Lay the remaining pancetta slices over the top of the veal. Roast at 375°F for 1 hour. Raise the heat to 425°F and continue roasting for 1 hour longer, for a total of 2¼ hours, or until an instant-read thermometer inserted into the center registers 160°F for medium or 170°F for well done. Meanwhile, coarsely chop the remaining parsley sprig. Set aside.

4. During the last 35 minutes of roasting, add the mushrooms, chopped parsley, chicken broth, wine, 1 teaspoon salt, and ¼ teaspoon of pepper to the pan juices. In a small cup, combine the flour and hot water, whisk until all lumps are dissolved, and stir into the pan juices. Taste and adjust all the seasonings as necessary.

5. Transfer the roast to a platter and let stand for 10 minutes before slicing. Surround with all the vegetables. Top the veal slices with the mushroom sauce.

Secrets of Success

Make sure to keep changing the oven temperature as directed, and the veal will come out extremely tender.

The Temptation of the Devil

ONCE UPON A TIME in Ciminna, there was a sixteen-year-old boy named Filippo, who dreamed of *la fortunata* (luck). In his sleep he saw a treasure chest of gold coins behind the altar in the abandoned church near where my grandma Josephina lived. He told his friends about the dream, which he shouldn't have done, since according to legend to tell another is to break the spell. Together they sneaked into the church and destroyed the wall and the altar with axes. They then pulled up the floor and found a chest. Eagerly they opened it, only to find dried sheaves of barley and wheat that were used for horse feed. When Filippo returned home and told his mother what he had done, she was furious. She, in turn, became terrified because her son did not have the courage to do the deed alone. She was convinced that the devil himself had turned the gold into worthless wheat because of her son's cowardice, and prepared for God, in his anger, to seek revenge.

Two weeks after the boys destroyed the altar, they were having fun playing ball on the little street outside Filippo's home, one block away from Grandma's house. Out of nowhere, a serpent appeared, coiled itself around Filippo's leg, and ferociously stuck its fangs into him. Everyone panicked, and the boys around him started to scream. They grabbed stones and branches to club the snake to death, but the snake remained unharmed and managed to slither away into the bushes. Filippo began to convulse badly. The neighbors ran to get his mother, but by the time she arrived, only moments later, her son lay dead, sprawled out and limp, on the narrow street outside Grandma's home. The mother grabbed his body and rocked it in her arms for a long time, screaming to God that he took her boy to have his revenge for destroying his altar in the church. After the funeral, although severely distressed, the mother accepted the boy's death as *la giustizia di Dio* (the justice of God). ✤

Custati di Vitella Marsala
VEAL CHOPS MARSALA

🍴 Dad makes this recipe. It comes from his mother, who made the dish only on special occasions.

Extra-virgin olive oil

4 veal or pork chops, each 10 ounces and about 1 inch thick

2 cloves garlic, cut into medium dice

½ cup sliced green onions (¼-inch-thick slices)

½ cup diced yellow onion (medium dice)

16 fresh basil leaves, 8 leaves torn into small pieces and 8 leaves left whole

1 can (16 ounces) whole tomatoes with juice, well crushed with a fork

1 tablespoon dried oregano, sticks removed, crushed until powdery

Salt, to taste

½ cup sweet Marsala wine

1 cup sliced fresh white mushrooms

1. Generously oil a large, deep frying pan with olive oil and place over medium heat until hot. Add the chops and cook, turning once, until well browned on both sides. Transfer the chops to a plate. Set aside.

2. Add the garlic, green onions, yellow onion, and 8 torn basil leaves to the same pan, reduce the heat to low, and cook, stirring often, until the mixture browns, about 10 minutes. Return the chops to the pan and spoon the onion mixture over them.

3. Stir in the tomatoes, oregano, and salt. Top each chop with 2 whole basil leaves. Cover and continue cooking until the chops are fork tender, 45 to 60 minutes. During the last 15 minutes of cooking, stir in the wine. During the last 10 minutes of cooking, add the mushrooms.

4. Transfer the chops to plates and spoon the sauce over the tops.

Secrets of Success

The Marsala permeates the veal, making it very tender. If you don't like sweet Marsala, substitute your favorite sweet red or Port wine. This same dish can be made with veal cutlets or pork chops.

Cutuletti di Vitella Fritte
BREADED VEAL CUTLETS

🔖 Here are the famous Sicilian fried veal cutlets coated with freshly made flavored bread crumbs. As a child, I ate this dish several times a week. Usually the cutlets were served after the pasta course, along with roasted sausages and fried potatoes with onions, but we also ate them for lunch, or even as an evening snack. They are as traditional to Sicilians as the seven-hour Sunday sauce is. In the movie *Goodfellows*, when Ray Liotta, although about to be arrested, keeps saying, "I have to bread the cutlets!" these are the ones he is talking about. You can't eat just one! Today, veal cutlets are extremely expensive; however, many people substitute chicken cutlets, which are boned, trimmed chicken breast halves, for the veal. See the variation that follows for chicken cutlets baked with wine.

1 cup bread crumb coating (page 14)

1 pound milk-fed veal cutlets

Extra-virgin olive oil

Salt

1. Prepare the bread crumb coating. Dip the cutlets into the egg bath, then coat with the bread crumbs.

2. Generously oil a medium-size frying pan with olive oil and place over medium heat. Add the cutlets and cook, turning once and sprinkling with just a dash of salt, until browned on both sides, about 3 minutes on each side. Veal cutlets cook quickly. If they are sliced very thin, cook them for only 2 minutes on each side.

Baked Chicken Cutlets with Wine

Preheat an oven to 375°F. Prepare as for Breaded Veal Cutlets, substituting 1 pound chicken cutlets for the veal. Arrange the cutlets in a single layer in a large baking pan. Sprinkle with ¾ cup sweet white, red, Marsala, or Port wine. Dot with 3 tablespoons butter, cut into bits. Cover and bake for 10 minutes. Then uncover and continue to bake until chicken is fork tender, 15 to 20 minutes.

Cutuletti di Vitella alla Parmigiana
Veal Cutlets Parmesan

Serves 6

Today, this dish is arguably the least respected dish in even the best restaurants. Most home cooks and chefs alike fry the cutlets first, pour a seeded marinara sauce over the top, cover each cutlet with a slice of mozzarella, and then bake them in the oven. Our family recipe may be unique for today's standard, but it's actually how veal parmesan—meaning the style of cooking, not the cheese—was made a century ago. The breaded veal cooks in the tomato sauce, rendering the cutlets soft and tender. Let's not forget that this is a rich sauce of strained tomatoes, precooked for 1¼ hours, and not a raw, seeded marinara-type sauce, which would not complement this elegant dish. And note that full-flavored provolone and grated *incanestrato* or romano cheeses are used rather than mozzarella. The latter may be excellent on pizzas, but it does not add any extra flavor to the blandness of veal. This is truly one of my favorites, a dish my family serves guests on special occasions.

(CONTINUED)

Secrets of Success

Thin veal cutlets cook quickly, and cannot be cooked twice with satisfactory results. Veal becomes greasy when fried and then baked.

1 recipe Sauce for Veal Cutlets Parmesan (see Weekday Sauce
variation, page 101)

2 cups bread crumb coating (page 14)

2 pounds milk-fed veal cutlets

½ pound provolone cheese, cut into ⅛-inch-thick slices and then
cut into 1-inch pieces

1½ cups grated romano or *incanestrato* cheese

1. Prepare the sauce and the bread crumb coating. Dip the cutlets into the egg bath, then coat with the bread crumbs.

2. Preheat an oven to 350°F. Spread a generous layer of sauce on the bottom of a medium-size baking pan, covering it completely. Arrange a layer of cutlets in the pan. Top each cutlet with a few pieces of provolone cheese, then sprinkle generously with romano cheese. Cover the cutlets generously with the sauce. Repeat the layering until all the remaining ingredients are used. Cover with aluminum foil.

3. Bake the cutlets until fork tender, 45 minutes to 1½ hours. The timing will depend on the type of veal purchased. Milk-fed veal from a calf 8 to 10 weeks old is the highest quality available and will cook in 45 minutes. Veal from calves older than 10 weeks is usually deep pink, has a grainy texture, and is of average quality. It will cook in 1 to 1¼ hours. Shoulder cutlets are generally not used in Italian cooking. In the strictest sense, cutlets must come from the thigh of the calf, not the shoulder. The latter are the poorest-quality cutlets available, are almost red and are quite tough. Shoulder cutlets will need to cook for 1½ hours.

A Stroll to Buy Meat in Little Italy in 1935

WHEREVER GRANDMA shopped in Little Italy for meat, she knew all the owners of the stores and could rely on the quality of their stock and their advice. She never shopped exclusively at any one butcher, of course. Instead, she visited several every week and chose the best of what she found at each shop. Let's take a walk with her, circa 1935, and look for good milk-fed veal cutlets, as well as some other meats.

First she might go to Mary and Moe's Butcher at 238 Elizabeth Street and chat about good veal and the proper cut of steak with the owner Marianina (Mary and Moe's still exists at this address). Then she would stop by Spataro's at 51 Stanton Street, before launching her search for a special cut of meat like London broil, a search that took her through the row of butcher shops that lined Christie Street near Houston and Elizabeth streets off Stanton. If all else failed and Grandma couldn't find what she wanted, she'd end up at Vito Orlando's at 16 Stanton Street. He always saved something special just for her. And for a truly exceptional cut of meat, especially for a holiday dinner, she'd travel east to Fiumefreddo at 91 East Third Street, where the best and priciest meat in all New York City was sold. I often recall her telling me at the kitchen table, *"Fren-zee, la carne parla* [a Sicilian expression meaning the meat is so fresh, it tells you to eat it]. You don't need a knife for the cutlets, just use your fork." That says it all. 🌿

Pizzaiola di Vitella
VEAL PIZZAIOLA

🍅 *Pizzaiola* is a popular sauce in which meat, poultry, or fish is cooked. It takes its name from being similar in taste to pizza sauce. This recipe was taught to my great-grandmother Maria by my great-great-grandmother Angelina, so it is two hundred years old. Grandma often ate this dish whenever her mother was able to buy good veal cutlets. She used her raw pizza sauce to top them, and they were then baked in her very large brick oven. Although this dish is simple to make, it was found only in upper-middle-class homes because veal cutlets were expensive at the turn of the century in Sicily as well as in America.

Veal *Pizzaiola* can be served alone or as a second course after pasta. A good vegetable and pasta would also be excellent with the veal, such as *Perciatelli* with Squash (page 123) or Pasta with Escarole (page 121). See the variations for directions on how to make steak, or pork or veal chop *pizzaiola*.

Secrets of Success

1 pound veal cutlets

⅔ cup flavored bread crumbs (page 14), made without the garlic but with
    an additional ¼ cup grated cheese

3 yellow onions, very thinly sliced

1 can (16 ounces) whole tomatoes with juice, well crushed with a fork

6 tablespoons extra-virgin olive oil, or to taste

6 tablespoons grated *incanestrato, cacio-cavallo,* or romano cheese

1 teaspoon dried oregano, sticks removed, crushed until powdery

½ teaspoon salt

Scant ½ teaspoon sugar

6 large fresh basil leaves

Never oil the
baking pan, or the
dish will be greasy.
The natural oils in
the meat, plus the oil
in the tomato sauce,
are sufficient.
Do not bake the
sauce longer than
20 minutes,
or it will dry up.

1. Preheat an oven to 400°F. In a large baking pan, arrange the cutlets in a single layer. Sprinkle each cutlet with some of the bread crumbs

and onion slices. If there are any leftover cutlets, use another baking pan. Do not stack the cutlets.

2. In a medium-size bowl, combine the tomatoes, 4 tablespoons of the olive oil, the cheese, oregano, salt, sugar, and basil. Spoon the mixture evenly over the cutlets, then drizzle with the 3 remaining tablespoons oil.

3. Bake until the cutlets are fork tender, 25 to 30 minutes, depending on the quality and thickness of your cutlets. Serve the veal directly from the baking pan and spoon a generous amount of sauce over each portion.

STEAK *PIZZAIOLA*

Prepare as directed for Veal *Pizzaiola*, but substitute club or prime rib steaks, each ¾ inch thick. Preheat broiler. Arrange the steaks in a single layer in a medium-size baking pan. Place the pan in the broiler about 6 inches from the heat. Just brown the steaks for 1 or 2 minutes on each side. Remove from the broiler and reduce the heat to 400°F. Reserve 2 tablespoons of the sauce. Top the meat with the bread crumbs, onions, tomato sauce, and oil. Cover with a few slices of provolone or fresh mozzarella cheese. Spread the reserved 2 tablespoons sauce over the cheese to prevent them from burning. Place the steaks in the oven and bake as directed. Prime rib steaks about ¾ inch thick take about 15 minutes to cook to medium-rare.

PORK CHOP OR VEAL CHOP *PIZZAIOLA*

Prepare as directed for Steak *Pizzaiola*, adjusting the baking time as necessary for the thickest of the chops. If the chops take 45 minutes to cook, only top with the bread crumbs, onions, sauce, and cheese during the last 20 minutes, or the sauce and cheese will dry up.

Spiedini alla Siciliana
STUFFED BREADED VEAL ROLLS

*Makes about
30 spiedini,
depending on
size; serves 6*

This rich man's version of *spiedini* was taught to my father by his mother, who came from the town of San Giuseppe. *Spiedini* means to cook on a spit. The Arabs, who invaded Sicily late in the ninth century, brought shish kebabs, the forerunners of this dish. At first, *spiedini* were just street food: grilled skewers of veal, beef, or lamb bought during the afternoon for lunch or a snack and eaten with a piece of bread. *Spiedini* were to Sicily what frankfurters are to America. Soon they became so popular, however, that other versions were made, including one that calls for veal cutlets pounded thin and stuffed with various ingredients. Thus, several towns have their own unique stuffing and style of cooking *spiedini*.

2 cups bread crumb coating (page 14)

2 tablespoons extra-virgin olive oil

2 large yellow onions, sliced ¼ inch thick

¼ teaspoon salt

⅓ pound Genoa salami, very thinly sliced

⅓ pound boiled ham, very thinly sliced

2 pounds veal *spiedini* (see note)

Salt and freshly ground black pepper, to taste

½ pound provolone cheese, cut into 1-inch squares ⅛ inch thick

Additional extra-virgin olive oil, if frying *spiedini*

1. Prepare the bread crumb coating. In a large frying pan, combine the olive oil, onions, and salt and place over medium-high heat. Sauté until the onions are golden, about 10 minutes. Using a slotted spoon, transfer the onions to a dish.

2. Cut or tear the salami and ham into pieces smaller than the *spiedini*. Sprinkle each piece of veal with a pinch of salt and pepper. Place a

Secrets of Success

Use milk-fed veal cutlets cut from the leg. They take less time to cook, which ensures moistness. Make sure the veal is pounded thin, since the thickness of a regular veal cutlet will ruin this dish.

piece of ham in the center of 1 piece of veal, leaving a ½-inch border around the edges. Top with a piece of salami, a few fried onions, and a piece of provolone. Roll up the veal tightly, and tuck in the ends. Secure in the center with a toothpick or two. The stuffing should not be sticking out of the ends or it will fall out during cooking. Repeat until all the veal and stuffing ingredients are used.

3. Dip the *spiedini* in the egg bath, and then coat them with the bread crumbs. Breaded *spiedini* may be baked or fried, as desired.

4. To bake the *spiedini:* Preheat an oven to 375°F. Lightly oil a large baking sheet with 1 inch sides, and arrange the *spiedini* in rows ½ inch apart. (Do not stack them.) Cover with aluminum foil. Bake for 15 minutes, then turn the *spiedini* over. Continue to bake for another 15 minutes. Remove the foil during the last 10 minutes of cooking to brown the *spiedini*. After 30 minutes, taste one veal roll for doneness. If it is not cooked through, bake for an additional 10 minutes.

5. To fry the *spiedini:* Generously oil a large frying pan with olive oil and place over medium heat. Add the *spiedini* and cook, turning once, until golden brown, about 3 minutes on each side. They cook quickly, so watch carefully to prevent burning.

STUFFING VARIATION WITH BREAD CRUMBS

A sprinkling of flavored bread crumbs (about ½ teaspoon per veal roll) can be added to the stuffing for additional flavor.

Note: *Spiedini* are available at Italian butchers. If you don't see them, ask the butcher to cut them for you. If this is not possible, then buy 2 pounds veal cutlets. Cut each cutlet in half horizontally. Gently pound each piece of veal with a meat mallet until it is very thin. One average-size veal cutlet makes 2 rolls. Once the rolls are cooked, they will keep in the refrigerator for about 4 days.

The Story of Cacaladritta, the Mass Murderer of Sicily

WHILE WE prepared a pork roast, Grandma insisted, "I can still remember my mother baking this roast in our ten-foot-wide brick oven."

"Ten feet! Grandma, that's bigger than the one in a pizzeria! You can't mean ten feet!"

"We had the house of Cacaladritta. He was one of the wealthiest men in all of Ciminna, and he was the biggest scandal Ciminna ever had. The scandal of Sicily!" She threw her hands up in the air. "A *vigliacco!* A bum, like that girl who axed her parents."

"Lizzie Borden!" I surmised. "What did he do in Ciminna, the hot spot of Sicily?" I nudged.

"Sit down, Fren-zee, and I'll tell you. He had a son and a wife. One day he said to his son, 'Let's go to the farm. We'll sleep there and get up early in the morning to finish cultivating the land.' That night, Cacaladritta waited for his son to fall asleep. He called his name a few times, and when he saw his son didn't answer, he took a big, big stone and mashed his head."

"What reason?"

"Reason? He was *pazzo* [crazy]! When he finished killing his son, he went back to town and stopped at his daughter-in-law's house. He wanted to kill his daughter-in-law and his grandchildren. He called his daughter-in-law, 'Come on down, I want to talk to you.' She said, 'No! I don't open no door to nobody at night.' So he went back to his own home to kill his wife. When he saw she was asleep, he took a hatchet and cut off her head. Then he dragged her body without the head down the steps and left the door open, so that when people walked by in the morning they would see her. Then," she clapped her hands, "he escaped and around that time a man started living in the church of San Antonio. There was no one there. No priests, no people. It was in ruins. In the morning, a man with a hood and a mask would beg for a piece of bread. No one saw his face, so they thought he was a hobo living alone."

"No one reported him and he wore an actual mask?"

"Don't you understand anything, Fren-zee! It was a veil! A disguise! No one saw his face, and with the long hood, who knew? After six months he moved near

Palermo and became a monk."

"A monk!" I became hysterical laughing.

"Could you believe that—a monk!" she continued, astonished at her own words. "He wore a long robe and hood and grew a beard down to his hips. One day a Ciminniti [someone from Grandma's hometown] was in the church in Palermo and recognized his voice. The Ciminniti spoke with him, but he pretended he didn't know him. He ran to *la giustizia* [the police department] and reported him. Cacaladritta was arrested immediately, and they took him to a cell where you had to wake up on time or the bed closed into the wall. One day they say he overslept, the bed closed in on him, and he was crushed to death. That was the end of Cacaladritta!

"Nobody wanted his house. It was for sale for a long, long time even though it was a mansion with running water, which was considered the greatest luxury at that time. No one had a house with running water! No one!" she slammed her fist on the table. "Finally, they asked my father if he wanted the house because he had ten kids. Everyone said the house was haunted. My father laughed, and said, 'The house is beautiful. I don't believe in ghosts.' He rented it for nothing. When we arrived, there was blood all over the walls and the stairs. We kids were so scared, we didn't want to live there. My father said. 'I don't want to hear any nonsense.' So we had to clean the bedroom, stairs, walls . . . all full of blood. I was only four years old and up in the loft when my brother Vito started teasing me. 'Josephina, run! Run! Cacaladritta *vien* [is coming]!' I ran and fell down the ladder and that's how I got the scar on my face. So not only did the bum kill his family, but I got a scar on my face because of Cacaladritta. I was afraid to hear his name for years."

"Wow! What a story. How long did it take you not to be afraid of him? A couple of years?"

"Are you crazy! When I was about seventy-five years old, then I wasn't afraid anymore."

"So Cacaladritta was rich and probably had the house built to his specifications."

"Exactly! And that's how my mother got a ten-foot brick oven! Don't argue with me, Fren-zee. I'm old, but I know what I'm talkin' about! Now put the pork roast in the oven." 🐚

Carne di Maiale Arrostita di Nonna
GRANDMA'S PORK ROAST

Serves 4

🐖 This recipe dates back over 150 years. It was a favorite of my great-grandmother Maria, whose mother, Angelina, often made it for her. Whenever she found out that a good pig was being slaughtered at the butcher in Ciminna, she would purchase a piece of boneless pork. My great-grandfather Michele, who was born in 1864, would only eat sausage, thick pork chops, and this pork roast.

Grandma also makes this dish with roast beef, filet mignon, and London broil. She just adjusts the roasting time for each piece of meat. Serve with Sicilian bread, which should be dipped into the gravy, and vegetable side dishes such as Fried Breaded Vegetables (page 208) and Asparagus Egg Pie with Provolone (page 52).

1 boneless pork loin, center cut, 2½ pounds

Salt

6 medium-small new potatoes, peeled and halved

1 teaspoon dried oregano, sticks removed, crushed until powdery

6 fresh basil leaves

6 bacon slices or 3 pancetta slices, cut into strips

1 yellow onion, sliced medium-thin

1. Preheat an oven to 350°F. Rinse the pork under cold running water and pat dry with paper towels. Salt the pork on all sides. Transfer to a roasting pan and add the potatoes. Pour water into the pan to a depth of 2 inches. Add ½ teaspoon salt, the oregano, and the basil to the water, and stir. Arrange the bacon strips or pancetta over the pork.

2. Roast the pork until it is browned on top, about 30 minutes. Turn the pork over, then arrange the onion slices around it. Continue roasting until the pork is well browned, about 45 minutes, or until an instant-read thermometer inserted into the center registers 160°F.

During roasting, check the water level from time to time. If the water is evaporating too quickly, add 1 or 2 more cups water, or as necessary. Every 20 minutes, taste the pan gravy and adjust all the seasonings as necessary.

3. Transfer the roast to a platter and surround with the potatoes and pan gravy. Allow to stand for 10 minutes before slicing.

Custati di Maiale Pieni
STUFFED PORK CHOPS

Serves 4

🐾 I made up this dish when I was about twelve years old because I loved *spiedini*, little veal rolls stuffed with some of my favorite ingredients: salami, ham, fried onions, and provolone cheese. When my mother brought home one-inch-thick pork chops from Macy's, they were too bland for me. So I stuffed the chops for a little extra pizzazz and topped them with Lemon, Oil, and Garlic Dressing.

Secrets of Success

1 yellow onion, thinly sliced

1 cup bread crumb coating (page 14)

1 recipe Lemon, Oil, and Garlic Dressing for 3 pounds of meat (page 16)

4 pork chops or milk-fed veal chops, each ¾ pound and 1 inch thick

4 very thin slices boiled ham, cut in half

4 very thin slices Genoa salami

4 pieces provolone cheese, each about 2 by 1 inch and ¼ inch thick

4 teaspoons grated *cacio-cavallo* or romano cheese

4 tablespoons butter

When stuffing any meats, always slice the ham and salami extremely thin. If you can't fit 1 whole slice into the pocket, break it into smaller pieces first.

(CONTINUED)

1. In a small frying pan, combine 1 tablespoon of the olive oil and the onion. Place over medium heat and sauté until golden, about 10 minutes. Prepare the bread crumb coating and the dressing.

2. Preheat an oven to 400°F. With a sharp knife, cut a horizontal pocket in each chop, cutting toward the bone. Stuff each pocket with 1 slice of ham, 1 slice of salami, 1 piece of provolone, 1 teaspoon of grated cheese, and one-fourth of the fried onion. Close each chop tightly with a few toothpicks. Dip the chops into the egg bath, then coat with the bread crumbs.

3. Brush a medium-size baking pan with some of the dressing. Arrange the chops in the pan in a single layer. Top each chop with 1 tablespoon butter. Spoon half of the remaining dressing over the chops. Bake, uncovered, for 20 minutes, basting occasionally with the pan juices. Turn the chops over and spoon the remaining dressing over the tops. Continue to bake until the chops are fork tender, about 20 minutes longer.

4. Transfer the chops to a platter and spoon the pan juices over the top. Serve immediately.

Figato di Maiale
PORK LIVER WITH THE NET

Pork liver with the net is quite famous among Sicilians. It consists of small pork livers wrapped in a net of pork fat in which a bay leaf has been inserted. The pork basically cooks in its own fat from the net, and the leftover browned bits make a delicious gravy. Many people who won't touch liver, go wild over pork liver because it's so flavorful. Most Italian butchers carry it, although it can be difficult to find elsewhere. Faicco's at 260 Bleecker Street in New York City carries pork liver, as does Florence Meat Market at 5 Great Jones Street. Serve with bread that should be dipped into the gravy.

Extra-virgin olive oil

1½ pounds pork liver with the net, rinsed under cold water and patted dry

Salt

½ cup water

1. Lightly oil a medium-size frying pan with olive oil and place over medium-low heat. Add the liver and cook, turning once, until well browned, about 4 to 5 minutes on each side. Sprinkle with salt. Transfer the liver to a dish.

2. Add the water to the frying pan and stir to scrape up any browned bits. Cook over medium heat just until the gravy comes to a boil. Spoon over the liver and serve.

Secrets of Success

Don't overcook the liver, as it can become dry and rubbery. As soon as it's well browned, it's done.

Salsiccia Fritta con Spinaci
FRIED SAUSAGE WITH SPINACH

This old, rare dish is seldom made in America. The joke is that one day when I was in my early twenties, I created the dish because I love sausage and spinach together. When Dad came home, he was shocked. His mother had made the same dish in the 1930s, and he hadn't eaten it for forty years. In fact, he had forgotten about it. I had no recipe, nor knowledge of this, and I was conceited enough to think I had made up something special. But it goes to show that when you learn a style of cooking, you can unconsciously re-create the past.

The technique I use for cooking the sausages is strictly Sicilian and is called *fritta in l'acqua* (fried in the water). The sausage is actually steamed in the water, then pricked and allowed to fry in its own fat. The result is plumper sausages with crustier skins. In Sicily, you'll be asked how you want your sausages cooked, *al forno o fritta in l'acqua?* Although this method takes longer, I prefer it over cooking them in the oven, and the distinctive taste is worth the effort. If you wish to serve only 3 or 4 people, halve the recipe. Serve the sausages with warmed Sicilian bread, which can be dipped in the pan juices.

2 pounds sweet or hot Italian sausages, with links left attached

1 cup water

6 large cloves garlic, cut into large dice

1½ pounds spinach, carefully rinsed

½ teaspoon salt, or to taste

Secrets of Success

Never use prewashed or prepackaged spinach when making this dish. It is tougher than fresh spinach bought at the vegetable stand, and it never cooks down to the proper softness. Do not use cheese sausages for this recipe. The sausages must be pricked, which means the cheese would slip out.

1. In a large, deep frying pan, curl the sausages in a coil. Do not prick the sausages. Pour in water to a depth of ⅓ inch. Bring the water to a boil over high heat. Reduce the heat to low, cover the pan, and simmer until the water evaporates, about 20 minutes.

2. When the water has evaporated, prick the sausages with a fork. Continue cooking over low heat, covered, until the bottoms of the sausages are crusty and deep, rusty brown. Then, turn over the sausages, prick the other sides, and cover the pan. Cook until the sausages are well browned on the bottom, about 10 minutes longer. Now, stir in the 1 cup water and scrape up any browned bits.

3. Add the garlic and pile the spinach evenly on top of the sausages. Sprinkle with the salt. Cover and simmer until the spinach has wilted, about 15 minutes.

4. Transfer the sausages to a platter, arrange the spinach around them, and spoon the pan juices over the top.

Salsiccia alla Griglia
GRILLED SAUSAGE WITH POTATOES, ONIONS, AND PEPPERS

🐖 Many of my students ask me why the sausages of today taste awful and are hard. They remember the days when Sicilian sausages melted in their mouths. Now, everything is made quickly and improperly. Sausage making, in particular, demands special attention.

The best sausages in New York City were at Fretta's on Eleventh Street, off First Avenue. The store has long been closed, but everyone in Little Italy still talks about Fretta's sausages. His seasonings were superb, and there wasn't a Saturday morning that I didn't see limousines from Connecticut, New Jersey, and upstate New York lined up outside the tiny shop to buy sausages. Often people purchased twenty pounds at a time and froze them.

Here's what makes sausage delicious. The amount of fat in the filling should be about 20 percent, from a well-marbelized boneless pork butt. Without the proper amount of fat, sausage is hard rather than juicy and, in my opinion, not worth eating. The sausages must also include the proper seasonings of dark fennel, freshly chopped Italian parsley, salt, and freshly ground black peppercorns. If cheese sausages are bought, they must contain small chunks of provolone.

Furthermore, the pork must be ground with the proper sausage disk, which has much larger holes than the one used to grind meat for meatballs. If the sausage is made (as it is in most grocery stores) with a small-holed disk, the pork will be packed too tight and become dense in the heat, resulting in a hard sausage when cooked. The final aspect of a good sausage is the skin. Sicilian sausages must have very thin skins, which are hog casings made from the pig intestines. A thick skin is gummy and will easily ruin the delicate taste of the sausage as you bite into it. You should not even know that the sausage is encased in skin.

This recipe is a very common one in Sicily. Since the weather is often hot, Sicilians like to put their sausages on an outdoor grill for serving at picnics or at-home dinners. That custom makes this a perfect dish to prepare if you're having an outdoor celebration—just barbecue the sausage instead of broiling it and make the traditional accompaniment of potatoes, onions, and peppers on the stove top or on the grill. Serve with bread and a platter of cheese and olives.

Extra-virgin olive oil

2 large potatoes, thinly sliced

Salt

1 large yellow onion, cut into ¼-inch-thick slices

2 large green or red bell peppers, seeded and sliced lengthwise ½ inch wide

2 pounds Italian sausages seasoned with fennel and parsley or with cheese

1. Preheat a broiler. Generously oil a large frying pan with olive oil and place over medium heat. Add the potatoes, cover, and cook for 15 minutes, sprinkling with salt to taste. Uncover and add the onions and peppers. Continue to cook, turning occasionally, until the potatoes are browned and fork tender, about 15 minutes longer. Using a slotted spoon, transfer the potato mixture to a platter; keep warm.

2. Meanwhile, with a fork, prick the fennel sausages on the front and back. If using cheese sausages, do not prick them or the cheese will fall out during cooking. Arrange on a broiler pan and broil, turning as needed, until crusty brown on both sides, 5 to 7 minutes on each side. Arrange the sausages over the potato mixture and serve.

Grandma's Neighbor Pietro

IN THE 1930s in New York City, Grandma bought live chickens from her neighbor Pietro, a man so cheap that he shaved his head every day to avoid spending sixty cents on a haircut. His completely bald head and unshaven face matched his ornery disposition. Pietro didn't walk; he shuffled slowly. And if he didn't like you, he told you to your face. He seemed always to be picking a fight with someone, and his familiar raspy voice would echo throughout the halls in the building, "Eeeee no gooood! [You're no good!]"

Pietro carried his live chickens in large sacks on his slightly hunched shoulders up seven flights of stairs every week. Whatever he didn't sell was brought back to his apartment and stored in a cage for him to eat during the week.

Grandma recalled, "The chickens he sold were always spring chickens, which are young, tender birds usually weighing 2 to 2½ pounds, and never more than 3 pounds. He would pick up a chicken in his hands and weigh it by feel, then ask his price, usually seventy to ninety cents a chicken."

"Did you kill them yourself, Grandma?"

"No, Pietro used to kill them in his apartment. But *l'armaluzzo* [the animal] felt no pain. He used to take the neck of the chicken and pull it. In one second *l'armaluzzo* was dead. No pain, no nothing."

I grimaced. "I love chicken, but I don't think I could kill one."

"Fren-zee, stop acting like that. Animals are here to eat. What are they going to do? Have the cows and chickens running in the streets? People were starving in World War I in Sicily. They'd jump on a rat if they saw it. What's the cow and dog gonna do for you? Clean your house, cook your food, take care of you when you're sick? Bah! I'm ninety-four and an old woman, but I'm not crazy. I've lived off the land, lived on a farm. I've seen life and I've seen death! And remember what Grandma tells you, to live you have to eat." She raised herself excitedly from her chair, waving a finger at me, and opened the oven door. "Women need a little meat or chicken; it's got minerals, iron, and protein . . . *questi cosi* [these things]."

"How'd you know that?"

"I saw it on the television, on the Don-a-who [Phil Donahue] show. The one who got white hair before his time. Fren-zee, what do you think, I'm a dummy!"

"Well, all I know is that when I'm tired and sick, I just want a big steak or a piece of roasted chicken."

"That's right! And I don't need nobody, or no Don-a-who show, to tell me that."

"If Don-a-who ate your food, Grandma, his hair wouldn't have turned white so fast," I teased.

"You said it, Fren-zee, not me!" She opened the oven door, and turned to me, saying, "Chickens were on sale at the A & P for ninety-nine cents a pound. I made chicken with lemon, oil, and garlic. Oh, Fren-zee!" she smiled. "I love *u sciavuru* [the smell] of fresh lemon and garlic—the way it goes through the whole kitchen. You want some?" 🐌

CHICKEN WITH LEMON, OIL, AND GARLIC

🐦 This recipe hasn't changed for centuries. The use of lemon, oil, and garlic leads me to believe it arrived in Sicily with the Greeks in the eighth century B.C. It remains one of my favorite ways to cook chicken, and perhaps the best part of it is the potatoes, which are permeated with the flavors of lemon and garlic. We always used to serve this dish after the Seven-Hour Sunday Tomato Sauce (page 95). In the old days, the chicken was cooked whole, but today, we sometimes cut it up before cooking. Both methods are included here, with the whole chicken explained in a variation.

1 recipe Lemon, Oil and Garlic Dressing for one 3-pound chicken (page 16)

1 spring chicken, 3 pounds, cut into serving pieces

4 new potatoes, cut into ½-inch-thick slices with a potato cutter with ridges, then cut in half

1. Preheat a broiler. Prepare the dressing. Rinse the chicken quickly under cold running water. Pat dry. In a medium-size baking pan, place the chicken pieces skin side down and surround with the potatoes. Brush one-third of the dressing over the chicken pieces and potatoes.

2. Broil the chicken for about 15 minutes on one side. Turn over the chicken pieces and potatoes, and broil until the juices run clear when the thigh and breasts are pierced with a fork, another 15 minutes. Throughout the cooking, baste the chicken and potatoes every 10 minutes with the remaining dressing and pan drippings. Transfer the chicken to a platter and surround with the potatoes. Top with the pan juices.

Preheat an oven to 375°F. Prepare as directed, but substitute a whole chicken for the chicken parts. Roast the chicken on the middle rack of the oven, basting every 20 minutes with the remaining lemon dressing, for 1 to 1¼ hours, or until an instant-read thermometer inserted into the thigh registers 180°F. Alternatively, test the chicken for doneness by cutting a slit in the leg joint; if the juices run clear, the chicken is ready.

Gallina Arrostita con Marsala
ROASTED CHICKEN WITH MARSALA SAUCE

Serves 4

🍗 Here's a recipe Dad and I created. I wanted a wine-based brown gravy, and since I prefer a whole chicken over parts because it's juicier, we fiddled until we came up with this recipe. This is great dish for entertaining because it has plenty of vegetables as well as chicken, and it's easy. Serve with Weekday Tomato Sauce (page 100) tossed with spaghetti for a first course, and you're done.

1 chicken, 4 pounds

Salt

4 carrots, peeled and sliced on the diagonal 1 inch thick

10 baby or small yellow onions (not pearl onions), peeled but left whole

2 tablespoons extra-virgin olive oil

6 potatoes, peeled and sliced 1 inch thick

1½ cups chicken broth

¾ cup sweet Marsala wine

(CONTINUED)

1. Preheat an oven to 500°F, then reduce the heat to 450°F just before placing the chicken in the oven. Rinse the chicken quickly under cold running water. Pat dry. Remove any excess fat from around the cavity and set aside. Salt the chicken inside and out. Oil a large roasting pan with the olive oil. Place the chicken breast side up in the pan and arrange the carrots and onions around the bird. Sprinkle the vegetables with salt.

2. Roast the chicken at 450°F for 15 minutes. Reduce the heat to 350°F and add the potatoes. Roast for 1 hour longer, then add the chicken broth and Marsala and raise the heat to 400°F. Roast for 15 minutes more, or until an instant-read thermometer inserted into the thigh registers 180°F. Alternatively, test for doneness by cutting a slit in the leg joint; if the juices run clear, the chicken is ready.

3. Transfer the chicken to a large platter and surround with the vegetables. Skim off the excess fat from the pan juices and ladle the juices into a gravy boat. Serve the gravy on the side.

Petti di Gallina Pieni con Marsala
STUFFED CHICKEN BREASTS IN MARSALA

Here's a recipe Dad and I created over the years that is great for company. Any sparkling white wine goes well with this dish. Accompany with Fried Squash with Basil and Grated Cheese (page 220).

1 cup bread crumb coating (page 14)

4 boneless chicken breast halves, skinned (about ¾ pound each)

Extra-virgin olive oil

1 large yellow onion, sliced

Salt

4 thin slices *each* Genoa salami and boiled ham

4 pieces provolone cheese, each 3 by 1 inch and ¼ inch thick

4 fresh Italian parsley sprigs, large stems removed

3 potatoes, peeled and cut into 2-inch-thick pieces

Wine Sauce

3 tablespoons extra-virgin olive oil

1 pound fresh white mushrooms, rinsed, wiped, and quartered, or portobello
    mushrooms, cleaned and cut into ¼-inch-thick slices

1 large yellow onion, cut into medium dice

3 cloves garlic, thinly sliced

½ cup sweet Marsala or tawny Port wine

¼ cup sweet white wine

½ cup chicken broth

1½ tablespoons butter

2 tablespoons hot water

¼ teaspoon all-purpose flour

3 fresh Italian parsley sprigs, chopped medium-fine

Salt, to taste

Secrets of Success

Pouring the sauce over the chicken during the last 10 minutes of cooking makes the sauce thicken properly and allows the flavors to blend.

(CONTINUED)

1. Preheat an oven to 375°F. Prepare the bread crumb coating. With a sharp knife, cut a deep horizontal slit along the side of each breast. (Do not cut all the way through.) Open each breast flat like a book and, using a meat mallet, pound it lightly just until it is flattened. In a small frying pan, heat 1 tablespoon olive oil over medium heat. Add the sliced onion and sauté until golden, about 10 minutes. Sprinkle with salt. Drain off any oil. Set aside.

2. Stuff the center of each breast with 1 slice of salami, 1 slice of ham, 1 piece of provolone, one-fourth of the fried onion, and 1 sprig of parsley. Roll up the breast jelly-roll style. Tuck in the ends, and secure each end with 1 or 2 toothpicks. Dip the chicken breasts into the egg bath, then coat with the bread crumbs.

3. Lightly oil a very large dutch oven and place it on the stove top, positioning it lengthwise over 2 burners. Turn on both burners to medium, add the chicken breasts and potatoes, and brown for about 3 minutes on each side. Cover, transfer to the oven, and bake until the juices run clear when the flesh is pierced with a fork, about 40 minutes.

4. Meanwhile, make the wine sauce: In a large frying pan, heat the oil over medium heat. Add the mushrooms, onion, and garlic and sauté until the mushrooms are browned, about 10 minutes. Stir in the Marsala or port, white wine, chicken broth, and butter. In a cup, using a fork, beat together the hot water and flour until no lumps are visible. Then stir the flour mixture into the sauce. Add the parsley and salt and bring the sauce to a boil over high heat. Reduce the heat to medium and cook for 20 minutes.

5. During the last 10 minutes of cooking, ladle the sauce over the chicken and vegetables in the baking pan and stir well with the pan drippings. When the chicken breasts are ready, transfer them to a platter along with the potatoes. Skim off any excess fat from the pan juices, pour into a gravy boat, and serve on the side.

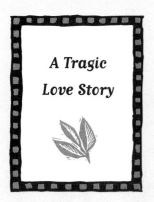

A Tragic
Love Story

WHILE GRANDMA was adding the sugar to the sauce for the chicken cacciatore, she told me about a man named Vincenzo who lived in Ciminna and who was very, very much in love with his wife. When World War I broke out, he, along with the other young men in the town, went off to war. While he was away, his wife died of the plague. When the war was over, Vincenzo returned and went to his mother-in-law's house, asking for his wife. His mother-in-law did not have the heart to tell him that his wife had died, so she pretended that she was still alive. She told him his wife was staying at his mother's house. When he arrived at his mother's house, his mother didn't have the nerve to tell him the truth either, and she told him to go over to his cousin's house, explaining that his wife had gone there to pick up some material to make a dress.

Vincenzo, annoyed and impatient, burst into his uncle's home seeking his wife. But the uncle was so mortified that no one had told Vincenzo that his wife had died, he, too, could not find the words to break the news to him. So after evading the soldier's questions, the uncle finally blurted out, "You want to find your wife . . . I will tell you then . . . go to the cemetery near the corner of the church, for that was the last place I saw your wife." The young man ran to the cemetery and questioned the caretaker, who immediately took him to his wife's grave. Vincenzo began to scream uncontrollably, crying and repeating over and over again, "How could you leave me?" All did their best to console him, but nothing worked. After five days, Vincenzo refused to eat. After ten days, Vincenzo refused to see his children. After fourteen days, Vincenzo completely lost his mind in sorrow. Two weeks to the day after he laid eyes on his wife's grave, Vincenzo died of a broken heart.

Grandma's moral: "Instead of passing the buck, the family should have sat Vincenzo down and explained the situation. Their lies made him find out in such a way that drove him insane. Don't play games. Tell the truth!" 🍃

Gallina Cacciatore
CHICKEN CACCIATORE

🐾 Grandma made this dish for Grandpa Natale at least once a month. It was one of his favorites and true to his fussy nature, he wanted it made the same way his mother Maria had made it. In fact, Grandpa taught Grandma how to prepare it, so this dish originated in Ventimiglia, next door to Ciminna. Grandpa always bought Grandma a spring chicken, which she cut into serving pieces for this dish, since larger roasting chickens are too tough for this recipe.

Extra-virgin olive oil

1 spring chicken, 3 pounds, cut into serving pieces

3 medium-large cloves garlic, sliced

1 can (35 ounces) whole tomatoes with juice, well crushed with a fork

1½ teaspoons dried oregano, sticks removed, crushed until powdery

1 teaspoon salt, or to taste

6 fresh basil leaves, torn into small pieces

¾ cup white or red wine vinegar, or as needed

Sugar to taste

4 fresh basil sprigs

1. Generously oil a large, 3-inch-deep frying pan with olive oil and place over medium heat. Brown chicken pieces about 3 minutes on each side. (Do not completely cook the chicken.) Transfer the chicken to a plate lined with paper towels to drain, then pour off the excess oil from the pan, leaving just enough to coat the pan generously.

Secrets of Success

Most people cook the chicken completely, then recook it in the sauce. That's why the chicken comes out dry and tough. The chicken must be cooked in the sauce and only browned in the oil!

2. Return the pan to medium heat, add the garlic, and sauté until golden, about 1 minute. Stir in the tomatoes, oregano, salt, basil, ¾ cup vinegar, and ¾ teaspoon sugar. Taste and adjust the sauce to a sweet and sour balance to your liking. If the sauce is too bitter, add more sugar, ¼ teaspoon at a time. If the sauce becomes too thick during the first 15 minutes of cooking, add an extra ¼ cup vinegar. But if the taste of the vinegar is already too sharp, add ⅓ cup water to adjust the acidity. Otherwise, water is not to be added to this dish, for it will dilute the sweet and sour balance and you will have to adjust the flavors all over again, and then cook down the sauce.

3. Return the chicken to the pan. Bring the sauce to a boil over high heat, then reduce the heat to low. Prop a wooden spoon under the lid to keep the pot half covered and simmer until the juices run clear when a thigh is pierced with a fork, 30 to 45 minutes. The chicken should fall off the bone easily. If the chicken pieces are small, this dish should be done within 30 minutes. If the chicken pieces are large, the dish will take 45 minutes. Every 20 minutes, taste the sauce and adjust all the seasonings as necessary.

4. Transfer the chicken to a platter and ladle the sauce over the top. Garnish with basil sprigs.

Secrets of Success

Do not use crushed tomatoes in this recipe, as they will make the sauce too thick too soon.

VERDURI E INSALATI

Vegetables

and Salads

 Vegetables in Sicily grow in rich volcanic mineral soil under an intense sun. Naturally sweet, they are one of the mainstays of the Sicilian table, where they appear as a side dish, a first course, an evening snack, or with pasta. The simplest and most common preparation for the majority of leafy greens is to combine them with extra-virgin olive oil and sautéed garlic. The second most popular preparation calls for breading and frying the vegetables, while traditional dishes like Eggplant Parmesan and Peppers Stuffed with Chopped Meat are meals in themselves, when served with bread.

When buying vegetables, I follow what I learned from Grandma: price doesn't necessarily have anything to do with quality. Experiment with different vegetable stands. It is unlikely that you will find just one that fulfills all your expectations, plus you will have the pleasure of shopping the old-fashioned way, from several different sellers. Getting to know the store owners, who will begin putting aside their best vegetables for their favorite customers, is part of the fun of becoming a discriminating shopper.

A second mainstay of Sicily is pasta, and for recipes on vegetables and pasta, see Chapter 5, page 85.

In Sicilian households, salads are served with lunch and dinner and accompany everything from roasted meats and fish to poultry. They are also eaten as an evening snack. A true Sicilian salad includes romaine lettuce and beautifully ripe red or green tomatoes tossed in a dressing made with extra-virgin olive oil, bits of garlic, oregano, and a good-quality red wine vinegar or distilled white vinegar. Other ingredients are added, too, including sweet red onions, the leaves of young escarole (which is often substituted for the romaine lettuce), chicken, tuna, and any leftover cooked meats or cheeses.

Grandma only uses distilled white vinegar in her salad. She feels its taste is closer to the strong red wine vinegar of Sicily. Because in Sicily she often made vinegar from fresh wine that had turned sour, she refuses to pay five or ten dollars a bottle for gourmet vinegar. Dad, on the other hand, uses only red wine vinegar. The choice is yours, but nothing in this country compares to the delicious red wine vinegar of Sicily. It is so strong that you must add more oil than usual to the salad to compensate for its acidity. I prefer salads where I can taste the vinegar, like those in Sicily, but since all vinegars and olive oils are different, it's impossible to give exact amounts for each. A good way to decide how much oil or vinegar to add is to mix equal amounts with your salad. Retaste once or twice, adding a little more oil or vinegar until the dressing is the way you like it. Several of the recipes in this book call for more vinegar than is customary. This is because I often use distilled white vinegar, which although closer to the taste of Sicily, requires using more vinegar for the proper balance.

In this chapter you'll find old Sicilian favorites, such as Olive Salad with Garden Vegetables, which is ideal fare for a party, buffet table, or the holidays, and Sicilian Potato Salad, a dish Sicilians are not known for because it is frequently made in the house and not found in restaurants. There are also classics like Grandma's Mixed Salad to which you can add leftovers, and Grandma's and my favorite, Green Plum Tomato Salad with Curls of Provolone. It's a meal or snack in itself.

The Legend of the Dancing Doll

WHILE WE WERE cleaning artichokes, Grandma told me the legend of *pupo che ballava* (the dancing doll). In Sicily there is a belief that this elfin is a representative of the devil. If the *pupo* appears to you, you must have strength not to be afraid. Instead, you must take a stone and throw it at him. If you do, the dancing doll will disappear and God will reward you with pots of gold for your courage.

One day my great-grandmother Maria was at the farm picking up olives off the ground and placing them in a large burlap sack that she dragged behind her. As she asked her husband, Michele, if she had enough olives to make oil, she glimpsed something out of the corner of her eye. It was a small man dancing on the side of mountain where her husband was harvesting vegetables. Frightened and excited at the same time, she called Michele to show him, but he replied that he could see nothing. Nervous, he took his wife by the hand and told her she must kill the *pupo* herself. Leading her up the mountain, he instructed her to pick up a stone and throw it at the vision. As she reached for the stone, the *pupo* laughed in her face and immediately disappeared.

When she told her husband, he was furious. "Why did you tell me?" he cried. "You broke the spell! We could have been millionaires!"

"I had a fortune in my hands, but I broke the spell by showing my fear and telling your father," she told Grandma. "The *pupo* was supposed to reveal his treasure to me—no one else! I'll always remember that day. I rode off slowly with the olive sacks tied over the mule, with tears in my eyes. Your father's sacks were full of peas, onions, eggplants, squash, and potatoes and he barely spoke to me. We were rich in vegetables but not in gold!"

Grandma's moral: "If you're in Sicily, Fren-zee, and you have a vision of a little man dancing on the mountain, shut your mouth and start throwing rocks!"

Cacociuli con Ovo e Formaggio
ARTICHOKES FRIED WITH EGG AND CHEESE

🐚 Whenever I buy artichokes, I look for small to medium-sized ones that are an even medium green without any black spots. If the leaves are crinkled rather than smooth, the artichokes are old. Although artichokes are available all year, they are only in season roughly from November to March. They may look good in the summer, but they are often tough, bitter, and stringy.

4 medium-small artichokes

Salt

2 large eggs

4 tablespoons milk

4 heaping tablespoons grated *cacio-cavallo*, provolone, or romano cheese

Extra-virgin olive oil

1. Trim and quarter the artichokes as directed on page 207.

2. Half-fill a medium-size pot with water, bring to a boil, and add salt to taste. Add artichokes and parboil until half cooked, about 5 minutes. They should be barely fork tender. Drain. Pat dry lightly with a kitchen towel to remove excess water.

3. In a soup dish, beat together the eggs, milk, grated cheese, and a pinch of salt. Generously oil a medium-size frying pan with olive oil and place over medium heat.

4. Working in small batches, dip the artichoke pieces into the egg mixture and add to the hot pan. Do not crowd the frying pan. Cook until lightly browned, about 2 minutes on each side. Serve immediately.

Secrets of Success

Do not buy the very small baby artichokes sold in gourmet shops. They are sometimes imported from other countries and can be ridiculously expensive. By the time you trim them, there is literally nothing left. Don't waste your money. And remember to invest in a sharp knife to cut the artichokes easily.

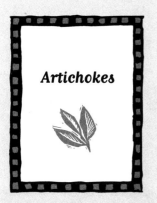

Artichokes

ARTICHOKES IN SICILY are very large, very tender, and very sweet. It is rare to see an artichoke with black spots on it. Most often they are cleaned, quartered, boiled in salted water, and then ladled into sterilized jars along with their cooking water. In Sicily, it is not uncommon to find a pantry full of jarred and dried foods, from figs and fava beans to tomatoes and artichokes. This enables the Sicilian to save his crops for the winter.

Here, in America, large artichokes are often tough, stringy, and expensive. Most people do not prepare artichokes because they have no idea of how to cook them. They rely instead on frozen or jarred hearts—many have never even eaten the artichoke leaves, which are my favorite.

Whenever I am in Sicily, evenings find me drinking wine and eating artichokes made in a variety of ways, from coated in bread crumbs or egg and cheese and fried to quartered, boiled, and dipped into equal parts of vinegar and olive oil well seasoned with salt and pepper. It is a perfect way to chat the night away.

To clean an artichoke that is to be stuffed whole: Remove the first layer of leaves from each row, from the top to the bottom of the artichoke, and discard. Only tender, green leaves should remain. You will end up removing at least one-third, or more, of all the leaves. With kitchen scissors or a sharp knife, cut off the top one-third of each artichoke leaf. Begin cutting the leaves at the top row and end with the bottom row, removing all the points. Next, cut off the bottom stem. (Peel, halve, and cook the stems along with the artichokes in water, or whatever sauce is being made for the recipe. The stems are similar in taste to the hearts.) Then remove all the leaves that surrounded the bottom of the stem and discard. The artichoke should now stand upright. Stop here and follow your particular recipe.

To clean an artichoke that is to be quartered, sliced, and fried: Prepare the artichoke as described for stuffing, then, holding it in one hand with the bottom facing you, hold a sharp knife in the other hand. Working on the diagonal, continue to cut several layers deep into the artichoke leaves, turning the artichoke slowly and removing about another one-half of the leaves. Quarter the artichoke lengthwise and remove the inner choke of small, white and light purple prickly leaves. ✿

Fritto di Verdure I
FRIED BREADED VEGETABLES

🐾 Dad says Grandma is the champ of breading. Give her anything and she'll bread it. Sicilians often have a table of "fried things," which they call a *frittura*. One of the most famous is a *fritto* of vegetables. It can be made with bread crumbs, as it is here, or with flour and eggs, as it is on page 211. This recipe can be adapted to almost any vegetable, but here I've included the most classic examples. The dish is at least three hundred years old and is well known among older Sicilians who live in the provinces surrounding Palermo. The most unusual and exceptional of the fried vegetables are the artichokes. Unfortunately, they are not popular in America anymore, and Grandma is the only person I know who still makes them. Sliced like a cutlet and fried, the artichokes take on a unique appearance and taste. They are delicious as hot snacks or as a side dish with a favorite meat entrée.

One *fritto* of vegetables serves 4; several *fritto*s of vegetables make a party, buffet, or holiday platter.

1 to 2 cups bread crumb coating (page 14), or as needed

Any one of the following: 4 artichokes; 1 head of broccoli or cauliflower,

    1½ pounds; 2 pounds medium-small eggplants or summer squashes

2 eggs

4 tablespoons milk

Salt

Extra-virgin olive oil

1. To make the artichokes: Prepare 1 cup bread crumb coating. Trim the artichokes as directed on page 207, leaving them whole. Position the artichoke in front of you with the leaves pointing up. Cut the artichoke through the stem end into ⅓-inch-thick slices. You should have 4 slices per artichoke. With a small knife, remove the inner choke of

small, white and purple prickly leaves. (If you clean the artichokes in advance, keep them in a bowl of cold water to which you've added the juice of 1 lemon. Refrigerate, covered, but cook artichokes the same day, or they will spoil.)

To make the broccoli or cauliflower: Prepare 1 cup bread crumb coating. Cut the broccoli or cauliflower head into small florets. Discard the tough ends of the broccoli stem, then peel and cut the cauliflower and broccoli stems into 3-inch pieces.

To make the eggplants or squashes: Prepare 2 cups bread crumb coating. Peel and cut off both ends of each eggplant or squash. Cut each eggplant lengthwise into slices ¼ inch thick, or cut each squash lengthwise into slices ½ inch thick.

2. Half-fill a medium-size pot with water, bring to a boil, and add salt to taste. Add the artichokes slices or broccoli or cauliflower pieces and parboil until half cooked, 5 to 7 minutes. They should be barely fork tender. Drain. Pat dry lightly with a kitchen towel to remove excess water. Do not parboil the eggplants or squashes.

3. In a bowl, beat together the eggs, milk, and ¼ teaspoon salt. Working in small batches, dip each vegetable piece into the egg mixture, then coat with the bread crumbs. Generously oil a medium-size frying pan with olive oil and place over medium heat. Add the vegetable pieces and cook, sprinkling with a little salt and turning once, until browned and fork tender, 2 or 3 minutes on each side. Transfer to a plate lined with paper towels to drain briefly. Serve hot.

Secrets of Success

Make sure to pat the vegetables dry after boiling and draining, or they will be soggy when fried. Do not overcook the vegetables when you boil them, or they will be mushy when fried.

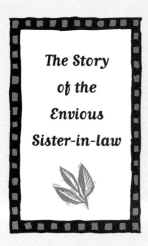

The Story of the Envious Sister-in-law

WHILE GRANDMA was breading broccoli, she told me that in 1938, her brother Mike traveled from his hometown of Chicago to New York's Little Italy without his wife, Caterina. He came to visit Grandma for one month, much to Grandpa Natale's dismay, since he detested company.

Mike was a wealthy man who was very sharp in business and owned a billiard ball store and several pieces of land in Chicago. A week after he left Grandma's home, the telephone rang. It was Mike's wife, Caterina. She arrogantly shouted, *"Chi ci mittisti ni cacociuli, ca tuo fratello non stapa mai dire che non averva mai mangiato—zucchero?* [What did you put in the artichokes that your brother never stops talking about them. He says he never tasted food like yours. Did you add sugar?] Because whatever I do now, it's not good enough to please your brother."

Grandma immediately understood her sarcasm and laughed, "Caterina, it's just the way I cook. If you ever want to learn, my door is open. When you come to New York, I'll teach you."

Caterina was what we Sicilians call *incazata* (so insulted that she had her nose up in the air). She was never really friendly with Grandma from that day on and often refused to speak to her. Grandma describes Caterina's cooking as "any old way, and she used to put lots of fennel seeds in everything. For some reason, she had an obsession with fennel. Probably because she didn't know what she was doing. My poor brother!" Grandma slapped her knee.

Grandma's moral: "A man should always marry a woman who's a good cook, then the family won't fight."

Fritto di Verdure II
BATTER-FRIED VEGETABLES

🔖 Here's the second way of making a table of "fried things" (see page 208). Today, batter-fried vegetables are often called tempura, and a hefty price is paid for squash or eggplants sticks. Sicilians have been making batter-fried vegetables for centuries, and it's easy and inexpensive.

The most interesting of these batter-fried vegetables is *cardune duce* (sweet cardoons), usually found in December. *Cardune amari* (bitter cardoons) are found in the summer, but they are very bitter. Cardoons can be fried in flour or bread crumbs and are equally good both ways.

For mixed vegetables

Any one of the following: 3 artichokes; 1 head broccoli or cauliflower,

1½ pounds; 2 pounds medium-small eggplants or summer squashes

1 to 2 cups all-purpose flour

For cardoons

1 bunch cardoons, about 2 pounds

1 cup all-purpose flour

1 cup pancake flour

2 eggs

4 tablespoons milk

¼ teaspoon salt, plus more for sprinkling

Extra-virgin olive oil

(CONTINUED)

Secrets of Success

Since sweet cardoons are rarely available, Dad mixes pancake flour with all-purpose flour to achieve a delicate, sweet taste for the normally bitter vegetable.

1. To prepare artichokes, broccoli, cauliflower, eggplants, or squashes, trim and slice the vegetables as directed in Fried Breaded Vegetables (pages 208–209). To prepare cardoons, cut off the leaves and remove the outside stalks; discard. Break the stalks apart and wash each one thoroughly to remove any dirt. Cut the stalks into 6-inch-long pieces.

2. In a bowl, beat together the eggs, milk, and ¼ teaspoon salt. Set aside.

3. Parboil and dry artichokes, broccoli, or cauliflower as directed in Step 2 of Fried Breaded Vegetables (page 209). Do not parboil eggplants or squashes. Following the directions in Step 3 of Fried Breaded Vegetables, substitute the flour for the bread crumbs, coat, and fry the vegetables. Drain on a paper towel–lined plate and sprinkle with salt.

4. To cook cardoons, parboil the pieces in salted boiling water as directed in Step 2 of Fried Breaded Vegetables (see page 209), allowing 10 minutes for sweet cardoons and 15 to 20 minutes for bitter cardoons. Drain and pat dry. In a bowl, combine the all-purpose flour and pancake flour. Dip the cardoon pieces into the egg mixture, then coat with the flour mixture. Fry as directed for Fried Breaded Vegetables, drain, and sprinkle with salt to taste.

Broccoli Rape con Olio e Aglio
BROCCOLI RAPE WITH OLIVE OIL AND GARLIC

Serves 4

🐟 I generally find broccoli rape too bitter. Grandma has a way of making it without the bitter taste, however (see Secrets of Success), and it comes out simply delicious. But many people like the bitterness, so in this recipe I've included three different techniques to satisfy everyone: boiled and tossed with olive oil, salt, pepper, and garlic (as in Step 2); cooked twice to make it sweeter (as in Step 3), or, if you like the bitterness, trimmed and then sautéed (as in Step 4).

1 bunch broccoli rape, 1½ pounds

Extra-virgin olive oil

Salt and freshly ground black pepper or red pepper flakes, to taste

5 cloves garlic, quartered lengthwise

1. To clean the broccoli rape: Remove the dark, stiff-feeling leaves from the lower half of each stem. You will always remove 2 to 4 leaves. Leave the top section with the broccoli head intact. Cut off 2 to 3 inches from the bottom of each stem, or until the stem feels tender. If the whole stems are tender, do not remove any portion of them. Peel each of the stems. Transfer the trimmed greens to a colander and rinse well under cold running water several times to remove any dirt.

2. To make with a half-bitter taste: Bring a medium-size pot half-filled with salted water to a boil. Add the broccoli rape and cook for 5 minutes. Transfer the rape and 2 cups of the cooking water to a medium-size bowl. Drizzle with olive oil and season with salt and black or red pepper. Add the garlic, and mix well. Serve immediately.

Secrets of Success

Make sure there are no yellow flowers on the broccoli rape, or the greens will be tough and hard. To remove the bitter taste, boil the greens first, and then simmer in olive oil and garlic.

(CONTINUED)

3. To make with a sweet taste: Prepare as directed in Steps 1 and 2, but reserve all the cooking water. In a small saucepan, combine ¼ cup olive oil and the garlic and sauté over medium heat until the garlic is golden, about 2 minutes. Add the greens and enough cooking water just to cover; discard the rest. Stir and simmer for 5 minutes. Season with salt and black or red pepper. Serve immediately.

4. To make with a bitter taste: Prepare as directed in Step 1. In a small saucepan, combine 6 tablespoons olive oil and the garlic and place over medium heat. Sauté until the garlic is golden, about 1 minute. Add one-fourth of the rape, leaving it very damp from its cleaning. Stir and cook until the greens wilt, about 1 minute. Repeat, adding and cooking in bunches until all of the greens are in the saucepan. Add 1 cup cold water, cover, and simmer, stirring occasionally, until tender, about 10 minutes. Transfer to a dish and sprinkle with salt and black or red pepper.

RAPE WITH PASTA VARIATION

Prepare in any one of the ways described, reserving all the cooking water and adjusting the salt, pepper, oil, and garlic to taste. Cut into 2-inch pieces; keep warm. Break 1 pound spaghetti in half, and then break each half in half again. (Or use *perciatelli* or *bucatini* and break into thirds.) Cook and drain the pasta. In a large bowl, combine the pasta and greens and its liquid. Serve with grated *pepato* cheese or your favorite grated cheese and red pepper flakes.

Scarola con Olio e Aglio

ESCAROLE WITH OLIVE OIL AND GARLIC

Escarole is popular in Sicily and in Little Italy, and it is one of my favorite vegetables. It can be extremely gritty, however, with sand hidden deep between the leaves. To clean the escarole properly, Grandma pulls all the leaves apart and places them in a very large pot filled with cold water. She tosses the leaves in the water and then throws out the water, and then repeats this three times with clean water. After the third bath, she removes the leaves in small batches, gives them a rinse under running water, and then puts them in a colander. She then gives all the leaves a final rinse, tossing them gently.

Serve dish with Sicilian bread for dipping into the cooking liquid.

1 pound young escarole, dry, tough leaves discarded and carefully rinsed

Salt

4 tablespoons extra-virgin olive oil

3 large cloves garlic, cut into medium dice

Freshly ground black pepper or red hot pepper flakes, to taste

1. To cut the escarole leaves, stack several of them and then cut them into 2-inch-wide pieces.

2. In a medium-size pot, combine the escarole, water just to cover, and 1 teaspoon salt. Bring to a boil, reduce the heat to medium, and cook until the leaves are tender, about 10 minutes. Transfer the escarole and 1½ cups of the cooking water to a bowl.

3. In small frying pan, combine the olive oil and the garlic and place over medium heat. Sauté until the garlic is golden, about 1 minute. Spoon the oil and garlic over the escarole and mix gently. Season with salt and black or red pepper.

Secrets of Success

Check the outer leaves of the head of the escarole. If the head is young and tender, it is not necessary to remove any of them. If it is large, the outer leaves will generally be tough. Remove and discard a couple of layers until the leaves feel tender.

Funci Fritte con Limone e Aglio
FRIED MUSHROOMS WITH LEMON AND GARLIC

🐟 These are the mushrooms that Grandma often makes as a side dish for our meat or poultry meals. Although many cooks do not believe in washing mushrooms, I feel they must be rinsed and wiped clean with a damp cloth. If not, they will always have a taste of dirt.

Extra-virgin olive oil

5 cloves garlic, cut in half lengthwise

1 pound small, fresh white mushrooms, rinsed and wiped one by one by hand, then halved

Salt and freshly ground black pepper, to taste

Lemon wedges

Secrets of Success

With a damp cloth, wipe each mushroom one by one. Any water they may absorb will be released and evaporated during cooking.

1. Lightly oil a medium-size frying pan with olive oil and place over medium heat. Add the garlic and mushrooms and cook, stirring occasionally, until the mushrooms are golden brown around the edges, 10 to 15 minutes. Sprinkle with salt and pepper.

2. Transfer to a serving dish and surround with the lemon wedges, which may be squeezed over the mushrooms for additional flavor.

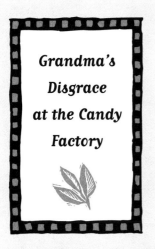

Grandma's Disgrace at the Candy Factory

AT NINETEEN, Grandma was single and was working in a candy factory on Hester Street in Little Italy. She had an older supervisor who liked her so much she used to call her "daughter" as a way of showing her love. One day the woman mentioned that she had a son who was in the navy and that she hoped that my grandma would marry him someday. Grandma didn't think anything about the incident until a few months later when the woman said her son had arrived in New York City on furlough and was waiting at the docks to meet her. Grandma panicked, then politely informed her friend that marriage was the last thing on her mind, and she soon hoped to return to Sicily to live with her parents. Throughout, Grandma was more than respectful about the refusal of marriage, but her friend turned on her like an animal. She refused to speak to her once-upon-a-time "daughter" and went so far as to pretend not to recognize her in front of friends. Grandma was disgraced and was forced to leave the candy factory.

Grandma's moral: "Beware of people who call you daughter, as they are often the biggest phonies. Only your mother has the right to do that."

Patate Fritte Tagliati a Pezzettini
FRIED POTATOES CUT INTO LITTLE TRIANGLES

Serves 4

🐟 My grandma and my mother have always said that these potatoes taste best fried in lard, just as they were prepared by a large woman who had a store at 210 Forsythe Street in Little Italy. Mom said, "All the kids used to run to her store after school to buy her special potatoes fried in lard. She'd put them into an Italian roll and make a sandwich. It cost only five cents in the forties, and the store was always packed. People used to stand in line for those delicious potatoes."

Here are two ways Grandma made potatoes for us, both of them popular preparations sold in grocery stores in Little Italy in the 1920s. I remember eating fried potatoes twice a day when I was a child. I ate them first when I came out of grammar school at three o'clock. My girlfriends and I would run down the block to the corner store that fried potatoes in olive oil. They were sold piled high in paper cones, with toothpicks. Then I would eat them again later on in the evening at Grandma's house.

1 pound potatoes, peeled

Extra-virgin olive oil or lard

Salt, to taste

1. Using a small paring knife, cut the potatoes into small triangles no larger than ¾ to 1 inch. To do this, cut off a ½-inch-thick section at one corner of the potato. Then cut around the edges of the potato to form a rough triangle. Finally, slice the triangle to form thinner triangles. Transfer the potatoes to a bowl of cold water to cover and let stand for 15 minutes to rinse off some of the starch. Drain well and pat dry with a kitchen towel. Alternatively, using a potato ridger (also known as a crinkle-chip cutter), cut the potatoes into French fries.

Secrets of Success

When frying in olive oil or lard, it's important to keep the temperature at 350°F. If you raise the heat higher, the olive oil and lard will begin to smoke. Do not allow potatoes to soak in water for more than 15 minutes, or they will become waterlogged.

2. To cook the potatoes cut into little triangles: Generously oil a medium-size frying pan with olive oil and place over medium heat. When hot, add the potatoes and cook, turning occasionally and sprinkling with salt, until well browned, about 15 minutes total. Serve hot.

3. To cook the potatoes cut into ridges: In a deep, medium-size frying pan, pour in olive oil (or melt enough lard) to a depth of 2 inches. Place over medium heat and heat to 350°F. In batches, deep-fry the potatoes, turning occasionally, until well browned, about 5 to 6 minutes. Transfer to a plate lined with paper towels. Sprinkle with salt and serve immediately. Or pile into large paper cones and serve with toothpicks for authenticity.

*Great-grandma Maria (right) at 87
and her daughter Vitina.*

Cucuzza con Basilico e Formaggio
FRIED SQUASH WITH BASIL AND GRATED CHEESE

🍴 Grandma makes this dish several times a week when squash is in season. Squash grows abundantly in Sicily and can be found in every small garden. Sicilians prefer *cucuzza*, a common green squash that resembles a cucumber. Zucchini, in contrast, are light mint green, about one foot long, and slightly curled. Many people are sentimental about cooking mint-green zucchini because they remember their grandmothers cooking them for them when they were children. But today zucchini is too often tough and not very sweet. On the plus side, zucchini will not fall apart as easily as *cucuzza*; therefore, many Sicilians use it when making stew.

Extra-virgin olive oil

1½ pounds medium-small green squashes, peeled and cut into
   ⅓-inch-thick slices

Salt

¾ cup grated *incanestrato, cacio-cavallo,* provolone or romano cheese

1 small bunch fresh basil leaves

1. Generously oil a medium-size frying pan with olive oil. Arrange the squash slices in a single layer in the pan; do not stack or crowd them. Place over medium heat and cook, sprinkling with a little salt, until golden brown, about 2 minutes total.

2. Turn over the slices and sprinkle generously with the grated cheese. Tear the basil leaves into small pieces, and top each squash slice with a few pieces of basil. Continue cooking until the bottoms of the squash slices are browned and the slices are tender, about 2 minutes. Transfer to a plate lined with paper towels to drain. Eat immediately, as they do not taste good cold.

Stu Rapido con Verdure
QUICK FRESH GARDEN STEW

🐦 Cooks in Ciminna make this stew often as a way of using up their fresh vegetables, and they serve it for lunch or an evening snack with sandwiches, frittatas, or leftovers. Whenever I cook this squash stew, I always make it red by adding ½ to 1 cup tomato sauce or 1 large tomato, peeled, seeded, and chopped. I also always make this stew with eggs, which is a Sicilian peasant tradition, and a way of making more of a meal. Serve with Sicilian bread.

1½ pounds medium-small green squashes (see description, page 220)

½ cup extra-virgin olive oil

1 medium-small yellow onion, thinly sliced

1 large potato, peeled and cut into ½-inch cubes

Salt and freshly ground black pepper

½ teaspoon oregano, sticks removed, crushed until powdery

10 large fresh basil leaves, torn into small pieces

4 large eggs (optional)

Grated *cacio-cavallo, incanestrato,* provolone, or romano cheese

1. Peel the squashes, leaving on thin strips of the skin to create a striped appearance. Quarter each squash lengthwise, then cut crosswise into 1-inch pieces.

2. In a medium-size pot, heat the olive oil over medium heat. Add the onion and potato and sauté, sprinkling with a dash of salt and stirring occasionally, until the onion is golden and the potatoes begin to brown, about 8 minutes. Add the squash pieces and continue cooking, stirring occasionally, until the squash is golden, about 8 minutes longer.

(CONTINUED)

3. Add water to cover (3 or 4 cups) along with the oregano, basil, 1 teaspoon salt, and ½ teaspoon pepper. Bring the stew to a boil, reduce the heat to low, prop a spoon under the lid to keep the pot half uncovered, and simmer until the stew begins to thicken, about 20 minutes.

4. If using the eggs, crack them one by one and gently drop them into the stew; do not stir. Taste the stew every 10 minutes and adjust all the seasonings as necessary. Continue simmering for another 15 to 20 minutes. Once the eggs have become hard-cooked and the potatoes are fork tender, the stew is done. During the last 10 minutes of cooking, add 4 tablespoons grated cheese. Serve with additional grated cheese.

Cacociuli Pieni con Mudrica

ARTICHOKES STUFFED WITH BREAD CRUMBS

Serves 4

These stuffed artichokes are not only a Sicilian favorite, but are also one of the most popular items in restaurants in Little Italy. They can be cooked in advance and kept in the refrigerator, covered, for 3 days, stored upright in the water they were cooked in. To reheat, place them upright in a pot with their water. Add more water as needed to reach halfway up the artichokes. Cover and simmer until hot.

Stuffing

¾ cup unseasoned freshly made bread crumbs (page 14)

4 heaping tablespoons grated romano or *incanestrato* cheese

5 cloves garlic, thinly sliced or cut into medium dice

5 fresh Italian parsley sprigs, coarsely chopped

¼ teaspoon salt

4 artichokes

4 heaping tablespoons grated *incanestrato*, provolone, or romano cheese

4 teaspoons extra-virgin olive oil

½ heaping teaspoon salt

1. To make the stuffing: In a bowl, combine all the stuffing ingredients and mix well. Set aside, or cover and refrigerate until needed.

2. Trim the artichokes as directed on page 207, leaving them whole. Spread open the center of each artichoke, then bang it upside down on the countertop a few times so it will remain open. Spread open all the surrounding rows of leaves.

3. Divide the stuffing into 4 portions. Place half of 1 portion of stuffing firmly inside the artichoke center; sprinkle the other half inside the surrounding leaves. Repeat with the remaining 3 artichokes.

4. In a 3-quart pot, stand the artichokes upright, leaning them against one another for support. Pour water into the pot to reach halfway up the sides of the artichokes. Sprinkle 1 heaping tablespoon cheese over each artichoke top and the surrounding leaves. Drizzle 1 teaspoon olive oil over each artichoke top. Add the salt to the water. Bring to a boil over high heat, then reduce the heat to low, cover, and simmer until the leaves can be pulled off easily, 30 to 40 minutes. Every 15 minutes, spoon water from the pot over the artichoke tops to moisten them.

5. Using a large slotted spoon, transfer the artichokes to a platter. If possible, serve on individual artichoke dishes, which have a section for discarding the half-eaten leaves.

Secrets of Success

Artichokes must be leaning against one another while cooking, so they do not tumble. If they fall on their sides, the stuffing will come out and the dish will be ruined.

Cacociuli Pieni con Carne Macinata in Salsa

ARTICHOKES STUFFED WITH CHOPPED MEAT

Here is one of our family's unusual dishes, because although you see meat stuffed inside peppers and other vegetables, I've never seen it stuffed into whole artichokes. This is a special dish that we make in November and December when artichokes are at their best. It combines three interesting eating rituals: First, you scoop out the center and enjoy the stuffing; second, you chat away and eat the inside part of the tender leaves; and third, you dip your bread into the luscious artichoke-flavored sauce. Although two of these small artichokes are a meal in themselves, one artichoke can be eaten as a snack or served as a side dish to accompany roasted sausages, beef, chicken, or pork.

4 medium-small tender artichokes

½ pound uncooked mixture for Meatballs (page 18)

Extra-virgin olive oil

2 large eggs, beaten

2 cloves garlic, thinly sliced

1 can (32 ounces) whole tomatoes with juice, well crushed with a fork

1 teaspoon dried oregano, sticks removed, crushed until powdery

4 fresh basil leaves

½ teaspoon salt

Secrets of Success

Do not prepare the meat stuffing ahead of time or pack it too tightly into the artichoke center, or it will become hard when cooked.

1. Trim the artichokes as directed on page 207, leaving them whole. Spread open the center of each artichoke, then bang it upside down on the countertop a few times so it will remain open. Spread open all the surrounding rows of leaves.

2. Stuff each artichoke center with about one-fourth of the meat, handling the stuffing as little as possible. Shape any leftover meat into a meatball and fry it for a snack.

3. Generously oil a small frying pan with olive oil and place over medium heat until hot. Drizzle about 2 tablespoons of the beaten egg over the center of 1 artichoke, covering the meat. Immediately turn the artichoke upside down into the frying pan, and cook for few seconds until the egg is set. Transfer to a flat plate. Repeat with the remaining 3 artichokes.

4. Generously oil the bottom of a medium-size saucepan with olive oil and place over medium heat. Add the garlic and sauté until golden, about 1 minute. Stir in the tomatoes, oregano, basil, and salt. Transfer the artichokes to the saucepan. (The artichokes must stand upright, so lean them against one another.) Next, pour water into the pot until the sauce reaches three-fourths up the sides of the artichokes. Taste the sauce and adjust all the seasonings as necessary. Bring to a boil, reduce the heat to low, cover, and simmer for 30 to 40 minutes. Baste the artichoke tops frequently with the sauce, and adjust the seasonings every 15 minutes. The artichokes are done when the leaves can be pulled off easily. If they offer resistance, the artichokes must cook a little longer.

The Eggplant Water Cure

"Fren-zee, guess what? I salted some *melanzane* [eggplant] and the water that came out worked again! Look, no mole on my face."

"*Melanzane* water? What are you talking about, Grandma? You don't have a mole on your face."

"Exactly! About six weeks ago I went to the druggist. I had something on my face. I asked him to give me medicine to make it go away. He gave me this cream— $6.75, expensive, don't you think? Anyway, he told me to put it on morning and night. Then, he said if it didn't go away in two weeks, I should go to a doctor because it looked like cancer. I got so scared! My heart stopped!" Her hands crossed her chest. "So I did what he said and nothing happened. Then I remembered what my mother told me in Ciminna about the eggplant water. 'Josephina, if you ever have anything on your face, splash the water that drains from the eggplant on it a few times a day for two weeks and it will go away.'"

"But Grandma," I said a bit annoyed, "what can the water from the eggplant do?"

She interrupted. "Shh! Shh! Would you let me finish? I put the eggplant water on for a few weeks and today I woke up and no mole! So I went back to the druggist and I told him off. I said I wanted my money back, that I had used the eggplant water instead. He looked at me as if I were crazy. 'Cancer!' I yelled, scolding. 'If people would go back to the old ways, they wouldn't need doctors or pharmacists! *Stupido!*' He reluctantly gave me back my $6.75, then I walked out the door with my nose in the air, a shopping bag with a gallon of olive oil in each of my hands, and my $6.75 secure in my coat pocket!"

"Is the poor guy selling his pharmacy, Grandma?"

"Well, I outfoxed him. My mother's smarter than him with all his degrees! Now, getting back to eggplant, Fren-zee, you said your father's making the parmesan today?" she asked inquisitively as she opened the door to let me out. I nodded yes. "He makes very tasty food, you know. When you come tomorrow, you bring Grandma a dish of the parmesan."

"Whatever you say, General!" I saluted.

"Well, at least you got my name right, Fren-zee." She shut the door. 🐚

Melanzane alla Parmigiana
EGGPLANT PARMESAN

🐦 This is the way parmesan was originally made, and it is an elegant dish. It was taught to my father by his mother, who came from San Giuseppe, where it was one of the town specialties. Since it serves a large group, Dad makes it for special occasions, and it's also a good buffet dish, as it is tasty lukewarm or hot. To simplify its making, prepare the sauce and fry the eggplant a day before serving. Serve with warmed *trezza* (braid) Sicilian bread.

1 recipe Sauce for Veal Cutlets Parmesan (page 101)

2 cups bread crumb coating (page 14)

3½ pounds eggplants, peeled and sliced lengthwise ¼ inch thick

Extra-virgin olive oil

Grated *incanestrato, cacio-cavallo,* provolone, or romano cheese

⅓ pound sweet provolone cheese, thinly sliced, then cut into 1-inch squares

5 or 6 hard-cooked eggs, peeled and sliced

1. One day before serving: Prepare the sauce, then store it in the refrigerator overnight. Prepare the bread crumb coating. Dip the eggplant slices in the egg bath, then coat with the bread crumbs. Generously oil a large frying pan with olive oil and place over medium heat. In batches, add the eggplant slices and cook, turning once and sprinkling with a dash of salt, until golden brown on both sides, about 2 minutes on each side. Transfer the slices to a colander set over a dish, cover, and let drain overnight in the refrigerator. The next day, discard the oil on the plate.

(CONTINUED)

Secrets of Success

Years ago, eggplants were very juicy and watery. Salt was sprinkled on each slice, then the eggplant was placed in a colander for 1 or 2 hours to allow its water to drain away. Nowadays, eggplants are dry. I suggest not draining the water from the eggplant, because it will make the vegetable drier and stringier. But make sure you drain the eggplant of oil for a minimum of 6 hours after frying, however, or the finished dish will be greasy.

2. The following day, reheat the sauce over medium heat until hot. Preheat an oven to 350°F. Cover the bottom of a medium-size baking pan with a ladleful of sauce, spreading it evenly. Lay the eggplant slices evenly over the bottom. Sprinkle generously with the grated cheese and top each eggplant slice with the a few pieces of provolone. Scatter the slices of 1 hard-cooked egg over the top. Repeat the layering process until all the ingredients are used. You will end up with 5 or 6 layers. Generously top the last layer with extra sauce and grated cheese.

3. Cover the baking pan with aluminum foil and bake until the cheese in the center layers is completely melted and the surface is bubbling hot, 50 to 60 minutes. Remove from the oven and let stand for 10 minutes before serving. Cut into squares to serve.

Melanzane di Ciminna
EGGPLANT FROM CIMINNA

Serves 4 to 6

🍆 At four o'clock on the dot, all the doors fling open in Ciminna, and the women scurry up and down the street to bring this eggplant to friends or relatives. The dish is made daily and quickly eaten up as an afternoon or evening snack. It is one of the dishes, too, that is left on the table for guests to help themselves, because it is equally good hot, warm, or cold. Whenever I've made it in one of my cooking classes, it's a big hit, but everyone thinks it is the Sicilian version of eggplant parmesan, which it isn't. (See page 227 for that recipe.) This is the classic eggplant preparation found in the area around Palermo, where it is known as *melanzane alla siciliana*. In America, I have never seen this dish other than at Grandma's table. Our family usually eats it as a one-dish meal with bread (see variation).

2½ to 3 pounds eggplants, each about 6 inches long and with a fat round bottom, peeled and sliced lengthwise ¼ inch thick

Extra-virgin olive oil

Salt

Sauce

1 can (32 ounces) whole tomatoes with juice, well crushed with a fork

1 teaspoon dried oregano, sticks removed, crushed until powdery

1 large bunch fresh basil leaves

3 cups grated romano, provolone, *incanestrato,* or *cacio-cavallo* cheese

½ teaspoon sugar, or to taste

¼ teaspoon salt

Secrets of Success

Don't stint!
Be generous with the
cheese, sauce,
and especially the
basil—you can't add
too much.

1. Quickly rinse the eggplant slices under cold running water. Pat dry with a kitchen towel.

2. Generously oil a medium-size, 2½-inch-deep frying pan with olive oil and place over medium heat. In batches, add the eggplant slices and cook, turning once and sprinkling with a dash of salt, until browned on both sides, about 2 minutes on each side. Transfer the slices to a colander set over a dish. Pour off and reserve 4 tablespoons of the oil from the pan.

3. To make the sauce: Using the same frying pan, discard any remaining oil and wipe the pan dry. Return the pan to medium heat and add the tomatoes, oregano, 6 basil leaves, 2 tablespoons of the grated cheese, ½ teaspoon sugar, the salt, and the 4 tablespoons reserved oil. Bring to a simmer, stir, taste the sauce, and adjust all the seasonings. If the sauce still has a bitter taste, add another pinch of sugar. Bring to a boil, reduce the heat to medium, cover partially, and cook for 12 minutes.

(CONTINUED)

4. Next, using a large spoon, move the sauce to one side of the frying pan. On the side of the pan without much sauce, lay down 1 slice of eggplant. Generously spoon the sauce from the other side of the pan over the top, covering the eggplant slice evenly. Generously sprinkle with some of the grated cheese, then tear a few basil leaves in half and arrange them over the eggplant slice. Repeat the layering process until you reach the top of the frying pan. When you finish this stack, make another stack next to the first one. Then make another stack, for a total of 3 separately layered stacks of eggplant.

5. When all the eggplant stacks have been made, reduce the heat to low, cover, and simmer until bubbling hot, 5 to 10 minutes. Adjust the seasonings again, if necessary. Grandma is able to hold the handle of her frying pan, tilt it forward gently, and slide the eggplant stacks into a deep rose dish that she uses for serving. She's the only person I've ever known that's able to do that without destroying the layers, however. Mom, Dad, and I cannot master it. I suggest using an extra-long, extra-wide spatula to carefully lift out 1 stack at a time and place it into a deep serving dish.

OPEN-FACED SANDWICH VARIATION

To use up leftover eggplant, reheat it in its own sauce over low heat. Then arrange the eggplant slices on top of Italian bread and spoon some sauce over the top. Sprinkle with grated cheese and torn fresh basil.

**A
Hometown
Story**

ALTHOUGH I THOUGHT *Melanzane di Ciminna* was a specialty of Grandma's, I was surprised to find an exact duplicate of the recipe from a century ago. When I was in Ciminna, more than one of Grandma's relatives made it for me, and they were shocked that this recipe existed in America, and that I'd been eating it since I was a child. In Sicily, every women prides herself on cooking better than the others. Even in the 1980s in Ciminna, it was considered a disgrace if a woman didn't cook well. So you can imagine my relatives' jealousy when I told them their cooking was almost as good as Grandma's. Their displeasure came out in snide remarks that were made when no one thought I was listening, or when they spoke and had no idea I could understand the Sicilian dialect. There was often a Sicilian foot tapping away in a plain black shoe, one hand on a plump hip, and an excitable voice blurting out something spoken so fast that only a trained ear could capture what was said: "She says it's almost as good as her grandmother's. No one cooks like her Grandma! Even the eggplant, too! I've been making it all my life. It's my specialty, and still Franca is never satisfied!"

"But Marietta," Vito, Grandma's brother, replied, trying to calm down his wife, "my sister is a great cook."

"Then go back to America and live with your sister!" she screamed, as she raised her wooden spoon over his head and her black shoes stomped up and down on the kitchen floor.

I laughed to myself and thought that even though nearly half a century had elapsed since Grandma had left Ciminna, Grandma's cooking was still envied enough to be causing a family fight. Some things never change, even across continents. 🐝

Torta di Melanzane

EGGPLANT PIE WITH EGG, PEPPERONI, AND CHEESE

🐟 This eggplant pie is made without tomato sauce and uses a mixture of eggs and cheese as a binder. It's a specialty of my father, who learned it from his mother, and is another dish I have never seen made by anyone except citizens of my father's ancestral hometown of San Giuseppe. Usually made in summer and great for a buffet, the pie can be served hot, lukewarm, or cold. In my opinion, it tastes best lukewarm, since a little warmth seems to bring out the flavors of the cheese and sausage. It's also good cold in a sandwich.

There are two types of eggplants, female and male. Sicilians always buy female eggplants, since they are sweeter. Female eggplants can be recognized easily because they are shorter, have fat, round bottoms, and contain fewer seeds. Male eggplants are larger, longer, and contain more seeds.

Secrets of Success

The more seeds the eggplant contains, the more bitter it will be when cooked. This is especially true when the seeds turn brown, which means your eggplant is old. Salting and draining the eggplant will never make a bitter eggplant sweet. It will just make it dry and tough when cooked.

2 cups bread crumb coating (page 14)

2½ pounds medium-size eggplants, peeled and sliced lengthwise ¼ inch thick

Extra-virgin olive oil

Salt

3 large eggs

3 tablespoons milk

¾ cup (12 tablespoons) grated *cacio-cavallo, incanestrato,* or romano cheese

⅓ pound provolone cheese, sliced ¼ inch thick and 1 inch long

1 sweet or hot dried sausage or pepperoni, ⅓ pound, sliced ⅛ inch thick

1. Prepare the bread crumb coating. Dip the eggplant slices into the egg bath, and then coat with the bread crumbs. Generously oil a large frying pan with olive oil and place over medium heat. In batches, add the eggplant slices and cook, turning once and sprinkling with a dash of salt, until browned on both sides, about 2 minutes on each side. Transfer the slices to a colander set over a dish. Cover and refrigerate for at least 4 hours (or as long as overnight) to drain off excess oil.

2. Preheat an oven to 350°F. In a small bowl, beat together the eggs and ¼ teaspoon salt. Divide the egg mixture, grated cheese, provolone pieces, and dried sausage into 6 equal portions, keeping each ingredient separate. Lightly oil a 2-quart round casserole with 3½-inch sides. Line the bottom of the casserole with a layer of eggplant slices. Pour 1 portion of the egg mixture over the eggplant, spreading it evenly. Sprinkle with 1 portion of the grated cheese, and scatter 1 portion of the provolone and 1 portion of the sausage pieces over the top. Repeat the layering process 5 more times. You will end up with a total of 6 layers.

3. Cover, place in the oven, and bake until the cheese has completely melted and is bubbling hot in the center layers, about 45 minutes. Let the pie stand for 15 minutes before serving. Slice into pie wedges and serve hot or lukewarm.

Melanzane Pieni di Mamma Grani Maria
GREAT-GRANDMA MARIA'S STUFFED BABY EGGPLANT

🔊 Here is an eggplant recipe that my great-grandmother Maria made only for special occasions. Taught to her by her mother, Angelina, it combines the richness of tomato sauce with a flavorful stuffing of onions and cheese, and serves them all over pasta. If you decide to make this without pasta, simply arrange the eggplants on a long platter, ladle the sauce over the top, and serve with bread for a beautiful presentation. This is a spectacular dish. Serve it when the boss is coming to dinner.

8 small eggplants, each about 4 inches long and 3 inches in diameter, unpeeled

Salt

4 cloves garlic, sliced

8 fresh Italian parsley sprigs, coarsely chopped

1 yellow onion, thinly sliced

½ cup grated *incanestrato, pepato,* or romano cheese

¼ pound provolone or *cacio-cavallo* cheese, cut into very small pieces

Extra-virgin olive oil

Sauce

¼ cup extra-virgin olive oil

2 cloves garlic, cut into medium dice

1 can (35 ounces) whole tomatoes with juice, well crushed with a fork and strained of seeds

¾ cup water

3 tablespoons grated *incanestrato, cacio-cavallo,* or romano cheese

1½ teaspoons dried oregano, sticks removed, crushed until powdery

4 fresh basil leaves

½ teaspoon salt

½ teaspoon sugar

1 pound spaghettini, spaghetti, or linguine

Freshly ground black pepper, to taste

Grated *incanestrato, cacio-cavallo,* or romano cheese

1. Cut off the stem ends of the eggplants. In each eggplant, make 3 deep lengthwise slits, being careful not to cut all the way through. Sprinkle the inside of each slit with a little salt. Stuff each of the slits with a few slices of garlic, some chopped parsley, a few onion slices, a little grated cheese, and a few chunks of provolone. Repeat with the remaining 7 eggplants.

2. Lightly oil a medium-size frying pan with olive oil and place over medium-high heat. Add the eggplants and cook, turning as needed, until browned on all sides, about 8 minutes total. Set aside.

3. To make the sauce: In a medium-size pot, heat the olive oil over medium heat. Add the garlic and sauté until golden, about 1 minute. Stir in the tomatoes, water, grated cheese, oregano, basil, salt, and sugar. Bring to a boil over high heat, then reduce the heat to very low. Gently place the eggplants in the pot. Prop a wooden spoon under the lid to keep the pot half uncovered and simmer until the eggplants are fork tender, 1 to 1¼ hours. Every 15 minutes, taste, and adjust all the seasonings, as necessary.

4. Cook and drain the pasta just as the eggplants are ready. Divide it into 4 equal portions in individual plates. Top each pasta portion with 2 stuffed eggplants and ladle on the sauce. Serve with grated cheese and top with black pepper.

An Abandoned Child

Eਅਚ TIME great-grandmother Maria (Grandma's mother) had a child, she would take care of the baby from morning until night—feeding and playing with him or her—never leaving the baby's side. Then, after a few months, she would go to the country to help her husband at harvest time. Her first son died. She gave birth to a second son, and when she left for the country, her second son died. She then gave birth to a daughter, Lena, and again left for the country, and her daughter died. The people of Ciminna said the infants were brokenhearted and felt abandoned by their mother. Maria called it *il discoragiamento* (the discouragement of life a child feels when a mother leaves). After her third child died, she never went to help her husband at harvest time again, and she told Grandma never to leave her children with anyone.

Grandma's moral: "If you work, work in the house, near your children, or your children, when left by you, may give up on life." As a result, Grandma always worked at home once she had her first child. ॐ

PEPPERS STUFFED WITH CHOPPED MEAT

🐚 This is my mom's recipe, one that she has made since she was a teenager. Whenever she finds very large green or red peppers, she makes this dish. The secret is the sauce, which is thin and takes on the unique, spicy flavor of the peppers. For years, we threw the leftover sauce away, but Dad felt it was a terrible waste. One day he tossed it with some pasta. Now this recipe not only makes a main dish, but a side dish as well.

4 large green or red bell peppers

1½ pounds mixture for Meatballs (page 18)

Extra-virgin olive oil

2 large cloves garlic, sliced

1 can (16 ounces) tomato sauce, or 2 cups homemade fresh tomato purée

¼ cup sweet Marsala or Port wine or vermouth (optional)

6 fresh basil leaves

Salt and freshly ground black pepper or red hot pepper flakes, to taste

⅓ pound *tubettini* pasta or your favorite small pasta,

 or 1 cup uncooked white rice

Grated *pepato, cacio-cavallo,* provolone, or romano cheese

1. Cut a ½-inch-thick slice off the top of each pepper, leaving the peppers whole. Remove the seeds and ribs. Rinse and pat dry. Prepare the meat mixture.

(CONTINUED)

2. Lightly stuff each pepper with one-fourth of the meat mixture; do not pack tightly. Generously oil a 3-quart pot with olive oil and place over medium heat until hot. Turn 1 pepper upside down into the saucepan and brown the meat. Then, turn the pepper on its side and continue browning, turning as needed, until the pepper is a golden brown and blistered on all sides. This should take about 10 minutes in all. Remove from the pot and transfer to a dish. Repeat with the remaining 3 peppers.

3. Add the garlic to the pot and sauté over medium heat until golden, about 1 minute. Return the peppers to the pot, standing them upright and leaning them against one another for support. Add the tomato sauce or purée, wine, and enough water to reach halfway up the sides of the peppers. Season with the basil leaves and salt and black or red pepper. Bring to a boil, reduce the heat to very low, cover with the lid slightly open, and simmer until meat is cooked throughout and the peppers are tender, about 2 hours. Every 30 minutes, taste the sauce and adjust all the seasonings as necessary.

4. During the last 30 minutes of cooking, cook and drain the pasta, or cook the rice. Transfer the pasta or rice to a large platter and top with half of the sauce. Arrange the stuffed peppers on top, and spoon the remaining sauce over them. Sprinkle the entire platter generously with grated cheese and black or red pepper.

Arancini
RICE BALLS

Makes 8
large rice balls;
serves 4

🐚 *Arancini* are a favorite street food in Sicily and are also served on every special occasion. This recipe was taught to my grandma Ciccina by her brother Benny, who owned a famous *fritturi* (fried-food store) where he sold *arancini* from the 1920s through the 1950s. Dad remembers going to the store when he was about eight years old to eat Uncle Benny's famous rice balls, *panelle* (chickpea pancakes), and *vastieddi* (ricotta and calf's spleen sandwiches). Unfortunately, his uncle closed the store and died many years ago, and those other recipes are lost. But Dad does have his mother's recipe for rice balls and insists it surpasses her brother's. Here is her original recipe, taught to her by her brother in the early 1920s.

1 recipe Sauce for Veal Cutlets Parmesan (see variation, page 101) made with

    1 pound Meatballs (page 18)

1 medium-small yellow onion, cut into medium dice

1 cup shelled fresh sweet peas, cooked and drained, or drained,

    canned petite peas

2 cups uncooked long-grain white rice

¼ cup water

2 teaspoons salt

1 tablespoon sugar, or to taste

2 large eggs, plus 1 small egg, if needed

1 cup flavored freshly made bread crumbs (page 14)

Extra-virgin olive oil

Secrets of Success

Do not use precooked or instant rice. Use only regular long-grain white rice. For every cup of uncooked rice, add 1 teaspoon salt to the water, or the cooked rice will be without taste. To shape the rice balls easily, keep your hands constantly wet or they will stick badly to the rice mixture. It's easier to have two people making rice balls, one to hold the rice ball and the other to pour the bread crumbs over it.

1. Prepare the tomato sauce, using only 1 medium-small onion and omitting the dried sausage. During the last 10 minutes, stir in the peas.

(CONTINUED)

2. Prepare the rice according to the directions on the package, adding an extra ¼ cup water to ensure moistness and the salt.

3. Transfer the cooked rice to a large bowl, add 1 tablespoon sugar, and taste the rice. It should taste slightly sweet; if not, add about 1 more teaspoon sugar. Let the rice stand, uncovered, for 15 minutes to cool. Add 2 large eggs and mix well. If rice mixture feels dry, add 1 more small egg. The mixture should be soft yet firm enough to hold together when shaped into a ball.

4. Using a slotted spoon, transfer the meatballs from the sauce to a medium-size bowl. Chop the meatballs into small chunks; do not mash. Gently stir in 2 cups of the sauce. Set aside.

5. Wet your hands well with warm water before shaping each rice ball. Spoon about ¼ cup of the rice into the palm of your hand. With your other hand, shape the rice into a half ball, making an indentation in the center. Fill the indentation with about 1 heaping tablespoon of the meatball mixture. Place another ¼ cup rice into your other hand, and cover the meatball mixture. Press both hands together, firming and turning the rice gently to form a ball. Next, hold the rice ball in one hand over the dish of crumbs. With your other hand, pour a small amount of bread crumbs over the ball, turning it as you work and coating it completely. Do not overcoat. Repeat to make 8 balls. Any remaining meatball mixture should be returned to the tomato sauce.

6. In a small deep fryer or heavy pot, pour in enough olive oil to reach at least halfway up sides of a rice ball. Heat the oil to 350°F. Working with 1 rice ball at a time, slip the ball into the oil and cook, turning once very gently, until well browned, about 2 minutes on each side. Using a large slotted spoon, transfer the rice ball to a platter lined with paper towels to drain. Repeat with the remaining balls. Cover the finished rice balls loosely with aluminum foil to keep them warm. Meanwhile, reheat the tomato sauce and pour into a gravy bowl.

Secrets of Success

Make sure you add the sugar before adding the eggs, or you won't be able to determine the correct amount of sugar needed.

7. To serve, cut each rice ball in half and place on a dinner plate. Spoon the sauce over the top. Leftover rice balls can be kept individually wrapped in aluminum foil in the refrigerator for up to 4 days. Reheat the rice balls in a 375°F oven until hot, about 20 minutes.

Insalata di Nonna
GRANDMA'S MIXED SALAD

Serves 4 to 6

🗲 My grandma and my great-grandmother Maria made this simple green salad in Sicily. The romaine lettuce can easily be replaced with the small leaves of young, sweet escarole or chicory. The salad can be served with almost any meal, but is particularly good with meat or poultry courses. Set out Sicilian Potato Salad (page 245) and Beet and Onion Salad (page 249) to increase the choices for your guests. The addition of chicken, steak, roast beef, or cold cuts can make this salad a complete meal (see variations). Simply halve the recipe to serve 4.

1 head romaine lettuce, about 1 pound

5 plum tomatoes, sliced

1 sweet red onion, very thinly sliced, soaked in cold water for 15 minutes,
     drained, and patted dry

1 small cucumber, peeled and thinly sliced

3 cloves garlic, cut into small dice

1 teaspoon dried oregano, sticks removed, crushed until powdery

2 tablespoons grated provolone, romano, *pepato, incanestrato,* or
     cacio-cavallo cheese (optional)

Salt and freshly ground black pepper, to taste

6 tablespoons distilled white vinegar

4 tablespoons extra-virgin olive oil

10 Sicilian black olives

1 red bell pepper, seeded and cut lengthwise into narrow strips

Secrets of Success

When making any
basic salad, I prefer
to mix the salad
ingredients without
oil and vinegar,
as is often done in
Sicily, and then place
carafes of oil and
vinegar on the
table so each person
can dress his
or her own salad.

(CONTINUED)

1. Working in batches, stack a bunch of lettuce leaves and cut them crosswise into 1-inch-wide strips. In a salad bowl, combine the lettuce, tomatoes, onion, cucumber, garlic, oregano, cheese (if using), salt, and black pepper. Add the vinegar and olive oil and toss gently. Taste and adjust the seasonings. Garnish with the black olives and strips of red pepper and serve.

RED WINE VINEGAR VARIATION

Substitute red wine vinegar for the white vinegar. Mix together equal parts olive oil and vinegar, about ⅓ cup of each. Taste, then add more oil or vinegar until the salad is the way you like it.

ROASTED CHICKEN VARIATION

Cut 1 pound boneless chicken meat, freshly roasted or left over, into narrow strips or bite-size pieces. Add to the bowl with the tomatoes. Adjust the dressing as necessary. If desired, add 2 medium-size potatoes, peeled, boiled until tender, and cut into bite-size pieces, with the chicken to make a complete meal.

MEAT VARIATION

Cut ½ to 1 pound steak or roast beef, freshly cooked or left over, into narrow strips or bite-size pieces. Add to the bowl with the tomatoes. Strips of ham, *capocollo*, or prosciutto, or slices of Sicilian hard salami, sweet or hot dried sausage, or pepperoni can also be added to the salad. Adjust the dressing as necessary.

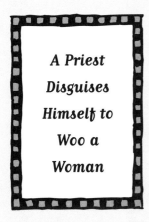

A Priest Disguises Himself to Woo a Woman

WHILE I WAS making olive salad, Grandma told me about a man in Ciminna who disguised himself in woman's clothing in order to romance a local woman, Ivana. Apparently, he and his lover were meant to look like two girlfriends, shopping, chatting, and dining out together—but no one in Ciminna was fooled. The two were having an affair! The people of the town were so outraged that they wrote letters to the Archbishop of Palermo, advising him that not only was Ivana's girlfriend no lady at all, but that he was the local priest from their church! The Archbishop immediately sent the "lady" in question to another town and church, thus avoiding a scandal.

Grandma's Moral: Without fail, at the end of this story, Grandma always shakes her head and says, "See, Fren-zee, there's nonsense that goes on in even the smallest of towns." 🍈

Insalata di Olive

OLIVE SALAD WITH GARDEN VEGETABLES

🍴 I made up this olive mixture from the Sicilian olive salads sold in Italian gourmet shops. I prepare it for Christmas and New Year's, and put it on the table with various cheeses. I do not remove it until dessert time, so guests can nibble on the olives and bread throughout the meal. If this salad is too large a quantity, simply halve the ingredients.

Extra-virgin olive oil

Distilled white vinegar or red wine vinegar

1½ pounds Sicilian green olives, or 1 pound Sicilian green olives and
    ½ pound small Sicilian black olives

½ pound cauliflower, trimmed, stems peeled, and florets halved lengthwise

½ pound broccoli, trimmed, stems peeled, and florets halved lengthwise

4 small celery stalks, cut on the diagonal into ½-inch chunks

2 large red bell peppers or 4 long, green, sweet Italian peppers, seeded and
    cut lengthwise into narrow strips

2 sweet red onions, thinly sliced, soaked in cold water for 15 minutes,
    drained, and patted dry

6 cloves garlic, cut into small dice

4 fresh Italian parsley sprigs, coarsely chopped

8 fresh basil leaves

Dried oregano to taste, sticks removed, crushed until powdery, to taste

Salt and freshly ground black pepper or red pepper flakes, to taste

Secrets of Success

If possible, make the salad 1 day before serving, so the vegetables and herbs have time to marinate. When seasoning the salad, always use a clean spoon to retaste, and do not touch the olives or any part of the mixture with your hands. Otherwise, mold will form on the surface.

1. Preferably 1 day before serving, mix together equal parts olive oil and vinegar in a large salad bowl, using ½ to ¾ cup of each. Taste, then add more oil or vinegar until the dressing is the way you like it. Add all the remaining ingredients, seasoning with the oregano, salt, and black or red pepper. Toss, cover, and refrigerate overnight.

Insalata di Patate
SICILIAN POTATO SALAD

Serves 6 to 8

🐾 While other kids in school ate potato salad with mayonnaise, I always ate potato salad with vinegar, onions, and fresh basil. Grandma never ate regular potato salad. In her mind, it was too bland. If anyone brought it over ready-made to her house, it usually eventually made its way to the table, followed by a query from her, "Well, taste mine, now which one is better?"

This salad goes well with any fish, meat, or poultry dish.

3 pounds new potatoes, peeled and cut into 1-inch chunks

Salt

1 sweet red onion, very thinly sliced, soaked in cold water for 15 minutes, drained, and patted dry

1 cup distilled white vinegar

½ cup extra-virgin olive oil

1½ tablespoons dried oregano, sticks removed, crushed until powdery

3 large fresh Italian parsley sprigs, coarsely chopped

8 fresh basil leaves, torn into little pieces

4 fresh basil sprigs

6 Sicilian green olives

Secrets of Success

Allow the potato salad to marinate overnight to absorb the full flavor of the vinaigrette. If this is not possible, allow the salad to stand for at least 3 hours, and it will still come out fine.

1. Preferably 1 day before serving, half-fill a large pot with salted water and bring to a boil. Add the potatoes and cook until fork tender, about 15 minutes. Using a slotted spoon, transfer the potatoes to a large salad bowl. Discard the water.

2. Add the onion, vinegar, olive oil, oregano, 1½ teaspoons salt, parsley, and basil to the potatoes. Toss well. Cover and let stand for at least 3 hours at room temperature or, preferably, overnight in the refrigerator. Serve in a beautiful ceramic bowl. Garnish with fresh basil sprigs and green olives.

Insalata di Patate e Fagioli

POTATO AND STRING BEAN SALAD

🐟 Here's a salad Dad learned from his mother. In Little Italy in the 1920s, she would grill lamb chops, porterhouse steaks, or pork chops over an open flame on her old coal stove and serve the salad as an accompaniment to them. At the turn of the century, Sicilians grilled most of their meats in this manner, and this salad provided a side dish of two vegetables. It was often served with a second salad, such as Grandma's Mixed Salad (page 241), and extra dressing was made for pouring over the grilled meat and for dipping bread.

Salt

3 pounds new potatoes, peeled and cut into 1½-inch chunks

1½ pounds string beans, ends trimmed

Extra-virgin olive oil

Red wine vinegar

2 large cloves garlic, cut into small dice

3 large fresh Italian parsley sprigs, coarsely chopped

1½ tablespoons dried oregano, sticks removed, crushed until powdery

Freshly ground black pepper, to taste

1. Half-fill a medium-size pot with salted water and bring to a boil. Add the potatoes and cook until fork tender, 15 to 20 minutes. Drain. At the same time, in another medium-size pot half-filled with boiling salted water, cook the string beans until tender crisp, 5 to 10 minutes. Drain.

2. In a large salad bowl, mix together equal parts oil and vinegar, using ½ to ¾ cup of each. Taste, then add more oil or vinegar until the dressing is the way you like it. Add the garlic, parsley, oregano, salt to taste, and pepper. Toss well, cover, and let stand for 10 minutes to allow the potatoes to absorb the vinegar. Toss again, then serve warm.

Insalata di Pomodori con Provolone

GREEN PLUM TOMATO SALAD WITH CURLS OF PROVOLONE

In general, I'm not a salad lover. A salad must have cheese in it for me to eat it, and it must be full of garlic bits. I also love cooked tomatoes and tomato sauce of any kind, but not lettuce and tomatoes. Green tomatoes are another story, however. Whenever Grandma and I can find them, we make this salad, my favorite. But since good green tomatoes are a rare commodity, we substitute very sweet red plum tomatoes, and the taste is just as satisfying. Grandma always made this salad with just the tomatoes and onions. Then, one day, I added more onion, garlic, and, of course, the cheese. She said, "It's a masterpiece and a meal in itself." We eat it with bread for lunch, then finish the leftovers that night for a snack. Often I add 1-inch strips of hard Sicilian salami, prosciutto, or *capocollo* for additional flavor.

1 pound firm green or red plum or beefsteak tomatoes

1 medium-small sweet red or yellow onion, very thinly sliced, soaked in
   cold water for 15 minutes, drained, and patted dry

3 tablespoons distilled white vinegar

3 tablespoons extra-virgin olive oil

3 cloves garlic, cut into small dice

3 fresh Italian parsley sprigs or 12 large fresh basil leaves, torn into small pieces

¾ teaspoon dried oregano, sticks removed, crushed until powdery

Salt and freshly ground black pepper, to taste

¼ pound provolone, romano, *incanestrato,* or *cacio-cavallo* cheese

1. In a salad bowl, combine all ingredients except the cheese. Toss gently. Using a vegetable peeler, shave thin curls of the cheese over the salad. Toss gently again. Cover and let stand for 15 minutes before serving.

Great-grandpa Paolo Dies in Little Italy

WHILE GRANDMA was slicing beets, she told me of how in 1915, when my Grandpa Natale was only eleven years old, his father—my great-grandfather—Paolo, died in Little Italy at two o'clock in the morning in the famous Yonah Shimmel Knish building on Houston Street. Natale was told by his mother to run uptown to inform his uncle and cousins. Grandpa, frightened and with tears rolling down his face, ran from Houston Street to Forty-second Street and First Avenue, over two miles, opposite where the United Nations stands today.

In the dark of night, and out of breath, Grandpa was grabbed by a large hand that dragged him to the corner. It was a policeman demanding to know what he was doing out in the middle of the night. Shouting, the policeman told Grandpa he was going to arrest him to teach him a lesson, but then he noticed Grandpa's face was swollen with tears. Touched by the little boy's story of witnessing his father's last breath, the policeman let him go.

Grandma's moral: "Two o'clock in the morning is no time for children to be out—in 1915 or now—or else they can end up in trouble with the law." 🐚

Insalata di Barbabietola e Cipolla

BEET AND ONION SALAD

🐦 Grandma never saw beets in Sicily, but she found them in New York in the 1920s. She quickly incorporated them into this salad. Dad usually serves it when he cooks steaks. Grandma often serves it with club steaks or roasted sausages, usually alongside roasted peppers. The beets need to marinate in the dressing, so plan on making the salad about 3 hours before serving.

1 bunch beets, about 1 pound

1 sweet red onion, very thinly sliced, soaked in cold water for 15 minutes, drained, and patted dry

2 small celery stalks, cut into ½-inch-wide slices (optional)

½ teaspoon dried oregano, sticks removed, crushed until powdery

Red wine vinegar

Extra-virgin olive oil

Salt and freshly ground black pepper, to taste

1. Trim off the beet greens, leaving about ½ inch of the stem intact. Be careful not to pierce the skin of the beets or they will bleed during cooking. Half-fill a medium-size pot with salted water and bring to a boil. Add the beets and cook until fork tender, about 20 minutes. Drain, then let cool for 15 minutes. Peel the beets and cut into ¼-inch-thick slices.

2. In a salad bowl, combine the warm beets, onion, celery, and oregano. Toss gently. In a small bowl, mix together equal parts olive oil and vinegar, using about ¼ cup of each. Taste, then add more oil or vinegar until the dressing is the way you like it. Add to the salad bowl and again toss gently. Season with salt and pepper. Cover and store in the refrigerator for 3 hours before serving.

DOLCI

Sweets,

Fruits, Nuts,

and

Ice Cream

To a Sicilian, a wonderful meal ends with a sweet. It may be a fruit soaked in wine or liqueur, a homemade pastry such as *cassatedri* (ricotta turnovers), or perhaps the famous, rich and elegant *cassata*.

In Little Italy, desserts are no less important, and every evening the cafes along Grand, Mott, and Mulberry streets are filled with people enjoying a sweet and a cup of espresso. So jealously guarded are dessert recipes that my grandma Ciccina, known in Little Italy for making the best *cuccidrati* (fig cakes) and *pignolata* (honey balls), deliberately gave my father hours of incorrect instructions so his *pignolata* would come out hard. She wanted to remain the Queen of *Pignolata* and take her recipe with her to the grave.

Centuries ago, pastries in Sicily were made by nuns and were ordered directly from convents for special occasions—birthdays, baptisms, weddings, Christmas, and Easter—thus providing the sisters with a livelihood. Bakeries grew out of these convent kitchens and eventually took over the art of pastry making, so that today there are only a handful of convents that still make the Old World pastries and candies. These venerable institutions closely guard their recipes, and when the nuns who make these sumptuous desserts die, their recipes, which have never been written down, will be lost forever. The nuns, it seems, are just as protective of their kitchen secrets as any home cook, and prefer their recipes be immortalized, rather than have another person make them. All Sicilians are alike!

Grandma recalls that in Little Italy from the 1920s to the 1950s, "you could walk down the streets and float on the smell of almond paste and vanilla. There was Monteleone's on Christie Street, Ferrara's on Grand Street, and Roma's on Broome Street. On Houston Street there was Casale, who had the best *cassata*. He'd sell it for half price the day after Christmas. Stronconi on Houston made the best butter cookies—he was famous for them. When I used to go into the store he'd laugh, 'Josie, the cookies I make, nobody makes. The butter I put in them is the best!' He was right! De Robertis on Eleventh Street made the best *sfogliatelle*, and Grandpa always went there to buy them. Fren-zee, no one had bad pastries. One was better than the other, and each had his own specialty. What people don't know is that the Sicilians in Little Italy in those days ate just as many German cakes as they did Sicilian pastries. There were German bakeries all over until after World War II. We used to buy the almond paste rings and the cinnamon crumb cakes, the mocha cakes and the chocolate eggs. Sometimes Uncle Mike would buy the seven-layer mocha cake filled with apricot jam and liqueur and say, 'Ma, forget the sauce, I'll have cake!'"

In this chapter, you will find such classic Sicilian recipes as *Pupa cu l'Ovo* (Easter Biscuits), *Niru di Uccelli* (Bird's Nest), and *Sfingi* (Fried Puffs). There are also Espresso Ice, a recipe for *cassata* from the renowned De Robertis Pastry Store on New York's Lower East Side, and an explanation of the famous ritual of *scaccio e biviri* (crush nuts and drink).

The Angel of Easter

As I dipped an egg into the food coloring, I realized that the American tradition of the Easter bunny giving baskets of candy to children on Easter Sunday is similar to the Sicilian custom of *l'angelo pasquale* (the Angel of Easter) giving baskets of gifts. Grandma, I think, still believes in the Easter angel. One recent Easter, just as she had risen out of bed and was securing a black stocking on her short, little leg with a trusty, old garter, I questioned her about it. As she finished her ritual, she recounted the story of Easter in Ciminna when she was just a girl of ten.

"What a joyous time it was—*Pasqua*—in Sicily. The Easter angel visited us and brought us *giocattoli di candi* [toys of candy]. You know, Fren-zee, little dolls made of candy, cookies, and *u pecura* [a special sheep of almond paste made only for Easter], *pupa cu l'ova* [Easter egg with doll bread], and *pupa cu l'ovo* [biscuits]," she continued, a contented expression on her face. "We were told to be good, and to go to bed early, but we were so excited we couldn't sleep. Our minds were on the candy! So as soon as the sun rose, we got up to see what the angel had brought. My mother used to say that all she could see on Easter morning were our feet and hands scurrying around the house looking for the angel's gifts, and all she could hear were doors banging as we ran from room to room and closet to closet."

"So the Easter angel is the Easter bunny," I remarked casually.

"Of course not," she retorted angrily. "How could you say a bunny rabbit is an angel . . . what's wrong with you, Fren-zee? Don't you know the difference between a bunny and an angel?"

"But Grandma, you're not going to tell me that if you throw rocks at bunnies, they turn into gold, too, like the *pupo che ballava* [a doll that dances on the mountains and leaves gold—see page 265]. Let's not start this nonsense again!" My eyes rolled upward.

"That was the chickens, not the bunnies! You have to get your stories straight. The Easter bunny is cheap! His gifts are nothing fantastic. But the Easter angel brings you big, big baskets full of everything. Money! Shoes! Toys! Material for clothes. Trays of little cakes, cookies, and candies. Whatever you needed, the angel brought if you were good. Why, I once got a two-foot-high doll made out of marzipan."

"Does he go to the bank and make a large deposit for you, too?" My eyes again rolled upward.

"No! Just keep quiet and learn for a change. Two months in advance my mother would begin preparing the large straw baskets full of gifts. There were many of us, so every day she would put a little something into each basket and each one had the name of one of us kids on it. I remember like it was yesterday. My brother Vito and I were crying because we searched the whole house and we couldn't find our baskets. We thought the angel had deserted us. Then my mother said, 'But you haven't looked everywhere. Maybe in that corner over there, or in the closet.' 'No!' we said. Our eyes were swollen and tears were running down our cheeks. 'The angel didn't leave us anything! Were we bad, mamma?' My mother laughed, and pointed us in the right direction, and like magic all sorts of gifts appeared. Once we got our baskets, we'd run to our other relatives, you know, like grandmas, aunts, and uncles, to see if the angel had left anything for us, and most times there were gifts there, too.

"Finally, all us kids from the neighborhood would run to the *chiazza* [the main square of the town]. Fren-zee, it was like a beautiful vision to see the Sicilian bread baskets, *pecura*, and the *pupa cu l'ovo* in all the bread stores and *pasticcerie* [pastry stores]. They were works of art. I can still remember the smell of vanilla, almonds, and sweetness from all the candies and cakes. It drove you crazy until you bought something to eat.

"And another thing," she said, pointing a scolding finger in my face. "*L'angelo pasquale* grants wishes and makes miracles for the sick and for people to get rich. If you pray to the angel on Easter, and if the angel wants, God willing, she'll make a miracle for you. Don't laugh!" Her finger was wagging vigorously. "The angel made plenty of miracles in Ciminna." Her voice screeched to a halt. "No bunny in America does that!" Should I have known that I would lose in this conversation, or what? 🐾

Pupa cu l'Ovo
EASTER BISCUITS

Makes 5 biscuit
baskets and
1 pound small
biscuits

During Easter week in Sicily, much food is prepared. The traditional Easter breads, cookies, and candies are all made, plus fresh pasta is either bought or made for the Sunday dinner of *pasta con salsa* and roasted leg of lamb. Not much has changed from a century ago, when both these recipes were standard in most Sicilian households.

In Sicily, many cookies, cakes such as *cassata* (page 263), and candies, especially those made of marzipan in various shapes and colors, are made for this most celebrated of all holidays. The best-known of the marzipan treats is the lamb-shaped *pecura*, which is sliced and eaten on Easter Sunday.

Pupa cu l'ovo means "doll with the egg." These delicious biscuits are what Grandma, her mother, and sisters made together in Sicily during the early mornings of Easter week. In the late 1800s and early 1900s, the biscuits were made with lard, since neither vegetable shortening nor butter was available. Many people still prefer them made that way, so feel free to experiment, using the same amount of lard as vegetable shortening. The dough is shaped into little oval baskets, and a hard-cooked egg, which may be colored, is placed in the center of each one. Each egg is then covered with a cross fashioned from dough. The egg and cross symbolize the Resurrection of Christ. After the biscuit basket is eaten, the egg is eaten with bread and cheese or stored in the refrigerator for a snack at another time.

I have been helping Grandma make these biscuits every Easter since I was three years old. I confess that although I have tasted hundreds of cakes and cookies all over Italy and France, these pure, simple, plain vanilla biscuits remain my favorite. I can eat them by the boxful. Today, with such convoluted recipes in baking, it's nice to know that this two-hundred-year-old recipe is still the best, and nobody makes these biscuits like Grandma!

Secrets of Success

If you make a mistake, adjust your ingredients—a little more egg mixture, sugar, or shortening—to perfect these biscuits the second time around.

(CONTINUED)

3 large eggs

¾ cup plus 2 tablespoons milk

1 tablespoon vanilla extract

4 cups all-purpose flour

3 heaping teaspoons baking powder

1 cup sugar

¾ cup solid vegetable shortening or lard, plus 2 tablespoons if needed

1 bottle (2 ounces) tiny multicolored sprinkles

5 hard-cooked eggs, dyed with food coloring if desired

1. To make the biscuits by hand: In a small bowl, whisk together the eggs, milk, and vanilla; set aside. On a well-floured work surface, sift together the flour and baking powder, then stir in the sugar. Add the ¾ cup vegetable shortening or lard, breaking it up with your hands until the mixture resembles little peas. If the dough feels hard, add an extra 2 tablespoons shortening or lard. Make a well in the center. Using a fork, slowly mix in three-fourths of the egg mixture. Knead the dough until soft and smooth, about 5 minutes. If the dough feels hard, add the remaining egg mixture. Cover the dough with a damp white kitchen towel and let rest on the work surface for 30 minutes. Then, knead again for another 3 minutes until completely smooth.

2. To make the biscuits with an electric mixer: Prepare the egg mixture as directed for the hand method. In the large bowl of an electric mixer fitted with a dough hook, sift together the flour and baking powder. Add the sugar and vegetable shortening and beat on low speed until the mixture breaks up into little pieces, about 2 minutes. Add the egg mixture slowly, and knead on low speed with the dough hook until the dough is soft and smooth, about 5 minutes. Remove the dough from the mixer and allow to rest as directed in the hand method, then knead by hand for 3 minutes.

3. Preheat an oven to 350°F. Roll a 3 inch by 1 inch piece of dough between your hands, shaping it into a log ½ inch in diameter and

about 7 inches long. Cut off 1 inch of dough. Set aside. Shape the log into an open oval, and seal the edges of the dough with your thumb. Dip the top side of the oval into the sprinkles. Securely press 1 hard-cooked egg into the center of the oval. Set aside.

4. Cut the reserved 1 inch of dough in half. Shape the pieces into 2 tiny logs, each about ¼ inch in diameter and 2 inches long. Form the 2 logs into a cross over the egg. Seal the edges of the strips to the dough basket to secure the egg. Decorate the cross with a few more sprinkles. Repeat, making 4 more baskets. Form any leftover dough into small biscuits in horseshoe and S shapes, then dip the top side of each into the sprinkles. You will make about 1 pound of biscuits with the leftover dough.

5. Transfer the baskets and biscuits to 2 large, greased baking sheets. Bake until the edges begin to brown and the bottoms are golden brown, about 20 minutes. Transfer to a platter and allow to cool completely before eating.

Biscotti di Giugiulena
SESAME SEED BISCUITS

Makes about 3 dozen biscuits

🐦 This centuries-old recipe is simple, and it is likely that you have all the ingredients, except the sesame seeds, already in your kitchen. Sicilian in origin, these biscuits have long been a standard in every Italian pastry store in Little Italy. *Biscotti di giugiulena* is the old-fashioned Sicilian name for them, although today they are more commonly called *biscotti regina*. Most professional bakers make them from leftover pasta frolla, which is the dough used to make *crostate* (tarts), *pasticciotto* (custard pastry), *cassata al forno* (baked cassata), and *cuccidrati* (fig cakes). Originally, this recipe called for lard, since butter was not available in Sicily until modern times. If you want to make the biscuits with lard, use 20 to 25 percent less lard than butter.

½ pound unsalted butter, at room temperature

1 cup sugar

3 large eggs

1 tablespoon baking powder

½ teaspoon salt

1 teaspoon vanilla extract

4 cups all-purpose flour

1 cup milk

2 cups sesame seeds

1. Preheat an oven to 400°F. In a large bowl, using an electric mixer set on high speed, beat together the butter and sugar until creamy. Beat in the eggs one at a time, then beat in the baking powder, salt, and vanilla. Stir in the flour, ½ cup at a time, until the mixture forms a smooth, pliable dough.

2. To form each biscuit, pinch off a small piece of dough and shape it into a log ½ inch in diameter and about 2½ inches long. Put the milk and sesame seeds into separate shallow bowls. Dip each log into the milk, and then coat with the sesame seeds on all sides.

3. Transfer the logs to a large, ungreased baking sheet. Bake until the logs are golden brown on the top and bottom, 15 to 20 minutes. Transfer to platters and let cool completely before serving. Store leftovers in an airtight container at room temperature for up to 2 weeks.

Dolce di Limone
LEMON ROLL CAKE

Makes 2 medium-small cakes; serves 12

🐚 This recipe was given to Grandma by a relative from Ciminna. It is an unusual cake in that it can be eaten warm or cold. For those who go crazy over lemon roll cake, this recipe is for you. It can be made on the spur of the moment, and the lemon filling can be the one included here, the one from your favorite lemon meringue pie recipe, or purchased lemon pie filling or lemon curd. (You will need two 16-ounce cans or jars.) Since this recipe yields two cakes, you can make it for large gatherings or give one cake away to friends or relatives. Wrapped in foil, these cakes will keep for about a week in the refrigerator.

Lemon filling

6 large egg yolks

1 cup sugar

½ cup freshly squeezed lemon juice

1 teaspoon lemon-flavored liqueur (optional)

¼ teaspoon vanilla extract

¼ cup unsalted butter, cut into small pieces

Dough

3 eggs

½ cup sugar

¾ teaspoon vanilla extract

2½ cups all-purpose flour

2 teaspoons baking powder

½ cup solid vegetable shortening

½ teaspoon ground cinnamon

¾ pound dark chocolate, cut into small pieces

½ cup sliced almonds

Confectioners' sugar

Secrets of Success

Make sure to seal the edges of the cake well or the filling will slip out during baking.

1. To make the lemon filling: In the top pan of a medium-size double boiler, combine the egg yolks and sugar. Place over (not touching) gently simmering water in the bottom pan and cook, stirring constantly, until just combined, about 2 minutes. Stir in the lemon juice, liqueur (if using), and vanilla. Continue to stir over gently simmering water until the curd thickens and coats the back of the spoon, about 10 minutes. Add the butter one piece at a time, stirring until melted before adding the next piece. Remove from heat and let cool to room temperature. (If not using immediately, transfer to a sterilized jar, cover tightly, and refrigerate for up to 1 week.)

2. To make the dough: In a small bowl, beat together the eggs, sugar, and vanilla. Set aside. On a work surface, sift together the flour and baking powder. Add the vegetable shortening, breaking it up with your hands until the mixture resembles little peas. Make a well in the center. Using a fork, slowly mix in the egg mixture until a dough forms. Knead until smooth, about 3 minutes. Cover the dough with a damp kitchen towel and let rest on the work surface for 15 minutes.

3. Preheat an oven to 375°F. On a well-floured work surface, cut the dough in half. Roll out each half into a 9-by-10-inch rectangle. Transfer the rectangles to a large, buttered baking sheet. Spoon half of the lemon filling lengthwise down the center of each rectangle, forming a strip. Then sprinkle each strip of lemon filling with ¼ teaspoon of the cinnamon, half of the chocolate pieces, and 2 tablespoons of the sliced almonds. To form each roll, fold in the sides, overlapping them. With your thumb, press together edges of dough at each end to seal.

4. Bake until the tops and bottoms are golden brown, about 35 minutes. (If the cakes are golden brown on the bottom and done, but the tops aren't browned, place them under a preheated broiler for just a few seconds to brown.) Allow the cakes to cool for 15 minutes on the baking sheet, then sprinkle with the remaining almond slices, confectioners' sugar, and a little cinnamon. Serve warm.

A Birthday Story

Turidru was Grandma's brother-in-law, the husband of her sister Vitina. When he arrived on Ellis Island in 1921, he got a rude surprise. His ship was quarantined and the passengers were refused entry because one of them had a contagious disease. For forty days, the ship remained out at sea. Turidru, a hard man, found himself lonely, without money, and unable to speak English. As the ship tossed in the rough waters and freezing December winds off Battery Park, Turidru was miserable and frozen.

One day a strange man began pacing hurriedly on the docks. Staring at the puzzled faces on the ship, he cupped his hands around his mouth, simulating a megaphone, and called out Turidru's name. Turidru cautiously inquired, "Who is this man looking for me?" The gentleman introduced himself charmingly as his sister's husband, a man Turidru had never met. Turidru was stunned and then concerned. "Where is my sister?" he asked.

The man shouted back, "She's with child. She can't come."

"How interesting?" replied Turidru, a note of apprehension in his voice. "My sister isn't even married! Who are you?" he demanded, frightened that someone was after him.

His brother-in-law laughed. "We sent the letters to Sicily, but by the time they arrived, you had already left. We've been married for a while. I assure you I am your brother-in-law."

Still very leery, Turidru questioned, "What do you want with me?"

The De Robertis pastry shop, 1938, with its windows dressed for Easter. They made one of the best cassata in New York.

"I have a present for you," he answered excitedly, then proceeded to put a very large box in a basket. "Pull it up, Turidru!" The two men worked the pulleys and the box finally arrived on the second deck of the ship. Turidru was shocked when he saw the lettering on it: De Robertis Pasticceria. Hastily he opened it. Inside was the largest *cassata* he had ever seen.

"Happy Birthday, Turidru! Your sister told me to make sure to buy you a big cake to surprise you for your birthday."

Overwhelmed with emotion, tears streaming from his eyes, Turidru waved good-bye to his brother-in-law with his white handkerchief. "I will always remember that when I was all alone in this country on my birthday, my sister sent over a *cassata* just for me," Turidru later recalled. "I was the ship's favorite person that day. But I still wasn't sure that man was my brother-in-law."

De Robertis has been in business at 176 First Avenue in New York City since 1904 (see page 263). 🐚

Here I am on my first birthday. Dad bought me a cassata from De Robertis. It looks like I enjoyed it.

Cassata di De Robertis
CASSATA FROM DE ROBERTIS

Cassata is considered the most spectacular of all Sicilian cakes, the island's pride and joy. It dates back over five hundred years. The word *cassata* is said to come from the Arabic *qas'ah*, the name of the slanted mold used for making the cake.

Many influences converge in this classic dessert. The sweetened ricotta filling is probably adapted from the sweetened yogurt and sour cream used by the Turks for their desserts. The Arabs invented almond paste, which nowadays is used for making *cassata*, although pistachio paste was traditionally used. The latter became prohibitively expensive, so almonds, which are abundant and inexpensive in Sicily, were substituted. But Sicilian cooks continue to add green food coloring to the almond paste, or marzipan, as a reminder of when pistachios were used. The Spanish, who ruled Sicily for hundreds of years, brought the soft *pan di Spagna*, or sponge cake, which recalls a French *genoise*. (Some books describe the original *cassata* cake as being hard rather than soft, but I have traced the story all the way back to great-great-grandmas, and all agreed the cake melted in your mouth.) Finally, *cassata* is topped with a fondant icing, stemming from the French invasion of Sicily. The addition of rum and liqueur was designed to keep the cake's texture soft and fresh in the absence of refrigeration, which I also believe was due in part to French cooks.

As you can see, this cake is the sum of many national traditions, all interpreted by the Sicilian cook. Many stories revolve around the invention of *cassata*, but I prefer the story of the wealthy man who requested a baker to make him a cake with cannoli cream because he was tired of cannoli. He asked for a cake topped with a sweet icing, lots of rum and liqueur on the inside, and pistachio paste on top. The baker came up with *cassata*, and it has been the traditional celebratory cake ever since, enjoyed by Sicilians, and many other Italians as well.

(CONTINUED)

Secrets of Success

The easiest way to make this spectacular dessert is to do it in stages. Prepare the cake and the icing 2 days before serving. Making the cake in advance allows time for it to cool completely so that it will stand up to the rum. Refrigerating the *cassata* overnight sets it properly. As the marzipan softens, the rum cake and cannoli cream blend together to give the dessert its unique flavor.

This very special recipe, from the famous De Robertis Pastry Store, is the Palermo version of *cassata*. Note that the vanilla powder; oils of cinnamon, lemon, and orange; and green marzipan can be found at any bakery supply store. Green marzipan can also be found at Italian and French bakeries, which will sell it to you by the pound. You will need 3 cake pans to make this cake: a 9-inch cake pan, a 10-inch cake pan with 3-inch sides, and a traditional *cassata* mold (sold at most bakery supply stores or at any Italian bakery supply store). If the last is unavailable, substitute a regular 9-inch cake pan with 3-inch sides. Also needed are a large cake stand and a 10-inch cake board.

Sponge cakes

10 large eggs

½ pound confectioners' sugar

¼ teaspoon vanilla powder, or 1½ teaspoons vanilla extract

3 tiny drops oil of orange, or 1½ tablespoons orange extract

2 tablespoons rum

1½ ounces baking powder (about 3 tablespoons)

½ pound cake flour

Cannoli cream

2 pounds fresh ricotta cheese

12 ounces granulated sugar

2 tiny drops oil of cinnamon, or ½ teaspoon cinnamon extract

1 tablespoon rum

1 tablespoon *crème de cacao* or coffee liqueur

½ cup diced mixed glacéed fruits (orange peel, citron, pineapple, and cherries)

½ cup tiny semisweet chocolate chips

Fondant icing

3 cups sugar

1½ cups water

½ teaspoon vanilla powder, or 1 to 1½ teaspoons vanilla extract, to taste

Secrets of Success

If you don't want to make the fondant icing, purchase it from an Italian or French bakery. The ricotta, flours, baking powder, and sugars must be weighed on a kitchen scale to ensure the best results.

Confectioners' sugar

1 pound green marzipan

1 cup rum

3 tablespoons *crème de cacao* **or coffee liqueur**

12 glacéed cherries, 6 red and 6 green

1½ pints mixed large glacéed fruits such as figs, pears, oranges, and cherries

1. Two days before serving, make the sponge cakes, cannoli cream, and fondant icing. To make the sponge cakes: Preheat an oven to 400°F. With an electric mixer set on low speed, beat together the eggs, confectioners' sugar, vanilla, citrus oil or extract, rum, and baking powder until the batter has tripled in volume, about 15 minutes. By hand, fold in the cake flour until just combined.

2. Grease a 9-inch round cake pan and a 10-inch round cake pan with 3-inch sides. Fill each cake pan three-fourths full with the batter. Bake until a toothpick inserted into the centers comes out with moist crumbs, about 55 minutes. Remove from the oven and let cool completely in the pans, then cover well and refrigerate overnight to firm.

3. To make the cannoli cream: Scoop the ricotta into a colander or large sieve placed over a large bowl. Cover well and refrigerate overnight to drain. (This step must be done or the cream will be watery and ruined.) The next day, in a large bowl, combine the drained ricotta, granulated sugar, cinnamon oil or extract, rum, and liqueur. Fit an electric mixer with a flat beater and whip the ricotta mixture on the lowest speed until it is completely smooth and free of any lumps, about 20 minutes. (Use only the lowest speed or the mixture can easily be ruined.) During the last minute, stir in the dried glacéed fruits and chocolate chips. Cover and refrigerate until needed.

4. To make the fondant icing: In a medium-size pot, stir together the sugar and water over low heat until the mixture comes to a boil.

(CONTINUED)

Reduce the heat and simmer until the mixture is thick enough to make a string between your thumb and index finger, about 10 minutes. Transfer to a medium-size bowl and allow to cool for 5 minutes. Stir in the vanilla. Fit an electric mixer with a flat beater and beat on low speed until the mixture turns snow white and develops a thick, pasty consistency, 10 to 15 minutes. Cover and refrigerate until needed.

5. To assemble the *cassata:* Butter a *cassata* mold or 9-inch cake pan with 3-inch sides. Dust the mold with confectioners' sugar and tap out the excess. Sift ½ cup confectioners' sugar on a wooden board and then generously sprinkle a rolling pin with more confectioners' sugar. Using your hands, flatten the marzipan into an 8-inch disk. Sift confectioners' sugar over the marzipan. Roll out the marzipan ⅛ inch thick and large enough to cover the bottom and sides of the *cassata* mold (about 12 inches in diameter).

6. Roll the marzipan around the rolling pin, then unroll it over the *cassata* mold. Press the marzipan into the bottom and up the sides of the mold. Trim the excess marzipan hanging over the edges of the mold.

7. Trim off all the brown edges from the sponge cakes. Then, using your hands, lightly lay your palms on the brown top crusts and rub back and forth to dislodge the brown crust. Discard the brown crumbs. Using a serrated knife, cut a ½-inch-thick slice off the top of the 9-inch cake. Place the slice over the marzipan layer. Set aside the 9-inch cake.

8. Cut the whole 10-inch cake into 3-by-2-inch slices, each ½ inch thick. Surround the sides of the mold with the cake slices, standing them upright and firmly pressing the slices against one another. Fit in as many slices as possible. The cake slices will rise above the rim of the mold. Trim them so that they are flush with the mold.

9. In a small bowl, combine the rum and coffee liqueur. Using a pastry brush, generously brush the rum mixture over all the cake slices and the large slice of cake in the mold. Be generous; if you don't soak the cake well, it will be dry. Spoon in enough of the cannoli cream to fill the mold one-third full. Sprinkle with the glacéed cherries and cover the cream completely with more cake slices. Generously brush the cake slices with more of the rum mixture, reserving some for the top cake layer. Fill the mold to the very top with cannoli cream (there will be some cannoli cream left over). Cut another ½-inch-thick slice from the top of the 9-inch sponge cake. Place it over the cannoli cream. Brush with remaining rum mixture. (Do not be alarmed; the cake will extend 1 to 2 inches above the mold. It will settle while standing overnight.) Cover the cake loosely with plastic wrap. Place a flat dish over the cake, then weigh it down with a very heavy pot. Store the *cassata* in the refrigerator overnight.

10. The next day, remove the weight, plate, and plastic wrap. Run a thin knife around the edge of the mold. Using a large knife, tap the bottom and sides several times to loosen the *cassata*. Invert it onto a 10-inch cake board and transfer the board to a large cake stand.

11. In a medium-size pot, heat the fondant icing over very low heat until it liquefies and pours easily from a spoon. Heat the blade of a large metal spatula in boiling water. Pour almost all of the icing over the *cassata* and, using the spatula, immediately spread it thinly over the top and sides of the cake, covering completely. Add more icing if it covers too thinly. (If any icing is left over, store it in a tightly sealed container for up to 1 month. It may be used on Dutch apple pies or other similar desserts.)

12. Using a damp towel, remove any fondant that has spilled onto the cake board. Decorate the *cassata* on the top and the sides with the large glacéed fruits.

(CONTINUED)

To store leftover *cassata,* freeze individual slices in aluminum foil. They will keep for up to 2 weeks. Allow the slices to thaw for 15 minutes before serving.

To store leftover cannoli cream, freeze in a tightly covered container for up to 2 weeks. Drizzled with a chocolate fudge topping, it will taste like the best ice cream you've ever eaten.

Torta di Ricotta
CONCETTA DI PALO'S RICOTTA CHEESECAKE

Serves 8

🐚 Concetta Di Palo, my friend Louie's grandma, made this cake for him every week for Sunday dinner. Today his mom, Viola, continues that tradition.

3 pounds fresh ricotta cheese

1 cup grated zwieback biscuits

1 tablespoon plus 1½ cups granulated sugar

¾ cup heavy cream

8 large eggs

1 teaspoon vanilla extract

4 teaspoons orange-flower water

½ pound semisweet chocolate, chopped into small pieces (optional)

2 tablespoons diced mixed glacéed fruits, such as orange peel, citron, pineapple, and cherries (optional)

Confectioners' sugar

½ teaspoon ground cinnamon

1. Spoon the ricotta into a large colander placed over a large bowl, cover, and refrigerate to drain for 2 hours.

2. Preheat an oven to 350°F. To make the crust: In a small bowl, combine the grated biscuits and the 1 tablespoon sugar. Butter a 10-inch springform pan and coat the pan with the crumb mixture, tapping out the excess.

3. To make the filling: In a large bowl, combine the ricotta and the 1½ cups granulated sugar. Using an electric mixer set on medium speed, beat until smooth and creamy. Add the cream, eggs, vanilla, and orange-flower water. Beat, scraping the sides of the bowl occasionally, until the ricotta mixture is smooth and creamy, about 5 minutes. Stir in the chocolate and the glacéed fruits, if using.

4. Pour the filling into the crust. Bake until the top is golden brown, about 1 hour. Transfer to a rack and allow to cool in the pan for 30 minutes. Then cover and refrigerate overnight.

5. The next day, remove the pan sides and slide the cheescake onto a serving plate. Dust the top with confectioners' sugar and the cinnamon.

Sam Di Palo poses in front of his store at 206 Grand Street, Little Italy, in 1948.

Ricotta Turnovers with Glacéed Fruits and Chocolate

Cassatedri are the homemade version of the *cassatini* (mini *cassata* cakes) sold in pastry stores. Grandma's sister Vitina taught her how to make them. Although this recipe serves a large number, it can be halved without any problem. Grandma always used her scale to measure the flour and I suggest you do the same for perfect results, although cup measurements are given for your convenience.

Filling

2¼ pounds fresh ricotta cheese

2½ cups sifted confectioners' sugar

Ceylon stick cinnamon, finely crushed between the palms,
    or ground cinnamon, plus extra for topping

½ pound diced mixed glacéed fruits (orange peel, citron, pineapple,
    and cherries)

6 ounces bittersweet chocolate, cut into large chips

Dough

2 pounds sifted unbleached all-purpose flour (8 cups)

¾ cup plus 2 tablespoons granulated sugar

2 teaspoons baking powder

¾ to 1 pound lard or solid vegetable shortening, chilled (1½ to 2 cups)

1½ cups water

1. To make the ricotta filling: Spoon the ricotta into a large sieve or colander placed over a large bowl. Cover and refrigerate to drain overnight. The next day, in a medium-size bowl, whisk together the ricotta, 1½ cups of the confectioners' sugar, and ⅛ teaspoon cinnamon

until the mixture is very smooth, about 3 minutes. Gently stir in the fruits until just combined. Transfer the ricotta mixture to a large platter and spread it evenly into a layer about ⅓ inch thick. Sprinkle the top of the ricotta generously with the chocolate. (Do not mix the chocolate and the ricotta together.)

2. To make the dough: On a large work surface, mix together the flour, sugar, and baking powder. Make a well in the center of the flour and add ¾ pound of the lard. Work it in the mixture with your hands, until little pieces of dough form. If the dough feels hard rather than tender, add the full amount of lard. Begin adding the water slowly while kneading, until it comes together easily in one piece. Then knead the dough for 10 minutes more. It should resemble a large oval loaf measuring about 11 by 7 inches. Cover the dough with a damp, white kitchen towel and let rest on the work surface for 30 minutes.

3. Preheat an oven to 400°F. Cut off about a 1-inch-thick slice from the dough and then cut it in half so that you have 2 pieces. Roll out each piece into an oval about 7 by 5 inches and ⅛ inch thick. (Extra flour is unnecessary while rolling the dough due to the lard content.)

4. Spoon 2 generous tablespoons of the ricotta–chocolate chip mixture into the center of each oval. Fold over the dough to conceal the filling, and seal the edges well with your thumb or a fork. Leave a ⅓-inch-wide rim around the edge and, using a ridged cutter, trim off the excess dough. Repeat until the dough and the filling are used up. As you make the turnovers, keep the unused dough covered with a damp, white kitchen towel so that it does not dry out. You will be able to make about 14 turnovers.

5. Transfer the turnovers to 2 large, greased baking sheets, leaving enough space around them to allow room for rising. Bake until the bottoms are browned and the tops are golden, about 30 minutes.

(CONTINUED)

6. Transfer the turnovers to a decorative platter and sprinkle each one generously with confectioners' sugar and cinnamon. Serve hot or lukewarm. Or let cool completely and store in an airtight container for up to 2 days. To keep them longer, refrigerate them for up to 6 days.

Niru di Uccelli
BIRD'S NEST

Serves 6

🐦 "This is the one thing I love to make and eat," says Grandma. She was taught how to make bird's nest by Carmella, whose daughter Dorothy was one of my mother's closest friends.

Carmella was from the Sicilian town of Recalmuto, and each year she made bird's nests for Easter, Christmas, and birthdays. She'd make six large nests and then give them away as gifts to family and friends. Grandma used to tell me the knots were called bird's nests because the mother bird has to make knots to entwine the little twigs when building a nest. This is Carmella's recipe from the 1940s.

1 large egg

4½ tablespoons milk

1 teaspoon vanilla extract

1⅓ cups all-purpose flour

1 teaspoon baking powder

2½ tablespoons granulated sugar

2 to 3 tablespoons solid vegetable shortening or lard

Extra-virgin olive oil

¾ cup honey

Confectioners' sugar

Ceylon stick cinnamon, finely crushed between the palms, or ground cinnamon

1. In a small bowl, whisk together the egg, milk, and vanilla. On a well-floured work surface, sift together the flour and baking powder, then stir in the granulated sugar. With your hands, break up 2 tablespoons shortening or lard with the flour until little pieces of dough form. If the dough feels hard rather than tender, add the remaining 1 tablespoon of shortening or lard. Make a well in the center and, using a fork, begin slowly adding the egg mixture to the flour mixture until the dough comes together in one piece. Then knead by hand or in an electric mixer fitted with a dough hook set on low speed until smooth, about 10 minutes.

2. On a lightly floured work surface, roll out the dough paper-thin (about half as thin as an average pie crust). Cut the dough into strips ¼ inch wide and 6 inches long. Tie the strips into medium-size knots. Transfer to a platter, arranging them in a single layer. Do not stack them.

3. In a medium-size frying pan, pour in olive oil to a depth of 1 inch and heat over medium heat to 350°F. In batches, add the knots to the hot oil and fry, turning once, until golden brown on both sides, about 45 seconds on each side. Transfer to 2 large platters lined with paper towels to drain for 1 minute, then transfer to 2 clean platters, arranging them in a single layer.

4. Meanwhile, in a small saucepan, heat the honey over low heat until it is warm; do not allow the honey to boil. Drizzle the warm honey over the knots, and sprinkle generously with confectioners' sugar and then with cinnamon. Eat while hot, as they do not taste good when cold.

Secrets of Success

Instead of rolling out the dough by hand, pass it through a manual pasta machine on setting number 6, where it will come out just the right thickness.

Little Italy's Queen of Pignolata

GRANDMA CICCINA guarded her *pignolata* recipe with her life. She felt, as did those who tasted it, that hers was the best—far better than any pastry-store version. She always insisted on making the honey balls herself and never told anyone the recipe, a typically Sicilian position. Every Christmas, she dutifully made *pignolata* and gave one dish to each of her children and close friends.

After my father married, he wanted to make these holiday treats himself. He never assisted his mother, but remembered most of the recipe from having watched her make it over the years. When his time came to make the *pignolata*, he questioned her about the recipe and the number of eggs used. She instructed him to use egg whites only, which my father argued against, since he specifically recalled her using whole eggs. After a lengthy discussion, she convinced my father to use the egg whites and, of course, poor Dad spent the whole day rolling, cutting, and frying the little honey balls, only to find their texture as hard as a rock. When he visited his mother again and told her what had happened, she denied, with a smile, ever having told him to use the whites only. Furious that he had wasted a whole day, he realized that his mother was jealous of his making a dish as good as she made it. Storming out of her house, he re-created her *pignolata* from memory, and much to her dismay, it came out perfect. She would have been ecstatic to see her recipe buried along with her reputation for making the best *pignolata* ever. 🌿

Pignolata
HONEY BALLS

Although these honey balls were traditionally made for Christmas, they are now also made in Little Italy for Easter, New Year's Day, and Saint Joseph's Feast Day. In Naples, they are called *struffoli*. The Sicilian version differs from the Neapolitan version in its more crunchy exterior and more cakelike interior. Neapolitans usually make honey balls that are lighter in texture and have a foamy consistency on the inside that quickly melts in the mouth. In the Sicilian town of Messina, there is a version of *pignolata* that calls for pouring chocolate rather than honey over the balls.

The fried pastries are shaped into pyramids and then customarily placed on the dinner table. Family and friends munch on them while chatting and sipping espresso throughout the night. Since this recipe makes six dishes, I suggest storing two dishes in the cupboard for your own family, leaving two dishes out for guests, and giving two away as gifts.

7 to 9 large eggs

About 4¼ cups all-purpose flour

½ teaspoon baking powder

Extra-virgin olive oil

1½ pounds honey, preferably golden orange blossom

2 teaspoons finely crushed Ceylon cinnamon stick or ground cinnamon

1 cup tiny multicolored sprinkles

1 cup Italian spice confetti candy (available at Italian pastry stores)

1 cup Jordan almonds (available at Italian pastry stores)

(CONTINUED)

Secrets of Success

Don't roll out the dough on a board or table. Rolling the strips between your palms is the only way to form them. While rolling, make sure your hands are well floured to prevent the dough from sticking to them. Keep the windows and doors shut, since any draft can cause the dough to harden. The most common mistake made in making *pignolata* is undercooking the pastry. Fry them until well browned.

1. To make the honey balls by hand: Into a small bowl, break 7 of the eggs; set aside. On a well-floured work surface, sift together 4 cups of the flour and the baking powder. Make a well in the center. Add 1 egg at a time, kneading well after each addition. If the dough feels too sticky to handle after all the eggs have been worked in, add an extra ¼ cup or more flour and knead until the dough becomes pliable. If the dough feels too dry, add 1 or 2 extra eggs and work in until the dough feels soft. With well-floured hands, knead the dough until all the air pockets are gone and the dough is smooth, about 10 minutes. Shape the dough into a medium-size loaf.

2. To make the honey balls with an electric mixer: Prepare as directed in Step 1, but sift the flour and baking powder into the large bowl of an electric mixer. Fit the mixer with a dough hook. Add the eggs one at a time and knead in on low speed, mixing well after each addition until fully incorporated. Add more flour or egg as directed in Step 1, if necessary. Then knead for 10 minutes and shape into a loaf.

3. Half-fill a medium-size deep fryer with olive oil and heat over medium heat to 350°F.

4. Meanwhile, cut off ½-inch-thick pieces of the dough, each 4 inches in length. Roll each piece of dough between your palms until it forms a log about ⅔ inch in diameter. Next, cut the log into ⅓-inch-thick pieces. After you have cut 3 or 4 logs into small pieces, add them to the hot oil in small batches and fry them until they are a crusty deep brown, 2 to 3 minutes. Do not cut all the dough in advance and leave the pieces out or they will harden and not fry properly. Keep the uncut dough covered with a damp, white kitchen towel so it does not dry out.

5. When the fried pieces are ready, using a slotted spoon, transfer them to a large colander placed over a dish to drain for about 10 minutes. Then transfer them to a very large bowl. Repeat until all the dough pieces are fried.

6. After all the dough pieces have been fried, heat the honey in an 8-quart pot over very low heat just until it is warm, then turn off the heat. (Do not cook the honey or it will become as hard as rock candy, and you will not be able to shape the pyramids.) Stir in the cinnamon, then add all the fried dough pieces. Using a large wooden spoon, stir vigorously until all the dough pieces are well coated with honey. Let stand in the pot for 5 minutes to absorb the honey.

7. Using a large slotted spoon, remove one-sixth of the honey-coated pieces and transfer them to the center of an 8-inch dish. Dampen your hands well with water and, cupping them around the bottom of the mass of fried dough, press them together gently, molding the pieces into a pyramid about 8 inches high. Keep dampening your hands and forming the pyramid until it takes on a nice shape. The top should come to a point. (The dish you use to shape the *pignolata* in will be the dish you serve it on, since there is no transferring the finished dessert once it is shaped.) Repeat the process 5 more times, until all 6 pyramids are finished. There will be honey remaining in the pot. Drizzle it over the 6 pyramids, dividing it evenly.

8. Decorate each pyramid with sprinkles, Italian spice confetti candy, and the Jordan almonds. To store, cover tightly with aluminum foil and keep in a kitchen cupboard for up to 1 month. To gift wrap, cover each dish with a large piece of gold cellophane paper, tie the top with a gold ribbon, make a large bow, and curl the ribbon ends.

CHRISTMAS FIG CAKES

🐦 *Cuccidrati* are Christmas cakes. They come in many shapes: large wreaths, small cookies, horseshoes, and logs. The latter are the most traditional for making at home. Interestingly, their styles haven't changed one bit over the last several hundred years.

In Little Italy at the turn of the century, and up to about ten years ago, the only way to make these cakes was to grind the figs and raisins in a meat grinder. In Sicily, before Christmas, the butcher did everyone a favor. After they bought his meat, he would clean his grinding machine, and then anyone from the town who wanted to make *cuccidrati* would bring sacks of figs and raisins to the shop and wait in line for them to be ground. Today, the figs and raisins can be ground in a food processor. Note that this recipe, which is from Grandma Ciccina, must be begun at least 3 days before serving.

Filling

Peel of 1 orange, removed in large pieces

1 Ceylon cinnamon stick, about 3 inches long, or 2 teaspoons ground cinnamon

¾ cup almonds

1 pound dried figs (buy a good soft variety)

½ pound dark or light raisins (about 1½ cups)

1⅓ cups sugar

¾ cup cold water, or ½ cup apricot brandy and ¼ cup sweet Marsala wine

½ cup diced mixed glacéed fruits (orange peel, citron, pineapple, and cherries)

**½ pound good-quality bittersweet chocolate, ¼ pound grated and
    ¼ pound cut into little chunks**

Dough from Ricotta Turnovers with Glacéed Fruits and Chocolate (page 270)

Glaze

2 large egg yolks

1 teaspoon water

Icing

1 tablespoon unsalted butter

1 tablespoon solid vegetable shortening

1 cup confectioners' sugar, sifted

¼ teaspoon vanilla extract

2 tablespoons milk

½ cup tiny multicolored sprinkles

1. To make the fig filling: Three days before serving, place the orange peel in a small dish and leave, uncovered, on the top of the stove to dry.

2. On the day you make the fig filling, combine the orange peel and cinnamon stick in a blender and grind until powdery. Transfer to a small dish and set aside. If using ground cinnamon, grind the orange peel and then stir in the cinnamon. Add the almonds to the blender and, pulsing for 2 seconds at a time, grind until the almonds are in tiny pieces but not powdery. Set aside.

3. In a food processor, combine the figs, raisins, and sugar. Pulse until the mixture is smooth but retains a little texture. The sugar ensures the fruits will grind evenly. (Or combine the figs and raisins, and grind them in a meat grinder with the disk used for making chopped meat. Then transfer to a bowl and stir in the sugar.) Transfer the fig mixture to a medium-size pot, add the water or brandy and wine and the cinnamon mixture. Cook over low heat, stirring constantly with a wooden spoon, until the figs are soft, about 10 minutes. Transfer to a medium-size bowl and let cool completely. Then stir in the almonds, glacéed fruits, grated chocolate, and chocolate chunks.

(CONTINUED)

4. Preheat an oven to 350°F. Grease 2 large baking sheets. Cut off a ½-inch-thick slice of dough. On a well-floured surface, roll out the dough into a 6- by 9-inch rectangle about ¼ inch thick. Using a pastry cutter, trim off the excess dough to even the edges. Spoon about a 1-inch-wide strip of the fig mixture down the center of the square. Fold the sides in to cover the fig mixture, then turn the log over. Using scissors, cut little slits in the dough at ½-inch intervals along both sides of the log. To make short logs, cut the log crosswise into pieces about 3 inches long. To make a horseshoe, cut the log in half and form a U shape, then cut little slits in the dough at ½-inch intervals. To make a wreath, shape the log into a ring and seal the ends together. Using scissors, cut along the outside edge of the ring at 1-inch intervals, forming slits about ½ inch deep. Transfer to a prepared baking sheet. Repeat with the remaining dough.

5. To make the glaze: In a small bowl, beat together the egg yolks and water. Brush over the tops of all the cakes. Bake until the top and bottom crusts are browned, 20 to 25 minutes.

6. Meanwhile, make the icing: In a small pot, melt together the butter and shortening over low heat. Increase the heat to medium and stir in the confectioners' sugar and vanilla. Keep stirring until the sugar melts and the mixture has a spreadable consistency. Then, stir in the milk.

7. As soon as you remove the little cakes from the oven, brush the tops with the icing. Return the cakes to the oven for 1 minute only, just to melt the icing. Transfer to a platter and, while still hot, decorate the tops with the sprinkles. Let cool and serve. Store any leftovers in an airtight container for up to 2 weeks.

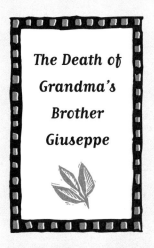

The Death of Grandma's Brother Giuseppe

GRANDMA'S SISTER-IN-LAW LUCIA was only fourteen years old and flirtatious when she married Grandma's brother Giuseppe. So immature and jealous was she of her mother-in-law, Maria, who was close to her son, that she refused to allow her husband to see his own mother or even speak to her on the street. Vitina, Grandma's sister, who was tougher than any Sicilian man, would not allow her sister-in-law to rule her, however, and she continued to see her favorite brother whenever she chose, often forcing herself through the front door and physically pushing Lucia aside in the process. Horrible arguments persisted nightly and the whole family was fighting over this issue. Vitina and Great-grandpa Michele used to say that Lucia would be the end of Giuseppe because he was too kind and weak to fight her.

One afternoon, Giuseppe told Vitina that he wasn't feeling well and had a headache, so Vitina placed a damp handkerchief on his forehead and left him to rest. Before she reached her home only a few blocks away, screams from the neighbors were heard throughout the town. "Giuseppe! Giuseppe!" Vitina picked up her long skirt and quickly retraced her steps, her black shoes thundering on the cobbled streets. But it was too late. Giuseppe had suffered a massive heart attack at the age of thirty-nine. From that moment on, Vitina lost her health and soon developed a heart condition from the shock. She remained brokenhearted over her brother's death, for he had been like a son to her—the son she never had. She died fourteen years later of a heart attack, always saying that her heart was tied with a string to Giuseppe's, and that it was her fate to die a similar death.

Grandma's moral: "Be very careful of whom you marry and allow into the family, for they can take your health away. Then you have nothing in life."

Sfingi

FRIED PASTRY PUFFS WITH CONFECTIONERS' SUGAR

Sicilians call them *sfingi*, while Neapolitans call them *zeppole*. Grandma never made them in Ciminna, but she ate them as street food in Palermo. Grandpa Natale loved eating *sfingi* so much that he asked her to start making them at home. This is her original recipe from the 1920s. If you're serving fewer people, halve the recipe. The texture and taste of these puffs recall hot, delicious vanilla doughnuts. Surprisingly, they are made with baking powder, not yeast! Although expensive to buy, they cost only pennies to make. Plan on preparing a batch when you are having a large gathering, and then have your guests assist you in the cooking. They will adore eating this old-fashioned treat.

2⅔ cups sifted all-purpose flour

1¼ to 1½ cups milk

4 large eggs

6 tablespoons granulated sugar, or to taste

3 tablespoons baking powder

2 teaspoons vanilla extract

Extra-virgin olive oil

1 cup confectioners' sugar

Ceylon stick cinnamon, finely crushed between the palms,
    or ground cinnamon

Secrets of Success

If it's a very cold day and/or the batter has not risen sufficiently, add 1 more heaping teaspoon baking powder.

1. In a medium-size pot, whisk together the flour, 1¼ cups milk, eggs, granulated sugar, baking powder, and vanilla until the batter is smooth. The batter should be the consistency of cake batter. Cover the pot with a clean, thick kitchen towel. Let the batter rest in a draft-free area for 30 to 60 minutes, or until it has risen by at least 50 percent in bulk.

2. Pour olive oil to a depth of 3 inches in another medium-size pot. Place over medium heat and heat to 350°F. Test the oil by dropping in 1 tablespoon of the batter (read Secrets of Success). If the batter instantly floats to the surface, the oil is ready.

3. Working in small batches, drop 1 tablespoon batter at a time into the hot oil. Do not crowd the pot. When the puffs turn a golden brown, gently turn them over to cook on the other side. Total cooking time is about 2 minutes. Using a slotted spoon, remove the puffs to a paper towel–lined plate to drain for a few seconds.

4. Immediately transfer the puffs to a large bowl and, using a sieve, sprinkle generously with confectioners' sugar and cinnamon. Serve hot. They do not taste good when they are cold.

Secrets of Success

If the batter does not puff up in the hot oil, or the *sfingi* are cooked on the outside but raw in the center, the batter is too thick. Remedy this by adding additional milk to the batter, about ¼ cup at a time and retesting until the proper consistency is reached.

If the batter is too thin, adjust it by adding 1 heaping tablespoon flour and ½ teaspoon sugar at a time, until the proper consistency is achieved.

Cudririuni Fritto
FRIED PUFFED DOUGH WITH SUGAR

🏮 Although this is a true Sicilian peasant dish, these are among the most delicious little pastries I've ever tasted. *Cudririuni* are usually made right after dinner for dessert. They can often be found on Mott Street in the local pizzerias, where they are called *pizza fritta* (fried pizza). This is one of Uncle Mike's favorite desserts.

1 pound bread dough, homemade (page 67) or purchased

Sugar

Extra-virgin olive oil

1. On a well-floured work surface, using a well-floured rolling pin, roll out the dough about ⅛ inch thick. Cut into 3-inch squares.

2. Spread about 1 cup sugar on a flat plate. Set aside.

3. Pour olive oil to a depth of ⅓ inch in a medium-size frying pan. Place over medium heat and heat to 350°F. Add 2 or 3 squares of dough at a time to the hot oil and fry until golden brown on both sides, about 1 minute on each side. Using tongs, transfer to a paper towel–lined plate to drain for a few seconds.

4. Using tongs, dip the hot squares into the sugar, coating them on both sides. Serve hot.

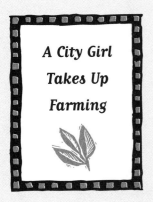

A City Girl Takes Up Farming

WHEN I VISITED SICILY, I'd often find Great-aunt Mica at her farm high on a hill, working in the wheat fields. It would be 110°F outside, and Mica would have already been cutting four-foot-high straw for six hours, wielding a large scythe out of an Ali Baba movie. Later, in the evenings, she would weave the straw into baskets. She was ninety-two, and I was twenty-five. One day I thought, well, if a ninety-two year old can cut straw, so can I. Attempting to look strong as the weight of the scythe tilted my body over was not easy. I took a whack at the straw and the momentum of the scythe turned me around 180 degrees. Mica quickly hit the ground to prevent her decapitation. "Mica, this is impossible! I'm so hot, and wet all over." I wiped the sweat from my cheeks, and then I noticed the blazing sun had transformed my mascara and lipstick into colorful liquids running down my face. I grabbed my compact to touch up my lipstick. Mica giggled, "Franca, why do you wear makeup? *Troppo colore!* [Too much color!]"

"I can see that not a soul wears makeup in Ciminna. Let me guess, they think I'm a *putana* [whore] because I wear lipstick and blush? Mica, I can't take it anymore! Let's go back to the house. I need to get something cold in my body before I pass out."

"If a girl wears too much makeup, people talk, Franca. What's that you sprayed yourself with?" she asked, pointing to the atomizer.

"Chanel 22—isn't it wonderful? You want to put some on?"

"Of course not!" Mica replied. "Look, there's my daughter Maria."

As we reached the door of the farmhouse, Maria yelled, "Close your eyes, Franca! Hot enough! Here, I made it just for you."

She handed me a slice of ice cream cake made with *savoiaridi* and chocolate and sprinkled with orange liqueur. There is a God! I took a big bite. The ice cream dripped down my chin. "Oh no! I have to put my lipstick on again!" ✍

Dolce di Gelato
ICE CREAM CAKE

Here's an ice cream cake that Aunt Mica's daughter Maria had made for me when I spent a summer in Ciminna. She took ordinary ingredients she had in her home—biscuits, liqueur, cream, ice cream—and molded the cake in an old tin she saved just for that purpose. Similar to a *tiramisù*, it's much simpler because you can substitute any ice cream for the marscarpone cream, and use almost any liqueur. It's an absolutely spectacular dessert that will impress guests for a special occasion. If you prefer to make a smaller cake, simply halve the ingredients and use a 5-cup freezerproof bowl.

30 *savoiaridi* (Italian ladyfingers sold in Italian bakeries); or

    60 regular ladyfingers

1 cup freshly brewed espresso, cooled

½ cup rum or brandy

½ cup crème de cacao

1½ pints pistachio ice cream, slightly softened

Ground cinnamon, for dusting

Cocoa, for dusting

½ pound dark chocolate, shaved into curls or grated

1½ pints butter pecan or butter almond ice cream, slightly softened

1½ pints coffee or chocolate ice cream, slightly softened

½ pound mixed large candied fruits such as pears, oranges, cherries, and

    figs (available at Italian bakeries or confection shops)

Whipped cream

2 cups heavy cream

½ cup sour cream, chilled

½ cup confectioners' sugar, sifted

1 teaspoon vanilla extract

1 tablespoon Grand Marnier or any apricot, cherry, or strawberry liqueur

1. Line the bottom and sides of a deep, 2½-quart freezerproof bowl with the ladyfingers. Combine the rum and crème de cacao. Generously brush the ladyfingers with the espresso, then the rum mixture. Spoon in the pistachio ice cream, patting it down. Dust generously with the cinnamon and cocoa. Top with one-third of the chocolate. Repeat the layering twice, using the butter pecan ice cream for one layer and the coffee ice cream for the other layer. End with a layer of ladyfingers. Cover and freeze until firm, at least 8 hours or as long as overnight.

2. While the cake is in the freezer, make the whipped cream: In a chilled medium-size bowl, combine all the ingredients. Using an electric mixer set on high speed, beat until the cream forms soft mounds. Cover and refrigerate until needed.

3. To unmold the cake, briefly dip the bottom half of the mold into hot water, then run a knife around the sides. Carefully invert onto a large, round platter. Using a spatula, frost the cake on the top and sides with the whipped cream, creating large swirls. Decorate with the candied fruits. Return the cake to the freezer for 30 minutes to allow the cream to stiffen before serving.

Granita di Caffè
ESPRESSO ICE

A family favorite, this simple, delicious ice is found in every home in Sicily and Little Italy on a hot summer's day. The espresso may be sweetened with anisette or sugar; both are traditional. To a Sicilian, espresso is always made in a Neapolitan drip pot. Every twenty years or so, our family invests in a new pot, although Grandma still has the one she bought when she married over sixty-five years ago. It seems that Sicilians never throw away old espresso pots.

Recently, while shopping for a new stainless steel drip pot in Little Italy, I had a good laugh with several shop owners. They all told me that the only people who buy the stove-top espresso coffee pot that runs on a burst of steam rising from the bottom are tourists—never Sicilian Americans. All the store owners refused to use this type of pot, insisting instead on the drip pot, sometimes called the Neapolitan flip-drip pot. Nor would any of them consider putting a drip pot directly over a gas jet, heating the water in the bottom of the pot, and then turning the pot over so the water drips through the ground coffee, as is instructed in most books. Instead, the water is always boiled separately and poured into the top portion of the pot, from where it drips down over the grounds.

As I left the store on the corner of Grand Street, the owner shouted, "You know, Francesca, I have this store and I sell all these pots, but I still use the drip pot I got when I married over fifty years ago. I take home a new pot every twenty years or so, but I never use it. My old aluminum one is still good, and it's seasoned with the taste of espresso. Full of scratches and little bumps, but still good. So the new one stays new, still in the box I brought it home in." His story sounded familiar.

Secrets of Success

The espresso should taste overly sweet before freezing. Once frozen, it will be just right.

1¾ cups (if using anisette) or 2¾ cups (if using sugar) freshly brewed espresso, prepared in a Neapolitan drip pot

¾ to 1 cup 30-proof anisette, or sugar to taste

6 lemon twists

1. To make *granita* with anisette: Allow the 1¾ cups espresso to cool to lukewarm, then add the anisette to taste. Remove the inserts from 2 ice-cube trays and pour the espresso mixture into the trays. Cover with aluminum foil. Freeze until firm, a minimum of 6 hours or as long as overnight.

2. To make *granita* with sugar: Prepare as directed in Step 1, but use 2¾ cups espresso instead of 1¾ cups. Add the sugar to taste while the espresso is still very hot, then cool to lukewarm, pour into ice-cube trays, and freeze.

3. Using a fork or knife, break the frozen espresso mixture into chunks. Scoop into champagne glasses and garnish with lemon twists.

Note: To make *granita* in an ice cream machine, prepare as directed with anisette or sugar. Then, pour the mixture into your ice cream machine and freeze according to the manufacturer's directions.

Granita di Limone
LEMON ICE

Our family always makes lemon ice in the summer nowadays. But a hundred years ago, lemon ice—indeed all flavored ices—were never made at home in the summer. They were a winter treat. Of course, there was no such thing as refrigeration in the old days, and even an icebox in the 1920s in America did not qualify as a way to make summertime ices. Ices and ice creams were bought at the local pastry store in Sicily or in Little Italy and they had to be consumed immediately. The only other place to get ices was from the ice man who sold them on most corners in Little Italy.

So why the winter? Because that is when it snowed. It even snowed occasionally in Ciminna. In the 1920s in Little Italy, there were several severe snowstorms, which gave everyone an opportunity to make ices by scraping the virgin snow off the windowsill or fire escape, and then pouring a fruit-flavored syrup such as cherry, lemon, strawberry, or even coconut over the top. All the syrups were either bought at the pastry store or homemade in the summertime when fruits were abundant.

The children of a hundred years ago awaited the snowfall to make their homemade ices. Today those century-old ices are known as snow

At the turn of the century, ices were found only at the local pastry store. Here is John De Robertis (right) at his store in 1938.

cones. With the invention of the home freezer in the early 1940s, ices could be made year-round at home. Everyone tells me, however, that nothing tastes as good as ices made with virgin snow.

1½ cups water

1½ cups sugar

1 cup fresh lemon juice, strained (about 6 lemons)

1 teaspoon grated lemon zest

1 teaspoon Italian lemon liqueur

¼ teaspoon almond extract (optional)

4 lemon or lime twists

1. In a medium-size pot, combine the water and sugar. Bring to a boil over high heat, and boil for 1 minute. Remove from the heat and let cool.

2. Stir the lemon juice, lemon zest, liqueur, and almond extract into the sugar syrup. Taste the mixture, and if the flavor is too sharp, add more sugar, 2 tablespoons at a time, until the tartness is the way you like it. Pour into a medium-size shallow metal tray, and freeze for at least 6 hours or as long as overnight. Using a whisk, stir the mixture every 30 minutes for the first 2 hours to break up the crystals. When frozen, transfer to a blender to make into a slush, or using forks or an ice cream scooper, scrape the ice into parfait glasses and serve immediately. Garnish with the lemon or lime twists.

Note: To make *granita* in an ice cream machine, prepare the lemon mixture as directed, then pour it into an ice cream machine and freeze according to the manufacturer's directions.

Uncle Mike's Army Days

MY UNCLE MIKE WAS in the military in the 1960s. One day the sergeant gave all the men a test to see how many of them could be assigned to take care of the barracks. To make it easy, the sergeant supplied the men with the answers to the test. My uncle and his buddies decided they weren't interested in working, so they devised a plan to fail. When asked what he would do in the event the furnace overheated in the building, my uncle answered: "Run the hell out!" When the sergeant saw the answers of my uncle and his friends, he was infuriated and shouted at the top of his lungs: "In all my life, I've never seen answers like this. You want to play games! Report at seven o'clock tomorrow morning to dig graves. Dismissed!"

Upon hearing the orders, Uncle Mike nearly fainted from fright. They did dig graves, but for only one day. Then they were assigned to afternoon KP duty, an absolute cinch. There was a machine to clean the potatoes, the dicing and slicing had already been done in the morning, and their work amounted to only a few hours a day. Meanwhile, they hung out and got to eat extra food. The guys had a good laugh at the expense of the sergeant.

Uncle Mike's moral: "Don't work if you don't have to!" The story went around, and the guys on Mott Street all had a good laugh, too. 🐦

Uncle Mike (right) with some of his Army buddies.

Insalata di Frutta
MIXED FRUIT SALAD

Serves 8 to 10

🐟 In Sicily as well as Little Italy, it is common to find a ceramic bowl filled with fruits on the dining table, with a plate of biscotti or pastries alongside. Often fruits are served with favorite cheeses and breads, too. This fruit salad is a classic combination that is still eaten in Sicily. It consists of many fruits, including some that you may not even associate with Sicily such as coconuts and watermelons. Both are extremely popular and frequently sold cut into pieces and priced according to size in resort areas like Cefalù and Taormina. The coconut pieces are placed on several tiers of ice, with water gently cascading over them. Although most fruits in Sicily are extremely sweet, they are still peeled, sliced, and dipped into a bowl of sugar for dessert.

Before I finish these thoughts on fruits, I am compelled to include a little tribute to four fruits: *nespoli giappone* (loquats), *scevusi* (mulberries), *ficurinii* (prickly pears), and *ficu* (figs). These particular fruits were among the most frequently eaten and adored by Sicilians from the late 1800s to the 1950s. Since the 1950s, all of these fruits have nearly disappeared in America. *Nespoli giappone* (loquats) were eaten in Sicily during the month of May; their taste is somewhere between an orange and an apricot. In their heyday, they were sweet, but now they are not only difficult to find, but their taste is bland and bitter. The sweetest loquats in Sicily are immediately consumed by connoisseurs who also make jam from them.

Mulberry trees were grown by every Sicilian who had property, and when Sicilians transplanted themselves to America, the berries came with them. In Brooklyn, where many Sicilians bought homes, rows of *scevusi* trees filled the backyards, just as they did on Mulberry Street. Unfortunately, only a handful of these trees have survived.

Unlike many other fruits, *scevusi* had many practical uses. Grandma recalls her brother, Turidru, writing home to Sicily from Chicago that he considered mulberries to be the most important of all the fruits

sweets, fruits, nuts, and ice cream 293

because he used their juice to make ink for his quill pen, to dye clothes, and to make wine and jam.

Prickly pears were popular because of their strong, sweet flavor. The fruits come in colors ranging from yellow and red to green. The yellow ones have the taste of banana; the red, the taste of strawberry; and the mainly green, the taste of pear with a hint of strawberry and banana. Today, *ficurinii* in the United States range in price from one to three dollars per fruit and are devoid of flavor. Ventimiglia, the town where Grandpa Natale was born, is famous worldwide for growing the sweetest prickly pears and figs in Sicily.

Figs, my favorite fruit, were a staple in every home in Sicily and Little Italy throughout the 1950s. It was common to purchase them by the crate and place them on the table for dessert at Sunday dinner. As a child, Grandma braided figs into a wreath and dried them for the winter. There were even fresh black winter figs in Sicily, a treat known to only a few. When I'm in Sicily, my relatives laugh at me because I walk down the streets of the little villages and steal figs off people's trees. One woman caught me, but she didn't seem to mind. *"Signora,"* I said, *"nu che questi cosi a America! Ca a Sicilia sono la bene di Dio!"* (Signora, there aren't these things to eat in America! Only in Sicily are there all the beautiful things that God created!) The plump, jolly woman smiled back, *"Certo! Mangia, signorina!"* (Certainly! Eat up, signorina!)

Although this salad is served at the end of a large dinner, the recipe is easily halved for four. A variety of roasted nuts (page 298) typically accompanies it.

2 apples, unpeeled, cored and cut into wedges

1½ cups blueberries, rasberries, or hulled strawberries

1 small cantaloupe or honeydew, seeded, halved, and scooped into balls

1 cup cherries

1 coconut, broken into pieces, served on the side

1 cup Concord grapes

6 yellow, red, or green prickly pears, served on the side

6 to 10 figs, served on the side

1 mango, peeled, pitted, and cut into cubes

1 cup muscat Italian grapes

2 oranges, peeled and sectioned

2 peaches or pears, peeled, pitted, and cut into wedges

1 small or ½ large pineapple, peeled, cored, and cut into wedges

½ pound Italian plums, unpeeled, quartered, and pitted

1 pomegranate, peeled

1 pint mulberries, served on the side

1 wedge watermelon, about 1 pound, seeded and scooped into balls or
cut into 1-inch chunks

Sweet Marsala or any favorite liqueur such as amaretto or Grand Marnier

Sugar, to taste

1. One day before serving, choose 8 fruits from the list. If you have selected fruits other than the coconuts, prickly pears, figs, loquats, and mulberries, peel and cut them as directed while holding them over a large bowl to capture their juices. As the pieces are cut let them drop into the bowl. Sprinkle the prepared fruits with wine and sugar to taste. Toss gently, retaste, and adjust. Cover and marinate for at least 8 hours or, preferably, for up to 24 hours. If using a coconut, break it into pieces right before serving and arrange over a bowl filled with ice. If using prickly pears, figs, or mulberries, place them in separate bowls to serve. (If mulberries are tossed with the fruit salad, they will break and stain the salad blue-black.) Mulberries can also be crushed, strained, poured over crushed ice, and served as juice.

PEACHES OR NECTARINES IN WINE

One or two days before serving, peel, pit, and slice 3 pounds peaches. Place in a large bowl and add 2 cups Italian red wine or sweet Marsala. Alternatively, add cold water to cover and 6 tablespoons sugar, or to taste. Toss, cover, and refrigerate for 1 or 2 days. Serve in large wineglasses. Accompany with biscotti such as Sesame Seed Biscuits (pages 257–258).

Secrets of Success

In my travels, I have never met a Sicilian who eats sweet oranges in a salad. Sicilians tell me that sweet oranges are a precious commodity, and they are always eaten plain. Bitter oranges, which the Spanish brought with them when they invaded Sicily, are abundant. When the bitter oranges become dry, they are used up in salads. They are also used in Sicily to make syrups and the island's famous orange marmalade, which was carried by Saks Fifth Avenue years ago and can still be found in many specialty food stores.

Aunt Mica Decides to Wear Makeup

ONE DAY AS AUNT MICA and I were roasting nuts, she asked me, "Why do you put all those things on before the lipstick?"

"Let me explain. First, there's the lip primer, that keeps the lipstick on. Then I color in the lips with the lip pencil, then the lipstick goes on. It works in New York, but in Sicily, the heat is too strong to keep lipstick on for long. Mica, let's put some lipstick and blush on you. Come on, we both have the same coloring."

"Are you crazy? I'll be the talk of the town. I'm an old woman, I'm eighty-nine."

"Grandma said you are ninety-two if you're a day!"

"Not true! Has my sister gone crazy. She's trying to make me old."

"Well, if you wore some makeup . . . please . . . please. Let's take down your hair from that stupid bun. How long is it?"

"It's forbidden. Only a *putana* looking for a man's pleasure . . ."

I took the pins out of Mica's hair as she fought me, and managed to put some lipstick and blush on her. "Mica, your hair is down to your hips, and it's gorgeous!"

"*Dio, Dio!*" She got up and stared at herself in the mirror. "Franca, you know, I'm still beautiful. I look like an actress."

"And not a day over eighty-eight."

"*Tu si una diavola!* [You're a devil!]" she yelled as she slowly chased me.

Suddenly the door opened. "Mamma, do you want me to drive you back? Your hair is down!" shouted her daughter Maria. "You have on lipstick and rouge!" She took out her handkerchief to fan herself and then wiped her bosom. "It must be the heat!"

"No, your mother has decided to date men again. You understand. And I'm going to get a bottle of Clairol and dye her hair jet black so she'll look twenty years younger."

"Francaaaaaaa! What are you saying? They don't understand you tease me!"

"Mamma! You're an old woman! You simply can't do such a thing. Why, you'd be the talk of the whole town. . . ."

"Why, you would think I put Maybelline on you instead of Chanel the way she's carrying on. And your daughter said you look old!" I smiled innocently.

"Old, did you say old? I thought you said old. Is that how you speak to your mother? Franca, buy the Clairol!"

"Come on, Mica, let's roast the *ciciri* [chickpeas]. Your dramatic daughter will survive. Has she fainted yet?"

"Maria!" Mica shouted to her sixty-eight-year-old daughter, "Stop fainting and help me boil the *ciciri*." Then she swung her lustrous hair over her shoulder and walked proudly into the kitchen.

Simply scandalous. 🐚

Scaccio e Biviri
CRUSH AND DRINK

Grandma once told me that her father used to plant everything. "In Sicily, we would keep a couple of hundred pounds of walnuts and almonds and thousands of pounds of favas on our farm. As you drank wine, you'd crush the nuts and eat them. We called it *scaccio e biviri* [crush and drink]. It was also a popular ritual in the bars of Italian neighborhoods in the United States. Since nuts were so abundant in Sicily, we substituted them for dessert when cake wasn't available. In America in the 1930s, I would go to the corner of Prince and Elizabeth streets to a *ciciraro* [store specializing in nuts]. The smell of the fresh almonds and nuts drove you crazy when you roasted them. Oh, Frenzee, those were days!"

½ pound almonds, pistachios, pumpkin seeds, sunflower seeds,
    or walnuts in the shell
2 pounds chestnuts
Salt
1 pound fava beans
¼ pound dried chickpeas

1. Select 2 pounds of the nuts, seeds, and beans in the ingredients list, in any combination.

2. To prepare the almonds, pistachios, pumpkin seeds, sunflower seeds, or walnuts, preheat the oven to 350°F. Spread the nuts or seeds on a large baking sheet. Roast until lightly browned, 15 to 20 minutes. Allow the nuts to cool, then serve.

3. To prepare the chestnuts, preheat an oven to 375°F. Cut a cross through the shell on the flat side of each chestnut. In a large, shallow baking pan, spread the nuts in a single layer. Add just enough water to cover the bottom of the pan barely. Sprinkle with salt. Roast until the chestnuts are lightly browned and soft in the center, 35 to 40 minutes. If the water evaporates before the nuts are ready, add a little more water. To serve, remove the shells and eat hot.

4. To prepare the favas, remove the pods but leave the skins intact. Fill a medium-size pot with salted water and bring to a boil. Add the favas, reduce the heat, and simmer until the favas are tender, about 15 minutes. Drain and transfer to a bowl. Eat warm or hot by removing the skin from each bean and sprinkling with salt.

5. To prepare the chickpeas, soak them overnight in a large bowl of cold water to cover. The next day, rinse the chickpeas 20 times in cold water to remove their musty odor. Half-fill a medium-size pot with salted water and bring to a boil. Add the chickpeas, reduce the heat to medium, and cook until slightly soft on the outside but hard on the inside, 10 to 15 minutes. Drain the chickpeas and pat dry with a towel. Preheat the oven to 400°F. Spread the chickpeas on a large, shallow baking sheet and sprinkle with salt to taste. Roast, stirring every few minutes, until lightly golden, about 15 minutes. Transfer to a bowl and serve warm.

Caution: Do not stick your head into the oven while checking on the chickpeas. They pop easily and can lodge in your eye. Stand back from the oven, open the door, and allow the hot air to cool down before checking them.

LIQUORI E BIVIRI

 Sicilians celebrate life by drinking espresso, liqueurs, and sodas. At the turn of the century in Sicily, coffee was only made in cafes and pastry stores, never in the home. Espresso was reserved for the wealthy, since only they could afford to purchase coffee. Whether it was a birthday, an anniversary, or the birth of a baby, Sicilians, both men and women, would go to their favorite pastry shop or local liqueur-maker to drink something with which to celebrate the occasion. At the turn of the century, liqueurs had to be ordered, since none were prepared in advance, and a minimum wait of two or three weeks was standard.

When Sicilians arrived in Little Italy in the 1900s, it was all the rage in the summertime to prepare these sought-after liqueurs, as well as vermouth and whiskey flavored with wine peaches. Few things are more festive than bringing out your own homemade liqueurs full of fresh fruit bits and strong alcohol (pages 304–311).

When I was a little girl, on hot days Mom and I would walk through Little Italy to the candy store to have an old-fashioned soda made from a flavored Italian syrup—cherry, strawberry, lemon-lime, coffee. The soda jerk would pour the syrup over crushed ice in a tall glass and then top it off with seltzer from a handheld spray bottle of crackled blue glass. The syrups are still available in pastry stores and Italian gourmet shops.

I've included nonalcoholic drinks made with syrups, such as a homemade Orangina, and a refreshing lemonade, as well as such alcoholic beverages as Whiskey with Wine Peaches and my grandpa's favorite liquor, vermouth. This way, everyone can celebrate!

Here I am (left) with Aunt Sue (center) and Mom (right) celebrating too much with liqueurs at a 1990s Sicilian wedding.

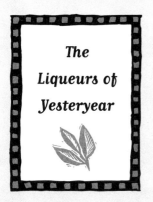

The Liqueurs of Yesteryear

AT THE TURN OF THE CENTURY when Sicilians arrived in Little Italy, they were forced to order their liqueurs well before the occasion in order to age the liqueurs in their homes, allowing them to grow stronger in flavor with time. The choices included *Strega*, a golden liqueur made with over seventy herbs and still sold today, *anisette* (anise), *caffè sporto* (espresso), and a variety of fruit flavors. They were served in liqueur glasses with or without espresso on the side, but usually with. The liqueurs of yesteryear were very strong, high in alcohol content, and very expensive. In the early 1900s, it was unthinkable for Sicilians to spend money on expensive liqueurs. They often held down two jobs just to pay the rent. It didn't take long to figure out these prized liqueurs could be made at home, however.

From late September through October on the Lower East Side and in Little Italy, making liqueurs in anticipation of the many holiday guests was a *smania* (a mania). In addition to liqueurs, vermouth and whiskey with wine peaches were also made. Most families, poor and rich, had a good stock of these beverages.

Although liqueurs with essences may be sipped only a few days after being made, they require at least one month to age to the point where they release their flavor, and three months for the most full-bodied bouquet. Essences cost twenty-five cents each in the 1930s, and until Prohibition was repealed, the alcohol had to be bought illegally.

A familiar scene at night would start with a knock on the door. "Who is it?"

"*Io.*" [Me.]

Grandma opened her door quietly. The neighborhood bootlegger would say nothing, never admitting he had alcohol with him. She knew him by sight and allowed him to enter her home. He pushed his five-gallon can through the doorway. The money was handed over—usually fifteen dollars during the Depression. The bootlegger glanced at it quickly, then stuffed it into his pocket. No other words were spoken. He left the apartment as quietly as he entered. Grandma would close the door and the fun would begin in the kitchen. 🌿

Liquori

LIQUEURS OF LITTLE ITALY

Makes 4 quarts

Here are Grandma's liqueur recipes from the 1920s. While she worked away in the kitchen, Grandpa would serenade her with this famous Little Italy ditty: *"Si imbriacaro e non ni vosiru qui, si imbriacaro e non ni vosiru qui, si imbriacaro e non ni vosiru qui. Abballa mugheri ca shurmi su."* (He got so drunk he didn't want her anymore. He got so drunk he didn't want her anymore. And the poor wife had to dance alone. Translation: The husband got so drunk, he couldn't have sex with his wife.)

Essences, or extracts, for making liqueurs can be found at most winemaking supply stores. Sometimes Italian pastry stores and gourmet shops carry them, too. See the sources for further information.

2 quarts water

1⅓ cups sugar

2 quarts (8 cups) 100-proof vodka or 190-proof pure grain alcohol

3 ounces (6 tablespoons) *anisette* essence

3 ounces (6 tablespoons) *crème de cacao* essence

3 ounces (6 tablespoons) *crème de menthe* essence

3 ounces (6 tablespoons) *Strega* essence

Crushed ice, for serving

1. In a large pot, bring the water to a rapid boil over high heat. Stir in the sugar until completely dissolved. Reduce the heat and simmer for 5 minutes, stirring frequently. Transfer the pot to a sink half-filled with ice water and let cool for 15 minutes.

2. When the syrup is completely cool, using a funnel, pour 2 cups of the syrup into a sterilized 1-quart bottle with a tight-fitting lid. Pour 2 cups of the alcohol and 3 ounces of the *anisette* essence into the

Secrets of Success

Nowadays, 190-proof pure grain alcohol doesn't have the body or taste it once did. I prefer making these liqueurs with 100-proof vodka.

bottle. Seal the bottle and shake well. Label with today's date. Store in a cupboard and allow to age for 3 months before drinking. Repeat the process 3 more times, using the remaining flavors. You will end up with 1 quart each *anisette, crème de menthe, crème de cacao*, and *Strega*. Serve poured over crushed ice in liqueur glasses.

CAFFÈ SPORTO

To make Grandma's 1930s version of *caffè sporto*, brew 2 cups double-strength espresso. While still hot, stir in 1 to 1½ cups sugar to taste until dissolved. Allow to cool completely. Pour into a sterilized 1-quart bottle and add 2 cups 100-proof vodka or 190-proof pure grain alcohol and 1 ounce (2 tablespoons) *caffè sporto* essence. Seal the bottle and shake well. Label with today's date. Store in a cupboard and allow to age for 2 or 3 months before drinking.

Caffè Sporto alla Francesca
ESPRESSO LIQUEUR OR ESPRESSO SYRUP

Makes 5 cups espresso liqueur, or 1³⁄4 cups espresso syrup

Since many liqueurs are made with a fresh syrup base, Sicilians often reserve some of the syrup for making sodas. Whenever I make this liqueur, I stir up an egg cream, substituting the espresso syrup for the usual chocolate syrup (see below).

4 cups brewed double-strength espresso

1¾ cups sugar

3 cups 100-proof vodka, for making liqueur

Crushed ice, for serving

(CONTINUED)

1. In a large pot, combine the espresso and sugar over medium-low heat and slowly bring to a rolling boil, stirring until the sugar is dissolved. Cover the pot and boil the syrup for 15 minutes, stirring frequently. Uncover and continue to boil, stirring frequently, until the syrup coats a spoon, about 15 minutes longer. Transfer the pot to a sink half-filled with ice water for 15 minutes to cool.

2. If making the syrup only, pour the syrup into a sterilized jar, cap tightly, and store in the refrigerator for up to 2 months.

3. If making the liqueur, using a funnel, pour the syrup into a sterilized 1½-quart bottle with a tight-fitting lid. Pour the vodka into the pot and stir up the leftover syrup. Pour the vodka mixture through the funnel into the bottle. Seal tightly and shake well. Label with today's date. Store in a cupboard and allow to age for 1 month before drinking. Serve poured over crushed ice in liqueur glasses.

ESPRESSO EGG CREAM

Fill a tall soda glass with crushed ice. Pour well-chilled espresso syrup to a depth of 1½ inches. Add 3 tablespoons well-chilled heavy cream. Slowly add seltzer until a high foam rises at the rim. Stir quickly. Serve immediately.

Secrets of Success

Espresso burns easily when boiled and can leave a rancid aftertaste if not cooked properly. Bring this syrup to a boil slowly over medium-low heat.

A Sad Story

AFTER MY GREAT-GRANDFATHER Paolo died, my great-grandmother Maria became more and more ill with each passing year. Natale, my grandpa, was her son, and he was often in and out of orphanages because she was too weak to care for him or any of her other four children. Many were the times when my grandpa, at only ten or eleven years of age, slept in the subway and sold newspapers on the train to make a little money to help support himself and his mother. His early life in Little Italy was a sad one, and a far cry from what he would have inherited growing up in his hometown of Ventimiglia. 🐦

Grandpa Natale as a young man, in 1926. He gave this photo to Grandma as a present after they were married.

Liquore di Mandarino
MANDARIN ORANGE LIQUEUR

Makes about
4 cups

The following two recipes came from discussions I had in Sicily with my great-aunt Mica, who made these liqueurs right up to the time of her death a few years ago. Often, she would make a fresh syrup, and then simply add the pure alcohol that was locally available to make an unaged liqueur. When I arrived home from Sicily, I began making these liqueurs and whiskey again with Grandma.

Mandarin orange liqueur is thick, but the more times you strain it, the thinner it will become. I strain the liqueur about 4 times for a medium-thick consistency. If you prefer a thinner liqueur, strain it 2 more times. As this liqueur ages, it will thicken. Simply add another 1 cup vodka, shake well, and age for another few days before drinking.

About 10 mandarin oranges

3 cups sugar

2½ cups 80-proof vodka

Crushed ice, for serving

Fresh mint sprigs, for garnish

Frozen mandarin slices, for garnish

Secrets of Success

Syrup boils over the pot rim easily, so stay near the stove to monitor the syrup closely.

1. Peel the mandarin oranges and separate into segments; do not remove the seeds. Reserve the peel of 1 orange and discard the rest. Transfer the orange segments and peel to a food processor and pulse until puréed. You should have 3 cups. In a large bowl, combine the orange purée and sugar. Cover and refrigerate for 2 days, stirring the purée twice a day.

2. Transfer the purée to a large pot and bring to a boil over high heat. Reduce the heat to medium-high and keep at a rolling boil, stirring occasionally, until the syrup coats the spoon, about 20 minutes. Transfer the pot to a sink half-filled with ice water for 15 minutes to cool.

3. Using a funnel, pour the syrup into a sterilized 1½-quart bottle with a tight-fitting lid. Allow the syrup to cool completely, then pour in the vodka. Seal the bottle tightly and shake it well. Label with today's date. Store in a cupboard and allow to age for 1 month before drinking.

4. Before serving, strain the liqueur through a sieve at least 4 times, or until it is as thick as you like it. Using a funnel, return the liqueur to its bottle. The liqueur may be served immediately. Pour over crushed ice in liqueur glasses. Garnish with mint sprigs and frozen mandarin slices. The longer it ages, however, the better it tastes.

Liquore di Fragole
STRAWBERRY LIQUEUR

Makes about
5 cups

🛱 Dad, as usual, was complaining one day. "The prices of liqueurs are enough to make me forget about drinking—period!" So for the next few days I tried to re-create Aunt Mica's recipe for strawberry liqueur, eventually coming up with an excellent version.

"Francesca," Dad exclaimed, somewhat surprised. "There's hope for you yet to become a good—not a great—but a good cook."

Ahhhh! Sicilian fathers have a way with words.

Although most homemade liqueurs need to age a minimum of a month, this one can be sipped on the first day. The leftover strawberries make a wonderful topping for pancakes, toast, or ice cream. Note that this is strong liqueur. If you prefer it sweeter, use less vodka. If you prefer it stronger, use 1 cup more vodka. If any large clumps of syrup remain in the vodka, do not be alarmed. In a day or two the alcohol will dissolve the clumps completely. *Cent' anni!* (That's a popular toast meaning we should all live happily for a hundred years.)

(CONTINUED)

5 pints slightly underripe strawberries, hulled

4 cups sugar, or to taste

½ cup water

5 ¼ cups 80-proof vodka

Crushed ice, for serving

Frozen strawberries, for garnish

Secrets of Success

Syrup boils over the pot rim easily, so stay near the stove to monitor the syrup closely.

1. If the fresh strawberries are large, cut them in half. In a large bowl, combine the fresh strawberries, 4 cups sugar, and the water. Cover and refrigerate for 2 days, stirring twice a day.

2. After the first day, taste and check the amount of juice the strawberries have released. The berries should taste overly sweet. If they have released 3 cups or more of juice and are very sweet, stir well and refrigerate for 1 more day. If the strawberries are dry, old, or overripe, however, they may not release enough juice or be sweet enough. Correct by adding enough water to the strawberries to measure 3 cups. If the strawberries are not overly sweet, add enough sugar until they are. In both cases, return the strawberries to the refrigerator for 1 more day.

3. After 2 days, you should have a total of 7 to 7 ½ cups strawberries and liquid. Transfer the strawberry mixture to a very large pot and bring to a rolling boil over high heat. Reduce the heat to medium and prop a spoon under the lid to keep the pot half uncovered. Keep the strawberries at a rolling boil, stirring occasionally, until thick, 30 to 35 minutes.

4. Place a large sieve over a large bowl. Strain the strawberry mixture into the bowl, pressing down on the strawberries to remove their juice. Set the strawberries aside. Taste the syrup for sweetness and add more sugar if necessary. Return the syrup to the pot, bring it back to a boil, and boil rapidly until the syrup coats a spoon, 5 to 10 minutes.

Meanwhile, stir the leftover strawberries vigorously with a fork. They will easily smash. Store in a sterilized jam jar in the refrigerator for up to 4 days and use as topping (see recipe introduction).

5. Transfer the pot to a sink half-filled with ice water for 15 minutes to cool. (If you prefer a clear syrup, strain it 2 or 3 times through a sieve. I prefer it with bits of fresh strawberry.) Then, using a funnel, pour the syrup into a sterilized 1½-quart bottle with a tight-fitting lid. Add ¼ cup of the vodka to the pot. Stir vigorously, picking up all the residue, and pour it through the funnel into the bottle. Allow the syrup to cool completely, then add the 5 cups vodka. Seal the bottle and shake it well. Label with today's date. Store in a cupboard and allow to age for 1 month before drinking. This liqueur may also be served immediately, although it tastes better aged. Pour over crushed ice in liqueur glasses. Garnish with frozen strawberries.

CHERRY LIQUEUR

Prepare as directed, substituting 6 cups pitted cherries (about 3 pounds cherries) for the strawberries.

CHAMPAGNE WITH STRAWBERRY LIQUEUR

Pour 3 tablespoons strawberry liqueur into a champagne flute, then fill with chilled champagne. Garnish with 2 frozen strawberries.

Grandma Josephina's Arrival in America

"SO GRANDMA, tell me when you arrived in America. I want to record it for the cookbook."

"I arrived here, Fren-zee, in 1922. It was on July 26, a little over seventy years ago," Grandma said. As she spoke, she leaned back in her old wooden chair and ran her fingers through her hair, just as she often does whenever she tells me one of her stories.

"But when did you actually leave Ciminna?" I asked curiously.

"Well, Fren-zee," she said, tilting her head back. Just then the sun shone through the window and made her hair sparkle like snow. "I arrived on July 26 at 1:00 P.M. on Ellis Island. They separated us. Whoever wanted to go to Chicago, New York, or Pennsylvania—all our *paesani* [people from the same town] went in different directions—and that's the last I ever saw of any of them. I looked for them years later, but it was finished!" She clapped her hands together, pulled her stocking up a little and rolled it around her garter tighter, then took a breath and wiped away the tears that were filling her eyes.

"I still don't understand why anyone would leave Sicily. I wouldn't. You were rich there next to what you are here! Why, I'm ready to go back now and you still like it here in America!" I snapped back.

"Fren-zee, you talk nonsense as usual. I came here because of my sister Vitina. My brother-in-law Turidru was here in America working at 35 Stanton Street, right where Roosevelt Park is now. They tore down the building in 1928. In 1920, Vitina told my father that she wanted to come to America to be with her husband, but she didn't want to come alone. She wanted me with her. She was sickly, and she felt if she got ill on the boat or in America, there would be no one to take care of her. So since we were very close, she asked our parents' permission to have me go along with her in case she got ill. Vitina was like a second mother to me. So my father, to make her happy, said, 'Okay. Let the sisters remain together.'

"I left Ciminna by horse and buggy on July 9. First I went to Baucina, a nearby town. Four hours later we took the train to Palermo. We stayed in Palermo for four days to wait for our visas and papers to be in order, then, on the thirteenth, we left for Napoli, and on the fifteenth, we left for New York. The doctors examined us. They looked at our eyes, hands, faces, and bodies to see if we had any rashes. If we looked okay, they allowed us to board the boat. The *sopragenti* [official who took the passports and tickets at the dock] was a rich man. He owned a pharmacy in Ciminna and took bribes from the wealthy people who wanted to leave for America immediately. While we were boarding the boat, he told my sister, 'I would like your place and your sister's because I have rich people that will give me a lot of money for them. I promise you'll leave on the next boat in two weeks if you give me this.' Vitina turned into an animal and started screaming at him. '*Questo vuole fare? Ci rompo la testa! Ci rompo la testa! Mio marito avuto la mia lettera et sta al pier aspettare il vapore!*' [This is what you're going to do to me! I'll break your head! I'll break your head! My husband has my letter and is waiting for me at the pier!] She didn't stop, Fren-zee! 'I have the trunks on the boat and we already said good-bye to my mother, who was on the couch hysterical that we were leaving! After all we went through, you do this!' Vitina was a tough one. No one started with her. She may have been sickly, but she had the personality of a tiger, and she could put any man in his place. She was just like you, Fren-zee . . . she told you off right to your face. She cursed the *sopragenti* up and down. She called him every dirty word you could think of in Sicilian."

"I thought Vitina was much worse than me, Grandma," I said, complimented.

"No! You're both about the same—with big mouths. So anyway, she refused to get off the boat! The *sopragenti* excused himself because she was screaming and went inside a room to speak to the doctor. I was waiting outside and,

Great-aunt Vitina and Great-uncle Turidru in New York's Little Italy. They waited for Grandma at the docks at Ellis Island in 1922.

when we boarded, they grabbed my sister by the arm and pulled her on board. Another two big men grabbed me and dragged me off the boat. I was so frightened, I started screaming. The *sopragenti* told me to go into his office. The doctor came out and told him that I had swollen, infected eyes. The doctor said, 'She must go back home to allow her eyes to heal.' It's true my eyes were red from crying over leaving my mother, but there was nothing wrong with them. But they made that the excuse, and the doctor got paid off as well. I ran off the docks to look for my brother Nicola, and we went back to Ciminna. When my mother saw me, she got up from the couch. She had been lying down, with a wet handkerchief over her forehead, almost dead from grief that her two daughters were leaving for America. She had been sick for over a week. Then the nightmare really started. To spite my sister for cursing him, instead of one month as he had originally said, the *sopragenti* wouldn't let me board the ship for six months. By that time, my father refused to let me come to America, and we had fights about it every night."

"Why? I thought you really wanted to stay in Ciminna. Your sister was already in New York, safe and sound . . ."

"Fren-zee, you don't understand as usual. They tortured me in Ciminna. Only people that were considered defective couldn't enter America. When I went outside, people would stare at me. There were rumors about me that I was a dummy, stupid . . . couldn't answer simple questions. Or maybe I had some contagious disease. Do you know what it's like to be in a small town and everyone whispers about you every time you walk by?

"Finally, my brother Nicola couldn't take the rumors that I was *difetti* [a defective person], so he had it out with my father. He said, 'Out of spite, she goes to New York, so the people in the town will shut their mouths about my sister!' No one started with my father. But that day Nicola was so angry, he won the argument. Six months later I got passage on the boat *America*. Now that boat is famous since it brought over so many immigrants, but in those days it was just another boat at the docks. About seven people from my town were aboard, and my father gave a little money to one of the neighbors to look after me since I was alone. It took thirteen days from Napoli to America. I was seasick the whole time." 🐚

Vermut
VERMOUTH

🐚 Vermouth was extremely popular in Little Italy in the early 1900s. It was Grandpa's favorite liquor, and he would drink it, as did most Sicilians, after a dinner with company. Various fresh roasted nuts (see page 298) were set out on the table at the same time.

2 quarts (8 cups) water

6 tablespoons sugar

4 cups 100-proof vodka or 190-proof pure grain alcohol

4 cups good-quality dry red wine

12 ounces (1½ cups) vermouth essence

Ice cubes, for serving

Maraschino cherries, for garnish

1. In a large pot, combine the water and sugar and bring to a boil over high heat, stirring until the sugar dissolves. Remove from the heat and allow the mixture to cool completely.

2. Stir the vodka or alcohol and the wine into the cooled mixture. Using a funnel, pour the mixture into 4 sterilized 1-quart bottles with tight-fitting lids. Pour 3 ounces (6 tablespoons) vermouth essence into each bottle. Seal the bottles and shake well. Label with today's date. Store in a cupboard and allow to age for 1 month before drinking. To serve, fill a short glass with ice cubes, add a few cherries, and pour in the vermouth.

Whiskey con Vraccochi
WHISKEY WITH WINE PEACHES

Makes 4 quarts

🎺 Dad enjoys telling this story: "One day when I was twenty-two years old and in the army, my mother sent me a large package that contained a whole salami, a big piece of provolone, and a bottle of her whiskey with peaches. How the bottle didn't break, I'll never know. I didn't care for whiskey much, so I gave it to the guys in the barracks. I watched them go to sleep one by one. That stuff was strong, but the guys loved it!"

A year later when Dad returned from the army, he found a rainbow of colored bottles on the dining room table. The liqueurs ranged from *crème de menthe* (mint), *fragole* (strawberry), *caffè sporto* (espresso), and *anisette* (anise) to his mother's specialty, whiskey with *vraccochi*. *Vraccochi* are a type of large, juicy wine peaches often weighing a half pound each or more. This tradition of adding fruit to wine stems from Sicily, where fruit in wine was substituted for pastries when pastries weren't available.

This whiskey, which is a Little Italy invention, needs to age at least 3 months before you can drink it. When Sicilians made it in the past, they added their large wine peaches to their wines, liqueurs, and whiskeys for an unusual taste. I'm told that in the old days you could not go to

Dad in 1942. The enemy couldn't defeat the aircorps, but Grandma's whiskey knocked them out!

a Sicilian American home without finding this whiskey. Note that the large wine peach remained in the jar until the whiskey was consumed, then it was eaten. Here's Grandma's recipe from the early 1920s. Fresh peach slices can be added to each glass for flavor and as a garnish.

6 cups water

2½ quarts (10 cups) 100-proof vodka or 190-proof pure grain alcohol

12 ounces (1½ cups) whiskey essence

4 large wine peaches, unpeeled, pitted and sliced into large sections

Ice cubes

Fresh peach slices, for garnish

1. In a large pot, bring the water to a boil. Remove from the heat and let cool completely. Then, stir in the alcohol. Divide the alcohol mixture evenly among 4 sterilized 1½-quart jars with mouths wide enough to slip a large peach through. Add 3 ounces (6 tablespoons) whiskey essence and 1 peach to each jar. Seal the jars and shake them well. Label with today's date. Store in a cupboard and allow to age for 3 months before drinking. To serve, fill a short glass with ice cubes, add a few fresh peach slices, and pour in the whiskey.

PLAIN WHISKEY

Prepare as directed, omitting the peaches.

Grandma's New Life in Little Italy

As I MADE WHISKEY with wine peaches, Grandma told me about her arrival in New York. "When I landed on Ellis Island, my sister Vitina and brother-in-law Turidru were waiting for me. I started crying and crying from the *contentezza* [joy and happiness]. We took the Third Avenue El back to Houston Street and walked to my sister's house. On our way, we went into the row of stores on Houston, and my sister bought me a hat, a dress, a pocketbook, and low-heeled shoes—not high heels, so the men wouldn't bother me. I remember saying that all the stores made this place look just like Palermo. I saw the fruit stands, pastry stores, the bread man, the milk man, all with horses and buggies. I told Turidru that I had thought things would be different here. But with all the horses and buggies, it looked just like Italy, and everyone spoke Sicilian, too!

"Turidru looked at me and laughed, 'So where do you think you're at? It should look like Italy. You're in New York, but you're in Little Italy!'

"When I got to Vitina's home, I dressed up in my new clothes, and then we went to our cousin Frank's house. My sister prepared sandwiches of *capocollo*, prosciutto, and all sorts of cheeses—provolone, *incanestrato*, *cacio-cavallo*, and mozzarella. Mozzarella didn't exist in Ciminna in my day, so that was my first taste of it. Where do you think we used to go for our cheeses and cold cuts? Di Palo's on Mott and Grand. I've been going to that store since 1926. My sister had all types of syrups to make fresh sodas—orange, cherry, even mint. I remember the mint soda like it was yesterday because I didn't like it.

"I didn't work for the first few months that I was in this country because I didn't speak English, so I took classes at night, and during the day I cooked and cleaned the house for my sister. Vitina worked on all the actresses' dresses from the opera and theater. She used to cut the patterns for the sequin gowns for the top stars on Broadway. I helped her make dresses for Helen Hayes, and I ended up sewing for two presidents, Roosevelt and Eisenhower. When Grandpa was alive, we used to watch the news and wait for the president to come on television and see the suit I made for him. I did all the finishing touches by hand. No sewing machine! I sewed the buttonholes, the pockets, lapels, everything by hand. Then I sewed for Mayor Lindsay, Cardinal Spellman, U-Thant [the head of the United Nations], so many famous people, I can't even remember anymore. So what else do you want to know for the *cook-ka-book*?"

"What did you like about the food here?" I asked.

"The meat!" she answered without hesitation. "What's this nonsense that Sicilians don't eat meat. Almost every night we had *verdure* [vegetables] and lamb chops, *verdure* and porterhouse steaks, *verdure* and pork chops. Meat was a big thing in Little Italy! We could buy meat everyday here, and not have to worry about the butcher running out of it—like in Sicily."

"What did you eat your first week here? What was different other than the meat?"

"Let's see, at dinner that evening we ate *pasta di casa* [homemade pasta]. My first week here my sister made me taste Mell-O-Roll vanilla ice cream and Sky-Rocket, the multiflavored fruit ice. The best American ice cream was from Louie who owned a candy store on Second Avenue and Fourth Street. Everyone from Little Italy went there. The ice cream was custommade for him—it was cream itself. Then in the 1940s and 1950s, there was Sammy's Luncheonette on Second Avenue and First Street. He made the best malteds. You could smell the pure vanilla a block away. People used to come from upstate, drive hours just to have his malteds. I'll always remember the sign he had at the luncheonette: 'If your wife can't cook, don't divorce her, just bring her to Sammy's Luncheonette.' They loved you, Fren-zee. Sammy always gave you something for free! And how about Austin's on Eighth Street and Second Avenue. He made the best egg creams. He had a secret formula for the chocolate syrup. The owner would never tell, but he said it had to do with semifreezing the syrup, and that it was a chocolate fudge syrup, not just chocolate. The *Daily News* once named Austin's egg creams the best in all of America. We already knew that. Oh! I fell in love with all these things, but my favorite was the Sicilian *granita di limone* [lemon ice], which I bought from Angelo, on the corner of Houston and Elizabeth streets. He rang a bell while he shouted, 'Lemon ice! Lemon ice!' as he walked around the neighborhood with his wooden cart.

"But the best thing, Fren-zee, was when I took a stroll to Delancey Street. There, I found a monkey and an organ grinder singing Italian songs. I was shocked! I handed a nickel to the monkey. He gave it to the organ grinder. Then, using his little foot, the monkey picked a fortune from his bag and gave it to me—such a smart animal. It made me so happy to receive a fortune that said, 'You will have a wonderful new life in a new land.'

"Anyway, that was America years ago, but it was also a little part of Italy. It will never be like that again. Those traditions are gone forever. Those were the days, Fren-zee. Mmmm . . . you made the whiskey with peaches good. I taught you well, didn't I?"

"But it's not your recipe. Dad taught me, and he got it from his mother."

"But if I didn't teach you how to cook, you wouldn't know how to make it right in the first place. I win the argument. Drink up!"

Okay, when she's right, she's right . . . 🐌

Caffè Espresso
HOT AND ICED ESPRESSO

When Grandma was a child in Ciminna, she would carry a little gray metal pail to the pastry store in the town square. The *pasticceria* owner would fill the pail with espresso, and then charge her according to the number of cups she had ordered.

Espresso is still an integral part of the lives of everyone in our family. We begin each morning with a cup of it, and in the summer we serve it ice cold in the afternoon. Every Sicilian knows that a bottle of ice cold espresso has its place of honor in the refrigerator door, where it sits just waiting to be sipped. Loving espresso as we do, we naturally make ices out of it, too. Espresso ice has never been as fancy as it is made to seem today. It has always been just a regular summer dessert, simply frozen in ice-cube trays and served with *biscotti* or pastries on the side (see page 322). Finally, to emphasize the importance of espresso in the Sicilian household is to know the first words I speak in the morning, after dinner, or on a hot summer's day: "Did anyone make the espresso?"

Italian espresso, French espresso, French mocha espresso, and Belgian mocha espresso are what I consider to be the best roasts available for making espresso. Of course, these roasts can vary in quality from coffee merchant to coffee merchant, so taste around until you find the roast that gives you the best flavor. But the quality of the espresso will suffer no matter how good the roast if you are not using the proper pot. Read the recipe for Espresso Ice (page 288) for information on making espresso properly in a Neapolitan drip pot. And remember, fill the pot only once with water for strong espresso.

The best part of drinking espresso for many Sicilians is flavoring it with sugar cubes. In both Sicily and Little Italy, our family traditionally sweetens with sugar cubes. The cubes never fully melt, and part of the cube remains on the bottom of the cup. So after we sip the liquid, we all suck on the little sugar cubes full of espresso. It tastes like the best hard candy you've ever had.

Ground espresso coffee (see recipe introduction)

Anisette, homemade (page 304) or purchased

1. Pour enough water into a medium-size pot to fill your espresso pot. Bring the water to a boil. Fill the section of the espresso pot that holds the ground coffee three-fourths full. Do not pack the coffee. Cover the coffee with the lid. Add 2 teaspoons ground coffee to the top section of the pot. Then pour the boiling water over the ground coffee until the water reaches the top of the pot. Cover the pot with its lid and let the espresso drip. When all of the water has dripped through to the lower section, serve the espresso. Discard the coffee grounds, as they cannot be used again.

ICED ESPRESSO

Prepare 4 cups espresso as directed. While the espresso is still hot, stir in sugar to taste; or wait until the espresso is lukewarm and add the anisette to taste. Store in the refrigerator until cold. Serve over ice. You can also double the recipe and freeze the sweetened espresso in ice-cube trays to make your own espresso ice cubes. They don't dilute the espresso like regular ice cubes do.

Limonata di Nonna
LEMONADE

Lemonade is one of the most common drinks in both Sicily and Little Italy. From the early 1900s through the 1950s, the streets of Little Italy in summer were lined with children selling glasses of lemonade for three cents. Mom throws her head back and laughs at the memory. "Fran-nee, Dottie and I thought we were in business. We used to be on the corner with our little table, and people would buy the lemonade. It was in a big, big glass, not like what you get today. We used to make some money, then run to Blah Blah's off Houston to buy penny candy by the Church of All Nations."

"Who on earth is Blah Blah's?"

"He owned one of the fanciest candy shops right off Little Italy. Whenever we had extra money, we would go there to buy the most delicious chocolates from Europe. We called him Blah Blah because he talked and blabbered all day long. What's wrong with you, Fran-nee, everyone had a nickname. Those were the good old days. . . ."

4 cups water

4 tablespoons sugar, or as needed

½ cup fresh lemon juice, strained (about 3 lemons), or as needed

Ice cubes

1. In a small pot, bring the water to a rolling boil. Remove from the heat and let cool to lukewarm. Stir in the 4 tablespoons sugar until dissolved, then stir in the lemon juice. Cover and refrigerate until cold.

2. Taste and adjust with a little more sugar or lemon juice, if necessary. Pour over ice cubes in tall soda glasses.

Secrets of Success

For maximum juice, choose lemons with a thin skin; thicker-skinned lemons are dry. Using your palms, roll the lemon back and forth on the counter about ten times to release its juice. Instead of using ice cubes, double the recipe and freeze half of the lemonade in ice-cube trays, then use the flavorful cubes for ice.

Arangiata
HOMEMADE ORANGE DRINK

🐾 Whenever Grandma finds good-quality juice oranges and it is a hot, humid day, she serves us grandchildren this easy-to-make orange drink. She's been making this drink for over sixty years.

1½ cups seltzer or water, chilled

Juice of 3 large oranges (1½ cups)

2 teaspoons sugar, or to taste

Ice cubes

1. In a sterilized 1-quart bottle with a tight-fitting lid, combine the seltzer or water, orange juice, and sugar. Seal the bottle tightly and shake well to dissolve the sugar.

2. Serve over ice cubes in a tall glass. This drink can be covered and stored in the refrigerator for a few days before it loses its freshness.

VARIATION

To make your own homemade version of the famous soda Orangina, proceed as directed, using half orange juice and half tangerine juice.

The Last Story of the Old Days in Little Italy

Mom, GRANDMA, and I were down on Mulberry Street shopping when I shouted, "I'm thirsty! Let's go to Ferrara's and have something to drink." We sat down outside the old cafe, and the sun began to withdraw into steamy clouds. The shadows of the evening were striking against the hundred-year-old buildings that surrounded us. In front of us stood a row of stores: Alleva Brothers, Little Italy Food Center, Piemonte Ravioli, and Di Palo's. Grandma sipped her espresso as she looked up. "I can't believe I've been in this country seventy-five years. When I look at these buildings, the walls talk to me. I can see Mikey as a little boy on my arm as I bought ravioli from Piemonte here on Grand. I remember taking Fren-zee down here in her stroller and shopping all along Mott Street. I remember the hard days of World War II. So my granddaugher is writing a *cook-ka-book*. You were the only one of the grandchildren who understood Sicilian, and the only one who liked my stories. Now you write about the old neighborhood. I was supposed to die with my recipes. We're breaking tradition, you know! I taught you too well. That's the problem." She turned to my mother, "Lee, remember the feasts?"

"Ma, remember here on Mulberry Street. The opera people used to come down from the Met and sing, and the kids used to throw the *vascile* [large pail of water] from the fire escape in the middle of a high note. Then, these five-hundred-pound women would scream, *'Fatense! Animale!'* [Louses! Animals!] Haaaa! Haaaa! Their beaded gowns were soaked, their bouffant hair all dripping wet. Those were great moments Fran-nee! Haaaa! The laughs we had! Everyone knew everyone. Doors were open. People were in and out of everyone's house. We were poor but happier then. We had each other. The characters that lived here. Ma! Remember Saint Gabriel? A real *stunata* [nut case]. She told us we'd go to hell if we didn't give her money, so we gave her a few bucks so she wouldn't put a curse on us. Everyone in the neighborhood knew her. She made a good living! Haaa! Haaa! We nicknamed everyone. There was Feet. He had big feet. Frankie the Nose. He had a big nose. Porky, he ate a lot, and Zumbie, he walked like a zombie. Haaa! Haaa! We tortured everyone equally. We saw Sinatra at the Paramount, Dean Martin and Jerry Lewis at the Roxy—I split my pants laughing—and Keely Smith and Louis Prima at the Capitol. Those were the good days, Fran-nee, good days!"

We left the cafe and walked down Mott Street. Louie Di Palo of Di Palo's Foods came out to greet us. "Hey, Francesca! Grandma! How's everybody?"

"We were just reminiscing about the old days," I replied.

"Funny, so was I. My store has been open on the corner of Mott and Grand since 1925. My grandparents Luigi and Concetta opened it when they came over from Puglia. They were cheese makers and had to make a living. Four generations later, here we are. If I ever close this store, nothing will be the same. The tradition will be lost forever. You know for me, I'm here because of the old days. I want people to be happy when they come into my store, and I want them to be even happier when they leave. There was something special about this place years ago. This is the biggest Little Italy in the country, where everyone landed. I can't think of the words ... there was a ... a ..."

I jumped in, "A magic to this place that can never be recaptured again."

"That's it. There was a *magic* here. That's the word I was looking for. Look at your grandmother. She's been shopping here for over seventy years. Where can I get customers like that again? Stop by next Wednesday. I'll have some good *incanestrato* and a sweet Sicilian oil I know you'll love—Barbera."

"Okay, Louie, see you next week." As we continued to walk home, I stubbed my toe. "Ouch! Ouch! My foot! Damn it!"

Grandma picked up my foot to examine it. "You should learn how to walk right, Fren-zee. You could hurt yourself with those high heels. Well, let's pray, and maybe we'll meet an angel that will cure you. Let me see if I can find a hobo."

"Are you nuts! What hobo? My foot's killing me and you want me to run into an angel in the middle of Mott Street. Maaaa! She's starting in again!"

"Didn't I ever tell you the story of how my sister Vitina was paralyzed in bed for seven years, then an angel came to our house and cured her? Lee, see if you find a hobo. I'll give him a dollar, then maybe Fren-zee will be able to walk."

"What are you talking about!" I shouted.

"Well, my mother once gave food to a hobo, and he granted her one wish. She asked him to cure Vitina, and she was able to walk. So if I give money to a hobo, it's said to be good luck in Sicily, and maybe he'll make a miracle and cure your foot. Fren-zee, what's wrong with you? Don't you understand anything anymore?"

"Now, why didn't I think of that?" I smacked my forehead. "Grandmaaaa! It's not possible! Maaaa! Tell your mother, it's not possible. How can someone who's paralyzed suddenly walk because great-grandma gave food to a hobo?"

"Stop screaming, Fren-zee. It's the truth!" She crossed her arms in front of her chest dramatically. "He was an angel in disguise."

"For God's sake! Maaaaaaa! I'm getting a migraine!"

"Just lean on your Grandma while we walk." She clutched my arm in hers. "Let's see, it was Ciminna in 1910. My sister Vitina had been paralyzed most of her life. Then one day this man appeared at our door dressed in torn clothes. He told my mother he hadn't eaten for a few days and asked her for some food."

As she chattered away, holding me up, I thought to myself, "Was it really such a long, long time ago in New York's Little Italy? Ahhhh yessss. Those were the days."

And Grandma's stories will always go on. ☙

Left: My Mom, Lena, with Grandma Josephina, circa 1970. Above: Grandma Josephina, 1994.

SOURCES

All of the mail-order businesses listed here ship throughout the United States. Call them and ask for products you're interested in, since the catalogs commonly do not include everything that is carried. If you can't find an item, call Di Palo's, Manganaro Foods, or Todaro Brothers. They have everything Sicilian.

Cheeses & Meats

Aidell's Sausage Company
1625 Alvarado Street
San Leandro, CA 94577
800/546-5795

Fresh and dried sausages. Catalog available.

Alleva Brothers
188 Grand Street
New York, NY 10013
800/4-ALLEVA

Sicilian cheeses, fresh ricotta, fresh and dried sausages, cold cuts, fresh pasta and ravioli, Sicilian bread. Catalog available.

Di Palo's
206 Grand Street
New York, NY 10013
212/226-1033

Sicilian cheeses, fresh ricotta and mozzarella, fresh and dried sausages, cold cuts, fresh pasta and ravioli, imported olive oils and vinegar, Italian tuna, Sicilian

salted anchovies and salted sardines, Italian espresso coffees. Catalog available.

Manganaro Foods
488 Ninth Avenue, New York, NY 10018
800/4-SALAMI

Sicilian cheeses, fresh and dried sausages, Sicilian olive oils, Italian espresso coffees, cold cuts, salted cod, salted sardines and salted anchovies, Italian tuna, fresh pasta and ravioli, dried pasta, Sicilian bread. Catalog available.

Todaro Brothers
555 Second Avenue
New York, NY 10016
212/679-7766

Sicilian cheeses, fresh and dried sausages, Sicilian olive oils, Italian espresso coffees, cold cuts, Sicilian salted anchovies and salted sardines, Italian tuna, salted cod, fresh pasta and ravioli, dried pasta. Catalog available.

Fish

For Italian tuna, salted cod and Sicilian salted anchovies and salted sardines, see Di Palo's, Manganaro Foods, and Todaro Brothers under Cheese and Meats.

Confections & Pastries

Ferrara Foods & Confections
195 Grand Street
New York, NY 10013
212/226-6150

Italian hard and soft candies, cannoli, *sfingi* St. Joseph, *cassata* cake, biscotti, Easter *percura* (almond paste sheep); special order cakes available. Italian soda syrups, Italian espresso coffees.

Perugina of Italy
636 Lexington Avenue
New York, NY 10022
212/688-2490

Italian hard candy, Italian chocolates, imported Italian cocoa, torrone.

Italian Espresso Coffees

Empire Coffee & Tea Company
592 Ninth Avenue
New York, NY 10036
212/586-1717

Italian espresso, mocha deluxe Italian roast, Neopolitan blend, Bialetti stove-top espresso makers, dried spices.

Northwestern Coffee Mills
217 North Broadway
Milwaukee, WI 53202
800/243-5283

Espresso roasts, decaffeinated espresso, coffee syrups, coffee flavors. Catalog available.

See also Di Palo's, Ferrara Foods, Manganaro Foods, and Todaro Brothers.

Dried Herbs & Spices

San Francisco Herb Company
250 14th Street
San Francisco, CA 94103
800/227-4530

Ceylon cinnamon, Greek oregano, sea salt, black whole peppercorns. Catalog available.

Mr. Spiceman
9-20 38th Avenue
Long Island City, NY 11101
718/472-5446

Fresh cinnamon flakes, sea salt, Greek oregano, Perugina candy discounted, Virginia Dare liqueur essences. Catalog available.

Herb & Vegetable Seeds

The Cook's Garden
P.O. Box 535
Londonderry, VT 05148
802/824-3400

Italian artichokes, Italian basil, broccoli rape, chicory, escarole, Italian parsley, rosemary, Italian sunflowers, tomato paste tomatoes. Catalog available.

Fratelli Ingegnoli
Corso Buenos Aires 54
20124, Milano, Italy

Italian oregano, Italian parsley, Italian rosemary, Italian eggplant, Italian squash. Payment by international money order. Catalog available, enclose SASE.

Shepherds's Garden Seeds
30 Irene Street
Torrington, CT 06790
800/482-3638

Italian basil, Italian onions, Italian garlic, Italian eggplant, fennel, romaine lettuce, sauce tomatoes. Catalog available.

Liqueur Essences

E.C. Kraus Wine & Beermaking Supplies
P.O. Box 7850-WC
Independence, MO 64053
816/254-7446

Wine- and liqueur-making supplies, how-to booklets, liqueur essences (extracts). Catalog available.

See also Mr. Spiceman under Dried Herbs and Spices.

RESOURCE GUIDE TO LITTLE ITALIES AND YOUR ITALIAN HERITAGE

Since the opening of the Ellis Island Immigration Museum in 1990, immigration centers throughout the United States are reporting that searches into family history and lineage are at an all-time high.

Studies based on the 1990 census indicate that about twelve million people in the United States are of Italian origin. The 1980 census found Italians to be the sixth largest ancestry group in the country constituting 5.4 percent of the total population. In other words, one out of every twenty people are self-reported as Italian or part Italian. More recent studies reported in the spring 1995 edition of *Sicilia Parra*—a Sicilian newsletter published by Professor Gaetano Cipolla of the Modern Foreign Language Department of St. Johns University, Jamaica, New York, put the number of Americans of Italian origin at twenty-five million, with 55 percent of that total of Sicilian ancestry. If these studies are correct, people of Sicilian background account for about fourteen million people in the United States, easily the largest group of Italians from any single region.

These large numbers are the result of immigration that began in the early part of the nineteenth century and increased dramatically during the Mass (or Great) Immigration of 1880 to 1920. The prosperous industrial cities of northern Italy were the primary sources of the settlers who arrived in the 1880s, while the less affluent farming areas of the south and Sicily were the major exit points in the first decades of the 1900s. The newcomers generally took up residence in large cities, first in the East in lower Manhattan, which was to become the largest Little Italy in the United States, in Boston's North End, and in South Philadelphia, and later in metropolitan communities across the country, including The Hill in St. Louis, neighborhoods in New Orleans, Chicago, and Omaha; and in North Beach in San Francisco. By 1910, over half a million persons of Italian birth lived in the United

States; with half of them of Sicilian origin. The immigrants lived close together, often in tenement neighborhoods. They re-created their own small-town life within these large American cities, and these enclaves soon became known as Little Italies. New immigrants moved into the same areas—areas where their language or dialect was spoken; where customs, religious traditions, and attitudes from the old country were still strong; and where feast days, folklore, and traditional music and games had not been forgotten. By the 1950s, a Little Italy existed in almost every state in the union.

Italian food was a daily way of life in these Little Italies, first with the arrival of the northern staple of polenta (cornmeal mush), and then later with the southern dishes of meat and pasta. Eventually, the cuisines of Campania and Sicily which feature tomato, onion, olive oil, cheese, and garlic, predominated. Local food establishments—bakeries, pastry stores, butchers featuring handmade sausages, pasta makers, pizzerias—grew up within these new neighborhoods, and in a few years, Sicilian food from such purveyors had become the standard. Much of what is recognized today as southern Italian food was first sold by these new shopkeepers.

This guide is designed to help readers find out more about the Little Italies of America and to guide them in tracing their heritage. First, there are four steps to get you started. They are followed by an alphabetical listing of museums, historical societies, and other institutions specializing in Italian-American history.

① Call your state historical society, which will inform you of any Little Italy or any Italian institution that may have existed in your area. Many historical societies have photographs and other archival material on food, culture, folklore, traditions, and types of work that Italians did upon their arrival in the United States.

② To trace your genealogical heritage free of charge, write the Church of Jesus Christ of Latter-Day Saints, Correspondence Unit Family History Library, 35 North West Temple Street, Salt Lake City, UT 84150 (see details, page 333).

③ Purchase *Italian Genealogical Records* by Trafford R. Cole (Ancestry Incorporated, 1995). This is the single best book available on how to search out your roots. It is published by the Church of Jesus Christ of Latter-Day Saints (see page 333).

④ Look for *Our Italian Surnames* by Joseph G. Fucello (Genealogical Publishing Co., Inc., 1987). It is the best book on searching out information on your surname. If you are lucky enough to find your name in this book, you'll find out its origin and meaning.

📖 Museums, Historical Societies, and Other Institutions

American Italian Historical Association
209 Flagg Place
Staten Island, NY 10304
718/499-7117

Holds forums every year on various aspects of the Italian American experience at which papers are presented by professors and historians. Among the past subjects are the Italian-American Woman, the Italian Family in America, Sex Lives of Italians, Sicilian Houstonians in Transition, and Arriving at Ellis Island.

The Balch Institute for Ethnic Studies
18 South 7th Street
Philadelphia, PA 19106
215/925-8090

Although it has limited genealogical information, this institute does have extensive resources on many of the prominent Italians who settled in the United States. It houses the manuscripts, papers, and correspondence of many Italian-American organizations; Italian-American newspapers from the 1890s to 1950s; papers of famed educator Leonard Covello of the Little Italy of Harlem; the records of Fiorani Radio Productions, which broadcasted Italian radio shows in the Scranton, Pennsylvania area from 1931 to 1975; and the records of the Italian Folk Arts Federation of America, along with the personal papers of one of its founders, Elba Gurzau.

Center for Migration Studies
209 Flag Place
Staten Island, NY 10304
718/499-7117

Here you'll find a complete library of the records of Italian arrivals. The center publishes several books, including *Italians in the United States*, which contain statistical information on the migration of Italians, their education, and their organizations throughout the United States. Among the center's other titles is *A Directory of Italian and Italian American Organizations and Community Services in Greater New York.*

The Church of Jesus Christ of Latter-Day Saints
Correspondence Unit
Family History Library
35 North West Temple Street
Salt Lake City, UT 84150
800/240-2331

The library will assist you in finding your ancestors for a minor fee. They maintain one the largest genealogical libraries of names in the world, and you do not have to be a Mormon to use their facility. Write to the address given for information and forms. A $3.75 charge covers shipping, handling, and a 30-day microfilm rental cost. Your records will then be sent to your local state Family History Center where the librarians will assist you.

For further information on how to get started and how to locate your state Family History Center, you can search their internet web page at: http//www.lds.org/Family_History/How_Do_I_Begin.html. You can also call the Family History Support line at 1-800-346-6044 for further instruction.

Ellis Island Foundation for The Statue of Liberty
52 Vanderbilt Avenue
New York, NY 10017
212/883-1986

With one phone call, the foundation will send you two free information packets compiled by the Immigration and Naturalization Service (INS) in Washington, DC. One is specifically on Italian immigration and the other is on all types of immigration to America. These packets will refer you to several government, ethnic, and genealogical organizations to assist you in tracing your genealogy.

Immigration History Research Center
826 Berry Street
St. Paul, MN 55114
612/627-4208

This center is an international resource on American immigration and ethnic history. Its archive and library document the history of twenty-four ethnic groups, including Italian Americans. The collection of the latter constitutes the most extensive body of original source material in the United States on Italian immigration and the history of Italians in this country. The material documents many kinds of activities, from daily household life and work to celebrations. Included are books, newspapers, manuscripts, photographs, and oral histories dating back to the 1880s. Among the unique holdings is the five-volume *Italians to America: Lists of Passengers arriving at U.S. Ports, 1880–1889.* The institute is currently gathering more passenger records. The center also houses the records of the Order of the Sons of Italy.

Italian-American Foundation
666 11th Street, NW, Suite 600
Washington, DC 20001
202/387-0600

A call here will lead you in the right direction, whatever your question. The foundation serves as a clearinghouse for information on the achievements and activities of Italian Americans, plus it publishes several books about Italian Americans, including the *Directory of Italian American Organizations*, which lists organizations in every state.

Italian-American Institute
John D. Calandra Institute
25 West 42 Street
New York, NY 10036
212/642-2094

The institute deals mainly with education and research on the Italian-American experience. It houses the original ship records of Italian immigrants from 1884 to 1890, and is awaiting the original ship records from the Mass Immigration era.

Italian-American Renaissance Museum and Library
537 South Peters Street
P.O. Box 2392
New Orleans, LA 70176
504/522-7294

This institution is the repository of ship records of Italians who arrived in the American southeast. It also, houses an extensive library and museum of the Little Italy of New Orleans, Louisiana.

Italian Cultural Institute
686 Park Avenue
New York, NY 10021
212/879-4242

The institute's focus is on all aspects of the Italian culture such as films, food, and music.

🐚 Books That Are a Must

Allen, James Paul, and Eugene James Turner. *We The People: An Atlas of America's Ethnic Diversity.* New York: MacMillan, 1988.

A large reference book that lists concentrations of Italian residents beginning at the turn of the century. Also lists the different types of work done by Italian immigrants upon their arrival.

Harney, Robert F, and J. Vincenza Scarpaci. *Little Italies in North America.* Ontario: The Multicultural History Soceity of Ontario, 1981.

Contains statistical and historical information on the first Little Italies in America and how they were formed. Call the Center for Migration Studies (see page 333) to obtain a copy.

Hobbie, Margaret. *Italian American Material Culture: A Directory of Collections, Sites and Festivals in the U.S. and Canada*. Westport, CT: Greenwood Press, 1992.

Currently in print and an absolute must! Lists collections of historical societies; photographic archives, festivals, museums, and Italian-American foundations. Includes a comprehensive list of Little Italies that have existed in the United States. Available in the reference section of large libraries.

Italian American Foundation. *Directory of Italian American Organizations*. Washington, DC: Italian American Foundation.

Guide to every Italian club or organization in the United States. See page 334 for address of foundation.

Williams, Phyllis H. *South Italian Folkways in Europe and America*. New York: Russell and Russell, 1969.

A great read! Written by a nurse who treated southern Italians and Sicilians in a New York City hospital during the great migration period, this is an in-depth look at the culture, folklore, foods, customs, marriage, and traditions of her patients. It is one of the best books ever written about Sicilian and southern Italian society in America. Out of print but available at the library.

᎒ Other Books

Bologna, Sando. *The Italians of Waterbury: Experiences of Immigrants and Their Families*. Portland, CT: Waverly Printing Co., 1993.

Brown, Mary Elizabeth. *From Italian Villages to Greenwich Village: Our Lady of Pompeii 1892–1992*. Staten Island, NY: Center for Migration Studies, 1992.

Chiumiento, Maria Ida. *Little Italy: 1890–1920*. Brooklyn, NY: America, Catholic Agency Inc., 1990.

Dolci, Danilo. *Sicilian Lives*. New York: Pantheon Books, 1981.

Fede, Frank Joseph. *Italians in the Deep South*. Montgomery, AL: The Black Belt Press, 1994.

Gumina, Deanna Paoli. *The Italian of San Francisco: 1850–1930*. Staten Island, NY: Center for Migration Studies, 1978.

Miranda, Edward, and Ino J. Rossi. *New York City's Italians*. New York: Italian-American Center for Urban Affairs Inc., 1976.

Orsi, Robert Anthony. *The Madonna of 115th Street: Faith and Community in Italian Harlem; 1880–1950*. New Haven: Yale University Press, 1985.

Schiavo, Giovanni. *Four Centuries of Italian American History*. Staten Island, NY: Center for Migration Studies, 1992.

Zucchi, John E. *Italians In Toronto: Development of a National Identity: 1875–1935*. Toronto: McGill-Queens University Press, 1988.

How to Find the Little Italy in Your Area

Below is a list of some of the Little Italies that could be found in the United States between 1860 and the 1950s. Although many of them no longer exist, you can still trace their origins. Each place listed has some type of historical society or photographic archive that will guide you to the original location, culture, and traditions. In her book *Italian American Material Culture*, Margaret Hobbie lists historical societies and photographic archives in nearly every state. She suggests from her extensive research that wherever these associations exist, there was once a Little Italy. For a quick and easy search, purchase Hobbie's book and look up your state to find local institutions that can help you research your Little Italy.

ALABAMA
DAPHNE

ARIZONA
GLOBE

ARKANSAS
TONTITOWN

CALIFORNIA
BRIDGEPORT
OAKLAND
SAN DIEGO
SAN FRANCISCO
SAN MATEO
SAN PEDRO

COLORADO
BOULDER
NORTH DENVER
PUEBLO

CONNECTICUT
GREENWICH
HARTFORD
MIDDLETOWN
NEW HAVEN

DELAWARE
WILMINGTON

FLORIDA
TAMPA

ILLINOIS
CHICAGO

INDIANA
CLINTON

LOUISIANA
HARVEY
NEW ORLEANS

MARYLAND
BALTIMORE

MASSACHUSETTS
BOSTON
LAWRENCE
NORTH ANDOVER
WELLESLEY

MINNESOTA
IRON MOUNTAIN
IRON RANGE OF
   MINNESOTA

MISSOURI
KANSAS CITY
ST. LOUIS

NEBRASKA
LINCOLN

NEW JERSEY
CAMDEN
HAMMONTON
MORRISTOWN
PATTERSON
VINELAND

NEW YORK
BINGHAMTON
BRONX
BROOKLYN
BUFFALO
DOBBS FERRY
ELMIRA
ITHACA
JAMESTOWN
NEW YORK CITY
OSSINING
OSWEGO
ROCHESTER
SENECA
STATEN ISLAND
SYOSSET

OHIO
CLEVELAND

OKLAHOMA
McALESTER

PENNSYLVANIA
PITTSBURGH
PHILADELPHIA
READING

RHODE ISLAND
PROVIDENCE

TEXAS
HOUSTON

UTAH
HELPER

VERMONT
BARRE

WASHINGTON
CHENEY VINCITY

WISCONSON
MILWAUKEE

FESTIVALS

 Italian food and folk festivals are held in many states. Contact the Center for Migration Studies (page 333) or seek out Margaret Hobbie's *Italian American Material Culture* for a complete list. This simple list is organized chronologically by month; all dates are subject to change.

March

March 19: Festival di San Giuseppe, Hackensack, NJ.

April

Late April: Little Italy Festival, Independence, LA.

May

Italian Festival, Allentown, PA.

Italian Festival, McAlester, OK.

Madonna di Sciacca Festival, Norristown, PA.

June

June 13: St. Anthony Festival, North Denver, CO.

Mid-June: St. Anthony of Padua Festival, New York, NY.

June 13: St. Anthony Festival, Wilmington, DE.

End of June: Fisherman's Feast of Sicilian Heritage, Gloucester, MA.

July

Italian Festival, Baltimore, MD.

Late July, early August: St. Lucia Festival, Little Italy of Omaha, NE.

August

August 15: Feast of the Assumption, Atlantic City, NJ.

Late August: Italian Heritage Festival, Waterbury, CT.

August/September: Little Italy Festival, Clinton, IN.

August 16: Our Lady of Mt. Carmel Festival, North Denver, CO.

August 15: Our Lady of the Assumption Festival, Cleveland, OH.

September

Last weekend of September: St. Rosalie Festival, Harvey, New Orleans, LA.

Labor Day: Feast of the Three Saints, Lawrence, MA.

Labor Day: Italian Street Fair, Nashville, TN.

Our Lady of Pompeii Festival, New York, NY.

September 19: San Gennaro Festival, New York, NY.

October

October 12: Columbus Day Festival, Federal Hill, Providence, RI.

Mid-October: St. Gerard Maella Festival, Newark, NJ.

INDEX

TABLE OF EQUIVALENTS

The exact equivalents in the following tables have been rounded for convenience.

LIQUID MEASURES

U.S.	METRIC
1/4 TEASPOON	1.25 MILLILITERS
1/2 TEASPOON	2.5 MILLILITERS
1 TEASPOON	5 MILLILITERS
1 TABLESPOON (3 TEASPOONS)	15 MILLILITERS
1 FLUID OUNCE (2 TABLESPOONS)	30 MILLILITERS
1/4 CUP	60 MILLILITERS
1/3 CUP	80 MILLILITERS
1 CUP	240 MILLILITERS
1 PINT (2 CUPS)	480 MILLILITERS
1 QUART (4 CUPS, 32 OUNCES)	960 MILLILITERS
1 GALLON (4 QUARTS)	3.84 LITERS

DRY MEASURES

1 OUNCE (BY WEIGHT)	28 GRAMS
1/4 POUND (4 OUNCES)	114 GRAMS
1 POUND	454 GRAMS
2.2 POUNDS	1 KILOGRAM

LENGTH MEASURES

1/8 INCH	3 MILLIMETERS
1/4 INCH	6 MILLIMETERS
1/2 INCH	12 MILLIMETERS
1 INCH	2.5 CENTIMETERS

OVEN TEMPERATURES

FAHRENHEIT	CELSIUS	GAS
250	120	1/2
275	140	1
300	150	2
325	160	3
350	180	4
375	190	5
400	200	6
425	220	7
450	230	8
475	240	9
500	260	10